b

The Gardener's
Guide to Growing
LILIES

A fine example of how much lilies enjoy company, this
is 'Grand Cru', a strong Asiatic hybrid, standing head
and shoulders above herbaceous friends

The Gardener's
Guide to Growing
LILIES

Michael Jefferson-Brown
& Harris Howland

David & Charles

NOTE

Throughout the book the time of year is given as seasons to make the reference sensible to all readers; those in the northern hemisphere can translate the seasons into months as follows:

WINTER	SPRING	SUMMER	AUTUMN
Early: December	Early: March	Early: June	Early: September
Mid: January	Mid: April	Mid: July	Mid: October
Late: February	Late: May	Late: August	Late: November

ACKNOWLEDGEMENTS

All photographs by the author except: pp1, 36, 43 Marijke Heuff, Garden Picture Library (G.P.L.); p2 Jerry Harpur (garden designed by Gary Keim and Peter Wooster); p9 Sunniva Harte, G.P.L.; pp25, 27, 38 Photos Horticultural; pp28, 30, 32 Harry Smith; p33 Stuart Hamilton (garden designed by Leila Aitken); p35 Jerry Pavia, G.P.L.; pp41, 95, 100, 105, 107, 110, 113, 115 Derek Croucher; p59 Henk Dijkman, G.P.L.; pp123, 125, 129, 149 Paul Biddle. Line illustrations by Rosemary Wise.

A DAVID & CHARLES BOOK

Copyright © Michael Jefferson-Brown 1995
First published 1995

Michael Jefferson-Brown has asserted his right to be identified as author of this work in accordance with the Copyright, Designs and Patents Act 1988.

All rights reserved. No part of this publication may be reproduced, stored in a retrieval system, or transmitted, in any form or by any means, electronic or mechanical, by photocopying, recording or otherwise, without prior permission in writing from the publisher.

A catalogue record for this book is available from the British Library.

ISBN 0 7153 0339 2

Typeset by ABM Typographics Limited Hull
and printed in Italy by Lego SpA
for David & Charles
Brunel House Newton Abbot Devon

CONTENTS

INTRODUCTION

On a warm, still summer's evening there is nothing to compare with the stunning perfume of lilies wafting across a garden. It is unmistakable, heady and almost narcotic, and it was the scent of lilies that first got me hooked on their cultivation. My grandmother had several stands of *Lilium regale* and *L. candidum* and I will always remember their wonderful scent and their stately grace. I, like many others, started with the faithful old *L. regale* which is relatively easy to grow, and did well for me. However, this early success was soon to meet with a setback. Lacking knowledge I rushed into buying *L. auratum* and planted the bulbs into chalky, clay soil, which only a few months before had been the building plot of my new house. They struggled to bloom and died. It could have been poor bulb material, it was certainly the wrong soil – so a little learning had to be undertaken. That was over thirty years ago when there were not so many varieties of lilies available, and of course I was green!

Today there is a whole host of lilies available, many of them providing easy-to-grow, long-lived garden plants. And they come in a wide range of flower shapes, sizes and colours: from the exotic Oriental hybrids derived from *L. auratum* and *L. speciosum rubrum* through the trumpets and upward-facing Asiatic lilies to the small-flowered *L. martagon* that are very long-lived and have naturalised in parts of Britain. There is also great variety in the flower shape, the arrangement of the inflorescence and the direction in which the flower faces. The Asiatic hybrids, which are the most numerous hybrid type, are mainly upward facing. There has been considerable hybridisation with these lilies because they lend themselves as commercial cut flowers and pot plants. An upward-facing lily is less likely to be damaged by transportation or wrapping. However, many of these lilies do make excellent garden plants, not only surviving a long time, but also increasing the number of bulbs in a planting.

There are then the trumpet lilies, which not only have wonderfully large flowers, but are also renowned for their beauty and scent. Between 3–6ft high, these promise a wonderful and graceful addition to the back of the border. Next, and probably the most numerous flower shapes, are the reflexed petal types more popularly known as turk's caps. These include *L. martagon*, many of the North American lilies and their hybrids together with some European and Asiatic species. From these various shapes the dexterity of the hybridiser has been at work to provide a combination of flares, bowls, semi-reflex, upward-, downward- and outward-facing flowers.

Being large, many lily flowers are easy to hybridise. The various parts are easily accessible and easy to handle, so it can be undertaken by amateurs as well as the commercial grower. This adds further excitement to the growing of lilies, increases a collection and offers security against unforeseen disaster.

When it comes to propagation, lilies are the most obliging of plants. Not only can they produce an abundance of seed, some like *Lilium lancifolium* (*L. tigrinum*), also produce small bulbils on the stem at the leaf axils. When ripe, these can be harvested and planted to produce quickly additional plants. The same applies to bulblets, which are produced below ground, around the lower stem and bulb. Left on the stem, they would naturally make further mature bulbs. The lily bulb can also be scaled. It is not of onion construction, such as tulips and

daffodils, but made up of numerous scales that are short, fat, modified leaves adapted as an energy store. Lastly, some large mature bulbs will naturally divide to provide up to four mature stems for the coming season. It is a joy to see them nosing through the ground every spring, greeting you like old friends with hopefully, a few new friends as well.

There is a fascination about lilies even for many who do not grow them. Thank goodness the days seem to have passed when if you mentioned the word 'lily' people would be reminded of funerals. I suppose this was because the word lily has been much abused and misused over time, particularly in the case of the Arum lily, which is not a lily at all!

The attraction of lilies has to be their stately grace, combined with the scent of the large, exotic blooms. They can be grown in the open garden, in pots and in greenhouses and are very easy to propagate. They offer a brilliant show

L. auratum, the main founder species of the glamorous Oriental hybrids, has heavily perfumed flowers up to 25cm (10in) across (p79)

which will stand out in any border whatever the competition. However, there is still the niche for those requiring a challenge in the more difficult and rare species. In fact in the whole lily spectrum there is something for everyone.

There are just a few tips to remember. Not all lilies will grow in all soils, but there are those that suit acid conditions, and those that will grow in alkaline soils. What they all like is a good free-draining site, and preferably a cool root-run. Keeping these few simple points in mind, everybody can have success with lilies.

HARRIS HOWLAND
Chairman of the Royal Horticultural Society
Lily Group

1

THE MAGIC OF LILIES

No one doubts their beauty. Lilies must be at the top of almost everyone's list as the most glamorous and diverse of flowers. You may wonder, 'Are they for me? Can anything so lovely grow for me?' Happily the answer is a resounding 'Yes'. This book argues an easy case, but it also points out such hazards and idiosyncrasies as there may be.

POPULAR AND VERSATILE

The lily is at the height of its popularity, as one of the leading cut-flowers all over the world. We see lilies in every florist's window. Potted bulbs greet us at the garden centre and the petrol station. They seem to be everywhere. This is the direct result of a breeding programme that should have disproven the idea that lilies are fleeting, difficult plants, a legacy of the introduction of many lovely species from Asia and elsewhere at the end of the last century and the first decades of this one. Some of these introductions proved easy, but quite a number maintained their wildness, a character adapted to the conditions in which they evolved in the wild. Today's hybrids, however, are hugely robust and are becoming even more so. It is the ease with which some of these can be grown in pots and in the garden that make them so popular.

The range of hybrids now on the market, or about to be introduced, includes cultivars for every garden, almost regardless of soils, and for every situation, for pots, containers, window-boxes, borders, rock garden, shrubbery or wild garden. They can be grown on the patio of a small suburban terrace house or in the more majestic surroundings of the gardens of a stately home.

THE HOBBY PLANT

Few ornamental plants have so much to offer the gardener who wants a speciality. There is such a diversity of types that there will always be fresh ones to try. They respond well to care, and some wild kinds offer a real challenge. One can have flowers most of the year. There cannot be another plant that can be propagated in so many different and interesting ways. If you enjoy the friendly rivalry of shows, lilies can form part of your repertory. A stem cut for the house instantly creates a picture. And, as you read on, you will realise that there is a strong sub-plot to this book: it is aiming to persuade those who have not yet tried to start breeding their own new lilies. This must be the gardener's purest delight: to see unique new flowers opening.

PAST LORE AND ROMANCE

This is a practical book, so we do not dwell on the history of the lily which has been so closely associated with human culture from earliest times. First valued as a fodder plant, it quickly became associated with domestic and religious decor. (What a shame the potato got in the way of the lily as staple diet, I could cope with the scent and sight of fields full of lilies.)

There is something unearthly, almost magic, about our lilies. They create an atmosphere of their own, rather as orchids may, suggesting difficulty with their astonishing loveliness.

In company with *Lysimachia* is the lily 'Destiny', one of the de Graaff Mid-Century hybrids introduced in the 1950s that played a major role in the huge renaissance of interest in lilies (see p102)

Myths and mystique flourished, fed on accounts of wealthy garden owners of the beginning of the century with their wide acres, expanses of glass and armies of gardeners. Yet lilies are the great horticultural surprise – they are for everyone.

FALSE LILIES

Our use of words can be very imprecise: 'lily' has been used almost without any discrimination. Sometimes it seems almost synonymous with 'flowers'. When used with a descriptive, such as Guernsey Lily, it is more usual for the plant to be something bulbous or knobbly underground. But not always – the day lily is a straightforward, herbaceous plant although the flowers look a lot more like proper lilies than arum lilies, toad lilies and many others. The water lilies are clearly not lilies in the more restrictive sense. It would be tidiest to keep our word for members of the Lilium genus, but perhaps it may be forgiven for related genera in the Liliaceae family. The giant lilies, the Cardiocrinums from the Himalayan rain forests, China and Japan, were once botanically Lilium members, but other close relatives such as the fritillaries, nomocharises and notholirions have not attracted the popular 'lily' name. (A list of typical 'non-lilies' is given on p152.)

I have been growing lilies since childhood, over fifty years ago, find them ever more exciting and aim to live till a hundred just to enjoy them. The present chairman of the Royal Horticultural Society's Lily Group, Harris Howland, whom I thank sincerely for his introduction, most obviously was infected with the lily-bug as early. Perhaps you think I am over-enthusiastic in my wonder at these flowers. That can only mean you have not tried growing lilies. Once you begin there is no stopping. Start now and grow younger!

A selection of upward-facing Asiatic lilies (*left to right*): 'Cote d'Azur, pink; 'Grand Cru' (*rear*), gold and maroon; 'Alpenglow' (*foreground*), pale pink; 'Menton', old gold (pp101–4)

2

ECOLOGY AND LIFE CYCLE

A lily is a herbaceous plant. It is a monocotyledon, that is, the seed germinates with a single cotyledonous leaf, like onions or grass. It forms a bulb enabling it to husband its resources through the winter in situations that can look very hostile. Its primary means of propagation is by seed, but bulbs may divide, and some species have other unusual adaptations for vegetative reproduction.

The genus *Lilium* is a member of the family Liliaceae. In main it is a clearly defined genus but the boundaries with the related genera *Fritillaria* and *Nomocharis* are blurred, especially those with the last.

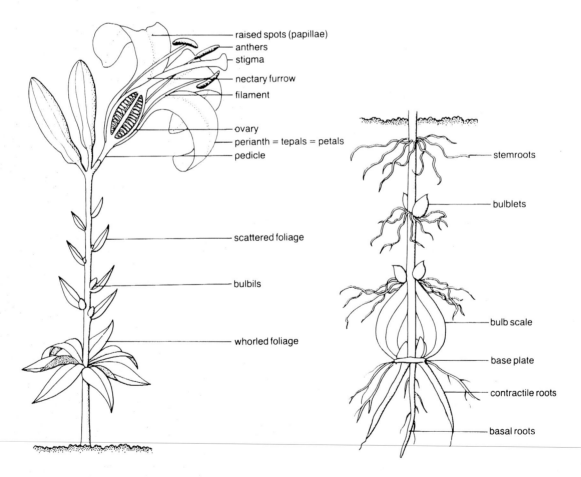

raised spots (papillae)
anthers
stigma
nectary furrow
filament

ovary
perianth = tepals = petals
pedicle

scattered foliage

bulbils

whorled foliage

stemroots

bulblets

bulb scale

base plate

contractile roots

basal roots

The parts of the lily

Lilies, unlike daffodils, have their ovaries enclosed by the perianth segments, an important distinction. The six perianth segments are composed of the three outer ones seen when in bud, these are botanically sepals; the three inner ones being petals. We shall follow the gardeners' lead and call them all petals. The three inner ones have more or less well defined nectary channels or furrows leading down the centre of the petal to the base where insects will find the nectar. A change of colour towards the centre of the flower and/or spotting is usual and is presumably an aid to insects' aerial navigation.

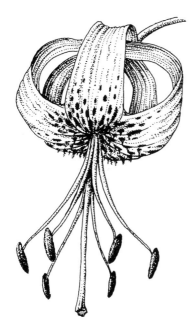

L. henryi, showing the flower parts

An unusual and distinctive feature in many lilies is the series of raised points on the inner surfaces of the petals. These fleshy points can be very freely produced, as in *L. henryi* and *L. speciosum* and are not undecorative. They are officially *papillae* (from the latin *papilla*, a teat).

The flowers usually face downwards, less often upwards, and the trumpet lilies are more or less horizontal. These flowers usually open in periods with little or no rainfall to offer their pollen. Some species have adaptions to protect pollen from rain. The role of the flower stalks, the pedicles, is an important feature for presentation of the flowers to the important insect visitors; horticulturally huge differences in floral appearance are governed by the length of pedicles, their shape and angles as well as their complexity can be observed. Pedicles can be almost any angle from vertical to the horizontal, and these are often curved towards their ends to give the requisite flower pose. Whilst pedicles may arise from one point to give an umbel, they may simply arise from the stem to produce a raceme. The pedicles are usually simple, carrying one flower, but some species such as *L. speciosum* and many hybrids divide to carry two blooms, and in very large heads even three.

Flower stalks, pedicles, can be of more or less uniform length resulting in an even umbel as in *L. bulbiferum* types or a narrow cylinder as in the tall spikes of *L. martagon*. On the other hand many Asiatic species vary the length of pedicles so that a spike forms a pyramid of bloom with the lower flowers being held much more widely from the stem than the upper younger ones. I welcome diversity in the genus but it is the pyramidal heads that are the most graceful.

LILIES IN THE WILD

Wild lilies belong to the northern hemisphere. In India they approach the equator, to the north they grow in Korea, Japan and Siberia. The genus is well represented in Asia, Europe and North America.

It is fitting that such a showy plant should have a dynamic lifestyle. Left to their own devices in the wild, many species form large populations and look almost incredibly wonderful in bloom – Ernest Wilson's descriptions of finding *L. regale* in flower in a precipitous mountain valley comes to mind. In the Caucasus ranges, hillsides can be turned yellow by masses of *L. monadelphum* (*szovitsianum*). In the past, North American lilies coloured valleys in

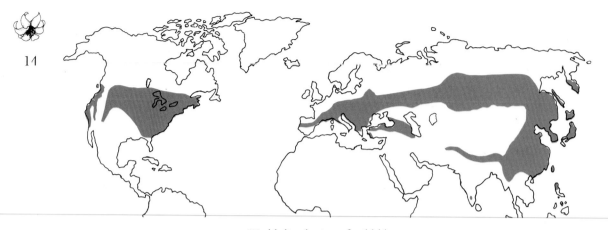

World distribution of wild lilies

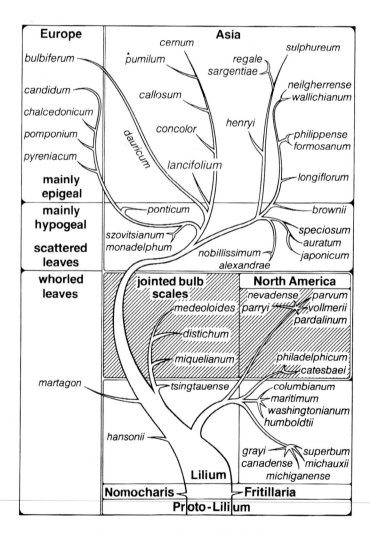

The suggested evolution of the lily family

California and Oregon. Such sights are much rarer nowadays as agriculture and building have eliminated populations. The lily's obvious beauty has proved a mixed blessing: collectors, both commercial and amateur, have grubbed up bulbs and destroyed many sites. What humans have left, goats and other animals may have devoured.

To survive, wild lilies have been driven to 'last resort' sites, banksides and scrubland. In fact such places can be ideal for many species. The bulbs love the perfect drainage of sloping ground and often rely on scrubby neighbours for root shade and the support of their flowering stems. Each species has its own preferred home. *L. arboricola* is the most extreme specialist – it grows in the debris collected in the nooks of tree branches in the forests of parts of northern Burma. In contrast, the widely known *L. martagon* can be found in a variety of sites from sea level to around 2000m (7000ft), on soils with varying pH values, some definitely alkaline.

Gardeners propagate bulbs vegetatively and tend to overlook the fact that in nature bulbs rely almost exclusively on seed for increase and to widen their distribution. The lily is ideally adapted to this task. A single pod may produce a hundred or more seeds, flat discs that can be whisked by the breeze to potential new sites.

STRUCTURE OF THE LILY

BULBS

Bulbs vary in form and size. Some species such as *L. concolor* and *L. pumilum* have bulbs little larger than marbles. Others, like some of the trumpet kinds, can be as large as a substantial artichoke. Unlike in daffodils and tulips, a lily bulb scale does not completely enclose the central growing point, although some have wide scales that may reach halfway round or even further. The bulbs of *L. concolor* consist of a few wrapped-round scales, while as a contrast those of *L. monadelphum* have a huge number of very narrow, upright scales making a large, loose – almost mop-like – bulb. While these are

clearly arranged around a central growing point, fixed on a round basal plate to form a concentric design, the North American *L. pardalinum* makes a spreading bulb with a wide basal plate having several growing points, and over the years is able to construct a wide, mat-like structure.

The more usual round, concentric bulbs may divide after flowering to form two or more new ones to the side of the base of the old flowering stem. The connecting tissue will perish relatively quickly. Rhizomatous bulbs can retain connecting tissue between growing points for a considerable time.

Bulb types are normally classified as below:

Concentric: This is by far the most usual form and normal orthodoxy is represented by the untold numbers of Asiatic and trumpet kinds sold each season in garden centres. A rounded, pyramidal basal plate is enclosed by a series of scales, more or less overlapping, according to their size and number. The flowering stem

The normal bulb form, erect concentric, seen for example in *L. henryi* and most Asiatic hybrids. The cross-section shows the flower stem base and new bulb forming beside it

16

emerges from the centre with the following season's stem, or stems, these being initiated in cells to the side of the base of the current stem.

Stoloniferous: These bulbs behave in the same manner as the concentric form but have the enterprise to send out one or more stolons from close to the base. These fleshy stems vary in length according to the identity of the bulb, its clone, its vigour and the soil conditions. The stolons have small, scattered scales but end with a perfect new bulb that can be a very useful size by the end of the growing season, when the connecting tissue begins to waste away. The attractive species *L. canadense* is the leading proponent of this lifestyle.

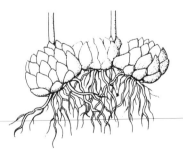

Stoloniferous bulb,
as in *L. canadense*

Rhizomatous: This bulb form is restricted to a few North American types, notably *L. pardalinum* and its hybrids. A wide basal plate is formed with upward-pointing scales in what appears at first sight to be a random arrangement, but branching of the rootstock is discernible and growing points can be identified,

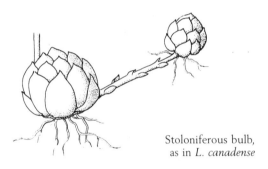

Rhizomatous bulb, as in *L. pardalinum giganteum*

Although one of the more rarely cultivated Asiatic species, *L. leitchlinii*, is well worth growing (p.83)

particularly towards the outer limits of an established plant. Scales of these types are very brittle and are often of waisted form, so that a scale may break off wholly, at the waist as a half, or as two halves (these can be used for propagation, see p.57). The somewhat scattered pattern of scales tends to become more concentrated at the growing points, in a half-hearted approach towards the concentric fashion. Bulbs of this type lifted for propagation need delicate handling, or you will be left with a thousand and one fractured scales. A strong, sharp knife can be used surgically to detach growing points with back-up sections of branching basal plate and scales.

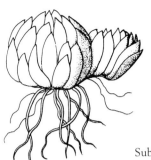

Sub-rhizomatous bulb,
as in *L. humboldtii*

Sub-rhizomatous: A few North American species are slightly schizophrenic in growth behaviour, for the most part acting out the respectable concentric role but suddenly producing energetic sideways growth, a veering towards rhizomatous activity. After a season, such an extension can be severed and grown as a separate individual. Such kinds are rare, *L. humboldtii* being one example.

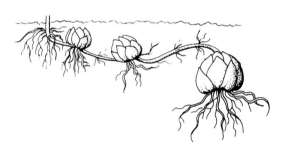

Stoloniform bulb, erect bulb with stoloniferous stem, as in *L. duchartrei*

Stoloniferous-stemmed: A couple of Asian species, while having bulbs that look ordinary concentric ones, behave idiosyncratically. A bulb planted in one spot can confound the gardener by having its stem emerging a considerable distance away, perhaps 30–60cm (1–2ft) adrift. Along the nomadic portion of the stem, between bulb and above-ground growth, one, two or three new bulbs may be formed. You need to work with caution when lifting all lilies – with these a little clairvoyance is also helpful! *L. duchartrei* is the main prankster, but

L. wardii has some deviant tendencies too. On occasion other species and hybrids not closely related will make attempts to ape the same behaviour.

17

ROOTS AND STEMS

New root activity is at its most intense in the early autumn after flowering and as autumnal rain falls. Most bulbs produce thick, fleshy roots that delve deeply, auger-wise, into the soil and these have the ability to pull the bulb down by contracting in a concertina manner. Bulbils that drop to the ground from the stem behave in the same way. Other busy, more fibrous roots also emerge as a ring around the basal plate. In addition, many lilies produce roots from the stem between the bulb and the soil surface. They may be scattered but are often massed as rings, and augment the feeding work of the basal roots as well as anchoring the stem securely. Flowering plants of *L. auratum* have been known to be supported entirely by stem roots, their bulbs having rotted away.

The stems of most lilies are upright and very strong, but some species have wiry, arching ones. Height may vary from a few centimetres (inches) to over 2m (6ft). Some of the little species have slender, wiry stems; those of the large ones can be like substantial bamboos. They need to be strong: some have to bear a burden of several dozen flowers. Colour can be any shade from pale green to almost jet black.

LEAVES

The cotyledon leaves of seedlings are narrow straps, with other seedling leaves narrowly spear shaped. The adult foliage of *L. lancifolium* is dark, very narrowly elliptical and crowded on the stem from bottom to top; that of *L. regale* is similar but paler and even narrower. The smaller leaves of *L. pumilum* are held rather upright or almost clasped to the stem. Others, such as *L. henryi* have fewer, larger and wider leaves. These are virtually stemless, but those of *L. speciosum* are very distinct with considerable stems (petioles) holding out broadly ovate leaves at acute angles from the main stems.

18

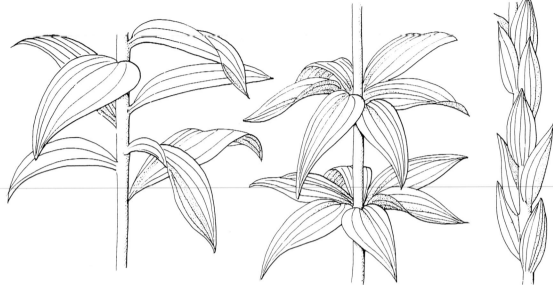

(*left*) Scattered foliage, as in *L. monadelphum*; (*centre*) whorled foliage, as in *L. martagon*; (*right*) scattered foliage close to the stem, as in *L. pumilum*

Alternate arrangement of *L. carniolicum* leaves, which sometimes become more scattered

The distribution of lily leaves can be an apparent scatter up the stem, may follow a spiral arrangement, can be alternate or can be restricted to a number of whorls, like the spokes of a wheel, with the intermediate stem devoid of foliage. A 2m (6ft) stem of *L. martagon*, for example, may have only three whorls, each with a dozen to seventeen or more leaves, and with three or four small, scattered leaves between the top whorl and the flowers.

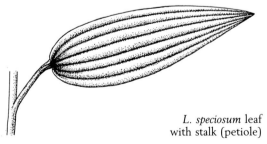

L. speciosum leaf with stalk (petiole)

Only few species retain their leaves through the winter. The flower stem of *L. candidum*, the Madonna lily, dies down normally, but the bulb produces a rosette of leaves to mark its site through the winter.

Whorled leaf arrangement of *L. superbum*, narrower than *L. pardalinum giganteum* or *L. martagon*

FLOWERS

It is the variation of form, size, colour and flower habit of lilies that can captivate gardeners. A few small species may have only one or two blooms but many have several dozen, sometimes over a hundred blooms, ranging in pose from an upright chalice through every degree to fully pendant.

The flower shape can be a slightly incurved cup, a rare form demonstrated by *L. mackliniae*. More common is a goblet shape, as in *L. parryi* or *L. dauricum*. Trumpet shapes are typical for *L. regale* and a group of Asian species, with some flared open and others, such as *L. longiflorum*, open at the mouth but with a long

L. longiflorum, the Easter lily, is often sold as a cut flower. A tender species it is naturalised in warmer climates such as those of South Africa and Australia (p.91)

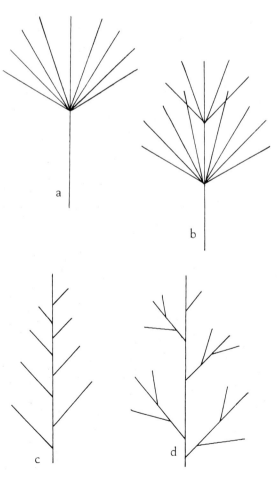

The arrangement of flowers: a) umbel; b) composite umbel; c) raceme; d) composite raceme

tube around the ovary. Many lilies are bowl-shaped, with petals spreading outwards and curving back; *L. martagon* is the most extreme example, with each petal curling tightly back to form cylinders, suggesting its common name, 'turk's cap'.

The flower colour may be uniform, but usually the main colour is augmented by others, especially in the centre. The exterior colour of the three outer 'petals' forming the bud may be partially or totally different, as for example in the white *L. regale*, with its buds painted a deep maroon. Inner surfaces may be spotted, splashed or lined with other colours or may be plain. Whites, creams, yellows, oranges and reds are comprehensively represented; greens, pinks,

mauves and maroon or purple shades also occur. Petals vary in width and surface: some are polished smooth, but many have ridges leading to the centre-base nectary, and a large number have raised points (papillae). The permutation of colours, sizes, forms and habits in both species and hybrids is incalculable.

The anthers and pollen are variously coloured and often play an important decorative role. The stigma can be a substantial three-lobed knob, as in the trumpet species, or a quite modest affair, as in many Asiatic lilies. The filaments holding the anthers are normally not very heavily coloured, but they may be suffused with shades of green, yellow or purple pink. Normally quite independent of each other, the filaments may be fused at the base around the ovary, as in forms of *L. monadelphum*.

SEEDPODS AND SEED

As petals fall and seed begins to develop, the seedpods are brought up to be held erect. Occasionally almost globular, they most often approach the shape of Grecian urns, very decorative in their own right. Pods split open to show three chambers, each with two rows of seeds neatly piled one upon another.

A ripe seed is a flat disc. Some lilies have notably heavier seeds, a feature helping identification. The vital centre of the seed containing the embryo and live cells is surrounded by a fringe of wasted tissue, a wing that helps the released seed to float away. There can be over a hundred viable seed in a pod. True seeds are formed when egg cells are fertilised by the male gametes that are brought down by the growing pollen initially adhering to the stigma. Unfertilised ovules are left as chaff – thin wafer tissue of similar disc outline. The radical of a viable seed can be seen clearly if it is held against the light, distinguishing it from the worthless, lighter, flaky chaff.

LIFE CYCLE

Seed pods burst open, and seed falls to the ground where, in contact with soil and moisture, it may germinate in one of four ways. It

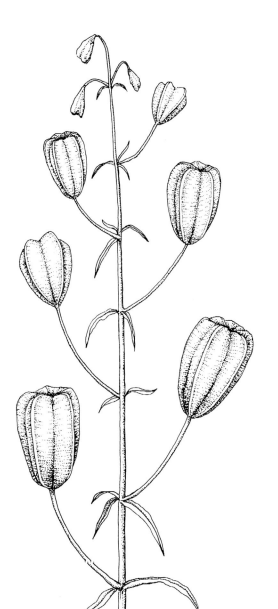

L. martagon seed pods.
Each may contain over 100 seeds

(*left*) Discovered in a remote valley in China in 1903, *L. regale* soon proved the most popular and easy species in European and American gardens (p90)

can start to grow quickly (immediate) or after a rest period (delayed). These two types of seed may both start germinating either above ground (epigeal) or below ground (hypogeal). Of the possible four methods the most frequent is epigeal immediate germination – most Asiatic hybrids and trumpet lilies germinate this way. Evolutionarily, hypogeal delayed germination is thought to be the most primitive method and occurs in the American species, the martagon group and the Orientals such as *L. auratum* and *L. speciosum*. Some kinds perform in two of these ways, possibly a 'belt and braces' approach to the vagaries of nature.

Above-ground germination (epigeal): The seed absorbs water, and the radical first root emer-

ges, extending downwards. A strap-like green leaf, the cotyledon, grows above ground, probably with the seedcase hung at the end like a flag. The radical first root plunges downwards and the growing point swells to begin the making of the bulb. As the little bulb begins to grow, the first true leaf pushes upwards from the bulb, this one being spear-shaped not a strap like the cotyledon. Other leaves follow as the bulb grows and gathers strength.

Under-ground germination (hypogeal): The growing point of the seed turns immediately downwards and begins to form a small bulb. This can be developing and forming a root system for some while before indicating anything above the soil surface. The small bulb

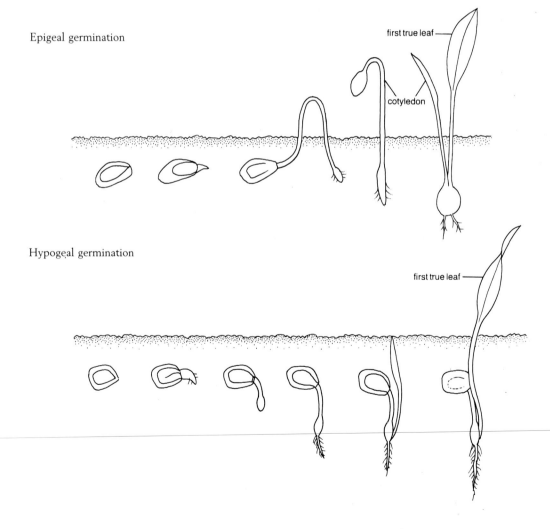

Epigeal germination

first true leaf

cotyledon

Hypogeal germination

first true leaf

then produces the first true leaf above ground, no cotyledon ever being in sight. In the soil the used seed case perishes.

Grown under controlled conditions, lilies can develop quickly from this early, tiny bulb, especially the Orientals, Asiatics, and trumpets. A succession of leaves appears till there is a cluster looking like a miniature aspidistra for a doll's house. Trumpet lilies, such as *L. long-iflorum* and *L. philippinense* grow bulbs so quickly that seeds sown in early spring will result in flower stems at the end of the summer! *L. regale* may produce stems, each with a bloom or so, the year following sowing. Similarly, I expect a significant proportion of my Asiatic hybrids sown one year to produce at least one bloom the next.

The bulbs expand by forming swollen scales around their potential growing points – the scales being modified leaves or the swollen bases of leaves. The time taken for a bulb to grow to flowering size varies considerably; *L. martagon* and *L. monadelphum* may take five or more years from seed. The initial basal leaves of seedlings are replaced by stems with leaves during the following seasons as the bulb gains strength. The stems will be without flowers until the lily has reached its mature size.

Basal and stems roots collect nutrients and send them for processing to the leaves which transpire any surplus water. The roots work most efficiently through the growing months, from the end of winter till after flowering time. The greatest number of fresh roots comes as a fresh flush after flowering, when the bulbs are in their seeding time. The plant establishes an invigorated rootstock before the onset of winter, which is especially strong in open, well-drained, gritty soil with a high humus content.

Leaves and stems begin to fail after flowering and, by the time seed is ripe, are likely to have died. For the winter most species have no foliage, and their stems are like dead sticks. Good drainage is important through these months; stagnant water is likely to cause disaffection and possible rotting, although I can well remember clumps of *L. pardalinum* flourishing in very heavy, wet clay!

VEGETATIVE REPRODUCTION METHODS

In several species and many hybrids, the section of the dead flowering stem below ground forms a number of small bulbs which by the end of the season are ready to start an independent life. A few species, such as the popular tiger lily, *L. lancifolium, L. bulbiferum*, the rare yellow trumpet *L. sulphureum* and *L. sargentiae*, produce a series of bulbils in the leaf axils. These ripen and fall to the ground where they root and grow into fresh plants. Usually bulbils fall before the parent plant's foliage shows any obvious sign of senescence. Some can be harvested by midsummer, potted up and grown to flowering size by the following summer. Admittedly they will have only one or two flowers per stem, but it still makes the idea of the lily as a difficult plant seem nonsense.

We can also propagate lilies by other means. Bulb scales, broken off and kept moist and protected from fungus attack, produce one or more small bulbils after a few weeks and these can be quickly grown on. Selected tissue can be induced to proliferate under laboratory conditions and then persuaded to form growing points and a huge number of cloned, identical plants. A number of species and a good proportion of Asiatic hybrids can be encouraged to form bulbils in their leaf-axils like the tiger lily. Such regeneration is achieved by growing bulbs strongly and cutting off the flowerheads well before they begin to show colour, to divert energy into bulbil formation (see p57).

3

LILIES IN THE GARDEN

THE RANGE

Every garden can benefit from growing lilies, from the tiny patio with potted bulbs to stately homes where some may grow naturalised in parkland and others set borders alight for the pleasure of the owners and visitors. The choice is so wide that there is no need for forcing or delaying tactics to have flowers on show from late spring until the frosts of late autumn. Some are small enough for the rock garden, others are perfectly suited to woodland or semi-woodland. Huge numbers of cultivars compete for space in borders, beds and shrubberies. There are colours to lead or augment almost every possible colour scheme, extrovert reds and oranges, charming pinks and mauves, delicate creams and whites.

EASY 'NATURALISERS'

All kinds of bulbs planted and established to grow in natural conditions without periodic lifting look 'right'. Snowdrops, winter aconites, daffodils, anemones and bluebells look their best when growing as if they owned the site. And there are lilies well disposed to such a lifestyle. In Britain, *L. martagon* and *L. pyrenaicum* have escaped over the garden wall and established themselves in a number of places alongside the native flora. At different times in parts of the southern hemisphere, especially in Australia and South Africa, one or two of the trumpet species have 'gone walkabout', led by *L. longiflorum*.

In climates like that of Britain, *L. martagon* and *L. pyrenaicum* are surefire naturalising kinds, although they may take a year to settle down. *L. hansonii* and *L. pardalinum*, together with its forms/hybrids, are just as reliable, and to this short list we may add *L. henryi*, which has been known to survive for decades in a non-flowering state when over-grown by scrub, then blooming again once the scrub was cleared. The site for this species and *L. hansonii* would be somewhere with light shade, not for health but for cosmetic reasons – in full sun the flower colour tends to bleach quickly.

The Madonna lily (*L. candidum*) still flourishes in cottage gardens. Perhaps it does well in isolation where it is unlikely to share the viruses of other lilies, and it may also benefit from a regime of benign neglect. A cottage just a hundred metres (yards) from our last garden had me more than a little envious with crowded heads of flowers, a couple of metres (six feet) of shining health.

Another easy naturaliser is the tiger lily, *L. lancifolium* (*L. tigrinum*). While the Madonna lily shows virus-induced distress quickly, with foliage becoming palely mottled and dying early, together with flower numbers falling and buds and flowers becoming distorted, species such as *L. lancifolium* can become infected without this initially appearing to affect growth and performance. The dark green foliage can almost mask the somewhat paler stripes that are virus symptoms, but while the plants may display an 'I'm-alright-Jack' attitude, they are a source of infection, carried by insect vectors such as aphids. Such sap-sucking, mini-vampire insects always pass some matter into the plants from which they are feeding, and if they have previously been dining on an infected plant the debilitating disease can be injected into their

Sturdy Asiatic 'Medaillon' surrounded by achillea, ivy and shrubs

new hosts, with disastrous effects. If you grow *L. lancifolium* or *L. candidum*, station them as far as possible away from any other lilies.

IN THE BORDER

Garden beds and borders are dynamic things. Books with border designs can give one the mistaken impression that all comes together at one time and the character of the border is predetermined when it is planted up. The fact of the matter is that the same border changes from day to day and from season to season. It is easy to be a little cynical when viewing some border designs calculated to give special colour effects. Despite the fact that it looks good on paper, like all plans made by mice and men not everything necessarily goes according to plan. All too often one plant will bloom earlier than it should and perhaps, others bloom later. Suggestions offered here are possible associations that may well blossom at the same time as the lilies but can also act as foliage foils, perhaps an even more important matter.

A single lily growing in the border is attractive but I rejoice when it has made proper increase and there are three or more stems to appreciate. Like so many plants and flowers, the increase in the effectiveness and beauty of a group seems to be based on some formula whose precise terms are not fathomable. Certainly three stems look more than three times as effective as one, and five stems become hugely more than five times as splendid.

The best lily cultivars to grow between herbaceous plants in beds or borders are the Asiatic kinds. They are easy to grow, tolerant of a range of soils, sturdy and showy. Ranging in height from 75cm (30in) to 1.8m (6ft), the colour choice of these hybrids is wide, and although the upward-facing kinds are by far the most numerous, there are plenty of outward-facing and pendant types from which to choose.

Some simple arrangements can work well. Groups of pale-flowered Asiatics are often accompanied very effectively by blue or mauve flowers. Sky-blue cornflowers can give lilies such as white 'Apollo', cream 'Mont Blanc' or pale yellow 'Medaillon' a very definite extra lift. Hardy geraniums are equally useful, their ground-covering foliage masses looking well as they shade the bases of the lilies and produce flowers of just the right cool contrast from late spring to late summer. 'Johnson's Blue' is a particularly good choice but the vivid magenta of *G. macrorrhizum* can be even more telling. More gentle patterns are achieved where plants of similar colours or hues are combined. For example, the soft yellow of 'Medaillon' looks well in early summer bloom with candytuft, achillea, lavender and the foliage of variegated *Deutzia* x *elegantissima*. There is little need of any shelter or support for this sturdy lily but, if there had been, then lavender and deutzia are useful shrubs to provide it.

Depending on what is planted, the early spring is likely to be dominated by bulbous flowers although these will not be lilies. Your garden will be filled with favourites, such as daffodils and is, perhaps, mainly yellow but this then may give way to the reds of tulips. Early doronicums with their yellow daisy flowers are succeeded by coloured pyrethrums before the early summer. As the new season beckons, the failing foliage of clumps of daffodils and tulips can be removed. A scattering of seed of annuals such as love-in-the-mist or candytuft around these clumps means any gaps are soon closed. Then suddenly, among this burgeoning spring growth, the lilies spike through the ground. If spikes appear early the value of the surrounding vegetation can be judged – it will help provide some frost protection.

Early summer is certainly one of the most exciting times in the garden. Just about everything seems to be in full growth and masses of plants are bursting in colourful bloom. All this with the days reaching their greatest length and the sun warm on one's back. Some of the species lilies are quick to get into floral action. *L. pyreniacum* is often fully out in late spring, in cooler spots it may be early summer. It is normally the first species to open outside, a

One of the graceful *L. lankongense* hybrids making an elegant addition to a bed of geraniums, roses and foliage plants

hardy customer, and will even manage in a hedge bottom or on the edge of a copse. It is nice to have lilies that manage themselves as this and the martagons will.

Another splendid species for early summer is *L. szovitsianum*, which can also be left to go its own way. With its large pendant soft yellow flowers with wide petals reaching out and curling back, it looks splendid naturalised in light grass or thin woodland edges and is aristocratic and altogether pleasing. If we can afford the time-scale, the fallen seed may germinate where it falls and begin the five or six

year stretch to fresh flowering bulbs. Other gardeners may have different ideas and colourful associates can be achieved with a little work. The border of *L. szovitsianum* with the bright company of candelabra primulas and meconopsis takes some care. *Primula beesiana*, *P. japonica* and *P. florindae* flourish in soil that is more moist than that preferred by the lily. It can use plenty of moisture while it is growing,

but will not want stagnant water around its bulbs. It is happiest in a warm gritty soil perhaps with a bias towards lime.

LIME HATERS AND EVERGREENS

Lime in the soil is likely to influence choice of neighbours for lilies. The Asiatics, most trumpet hybrids and European species can cope with some lime but the Orientals such as 'Star Gazer' cannot. Rhododendrons, camellias and heathers thrive in acid soils and these shrubs can make good companions for lime-hating lilies. Surrounding rhododendrons certainly give shelter and heathers and their low-growing relatives may be persuaded to give the lilies shade over their lower parts. All are dark evergreen bushes and serve to highlight almost all lily colours – the paler shades most obviously. Fiercer oranges and reds can also look very dramatic although some may find 'Enchantment' a little too strong for association with camellias and rhododendrons. By the time the lily flowers appear these shrubs will have passed their flowering period so there will be no conflict of extrovert colouring.

Whites, creams and pale yellows are a safe bet with evergreens and they look very effective. White trumpet kinds are particularly splendid with such a rich background. Among the stronger yellows a bold group of Asiatics, such as upward-facing 'Connecticut King', 'Sun Ray', or 'Luxor' with its richer-coloured throat, should not raise any objections. A note of refinement or less boisterous beauty can be introduced by using some of the pendant Asiatics, a suitable choice being bulbs of Citronella strain with lots of hanging bright yellow turk's-cap flowers.

Rock beds or special raised beds can provide the opportunity for arranging soil pH levels to suit particular lilies. In gardens with distinctly limy soils it will certainly be easier to restrict choice to those kinds tolerant of lime (see list on p45), although the roots of even the lime-tolerant and lime-loving types like to explore rich seams of leaf mould and such matter. If you live with very limy soils you can still enjoy the lime-haters by growing in containers (see p48).

LILIES WITH PERENNIALS

Gracefulness is the hallmark of *L. lankongense* hybrids and the species itself. Beautifully-formed flowers with swept back petals hang daintily and widely-spread in heads that are pyramidal in form. The colours are usually pinks and pastel shades, all very alluring and lasting well through mid- and late summer. These pale colours can look very attractive among darker flowers or can complement similar shades, such as yellow or cream roses. The elegant flower spikes and narrow leaves provide additional interest.

There is a series of named *L. lankongense* hybrids in cultivation together with some unnamed ones. Our illustration shows a typical hybrid, an unnamed seedling similar to but rather paler than 'Karen North' growing with geraniums, roses and a mix of herbaceous plants. In open humus-rich soils these *L. lankongense* hybrids can multiply fast, but they are probably best lifted every two or three years and given extra healthy well-rotted compost or leaf mould. Top dressing with peat or leaf mould certainly pays good dividends. These lilies, when successful, are outstanding but in less friendly soils they can peter out rather quickly.

Pink lilies can be very pleasing in the summer garden, and certainly take a leading role in the popular colour theme of lilacs, mauves and blues with ever-present greens. Although this may seem a very safe range of colours it is also very telling and charming in the summer months. Adding a touch of pink produces a highlight, and in a successful scheme you can afford to stray a little, making space for the mustard-yellow from *Achillea* 'Moonshine' or

An unusual early summer combination of candelabra primulas and meconopsis with *L. szovitsianum*

the frothy, similarly-coloured *Alchemilla mollis* as a complete contrast. A lot of yellow especially brassy golds would defeat the cool but pleasing medley of blue-mauve colours, but a hint of lemon or mustard gives just enough extra bite to enliven the whole picture. Of course these are matters of scale. An old-fashioned herbaceous border a hundred yards long can cope with extra flashes of contrasting colour without ruining an overall muted colour scheme and in this case groups of pink and white lilies might be punctuated by occasional lemon, gold or even orange ones.

'Cote d'Azur' is a sturdy, low upward-facing full pink Asiatic that might play a part close to the front of a bed or border and will look well associated with foliage plants such as ferns, grasses and *Alchemilla mollis*. Quite different in character is 'Tinkerbell' a pretty plant that looks like the rather tricky species, *L. cernuum*, with lavender-pink recurved flowers hanging in a wide pyramid form. It has thin grassy foliage similar to that of *L. cernuum* and has its tolerance of limy soils. While its flowering stems can be 90cm–1.20m (3–4ft) its daintiness makes light of the stature. The rather larger-flowered 'Ariadne', a *L. lankongense* hybrid, is bolder and its recurved, nodding flowers are a dusty-rose with some buff in the centre and marbelled, deep spotting. It opens a week or two later than 'Tinkerbell' which should be starting its display at the very beginning of early summer.

By midsummer and into late summer the trumpet lilies are opening and they bring their own ambience to the garden being fairly heavyweight performers. Trumpets are what most gardeners regard as 'real lilies' and, although they are most often thought of as white, there are plenty of other colours to choose from, including pink. Pink Perfection lilies are a closely-similar series of clones, more or less all are in rich pink colours, the richest

being rather unglamorously described as 'deep beetroot'. They certainly can be very impressive with stems often over 2m (6ft) and carrying one-, two- or even three-dozen large, trumpet blooms. Not only do they have visual appeal but their perfume will load the surrounding air. Even small bulbs with more modest stems make a big impact and are perhaps easier to fit into garden schemes. Try using other plants in shades of pink with greys and whites for an eyecatching but harmonious display.

These taller trumpet lilies are marvellous between shrubs. Pink Perfection will rear up besides cut-leaved elders, 'Royal Gold' is effectively backed by ceanothus hybrids and flanked by cultivars of *Hamamelis* and *Deutzia*. *L. regale* in standard form, and in its pure white manifestation *L. r. album*, stands tall when surrounded by berberis, escallonia, viburnum and some small forms of lilacs.

Our *L. regale* bulbs tend to stay put for three or four years and then get lifted and moved to some new site, more often because surrounding shrubs are encroaching too formidably over lily territory than because the lilies demand moving. However, it gives us a chance to divide crowded bulbs and give them a fresh start. You may garden differently, with us every plant fights for its place, nature almost in-the-raw working out survival of the fittest.

LILIES WITH ROSES AND OTHER SHRUBS

One of the most traditional of associations for *L. regale* is with roses. It may be old-hat and owing more than a little to nostalgia, but some of the old ideas are proven and cannot get overworked – they always look fresh. Think of *L. regale* with lavender at the front and honeysuckle, climbing up with clematis, through the rambling roses behind. There is something undeniably friendly about a classic combination such as the 1931 pink rose 'The Fairy', a polyantha still holding its own against the tide of floribundas, with *L. regale*. Its colour with its

The strong pink of Pink Perfection strain flowers is set off by the tall Campanula latifolia alba and a soft pink achillea

A traditional association of lilies and roses, this time with *L. regale* and the polyantha rose 'The Fairy' but also with an effective foreground including poppies, polyganums, campanulas and pinks

daintiness and glossy light green foliage goes so well with the lily.

Some shrubs are useful adjuncts to lily culture. Lavender is one being neither too large nor too robust. It provides support and shelter for many lilies, and lavender flowers and foliage are a complement to the lilies' colours and character. Another such useful auxiliary shrub is *Brachyglottis* (syn. *Senecio*) 'Sunshine'. Whatever the name, the shrub is a real splendid yeoman type with silvery twelve-month foliage and a summer bonus of drifts of golden daisies. It grows on all soils provided there is some drainage and sunshine; it can make a fine cover over patches of really desperately poor soil.

Like lavender the foliage colour of *Brachy-*

glottis is a fine foil to all lily colours. Silver and white, silver and gold, silver and pink, or silver and orange; each gains from the juxtaposition.

LILIES IN POTS

Surrealists make a big thing of juxtaposition. It is not my present thesis to argue that the incongruous has merit, but surprise and drama has its place in the garden as in other fields of endeavour. A piece of sculpture or artifact or an outstanding plant at some point in the garden can focus attention not only on the article itself but the surrounding part of the garden We can learn from the surrealists.

Lilies can be the leading players in dramatic

Lilies are wonderful container plants, here one of the Oriental hybrids, 'Casa Blanca', does noble duty on the patio

34

garden scenes. They may accomplish their act in beds or borders, dominating the stage, or they can be brought inside as cut flowers to transform a room by sight and scent. A most pleasing statement can be made by growing them in containers, brought to such focal points as the patio or range of steps. Some actors may involve themselves in various schemes to claim attention, the lilies have no need. They stand still and command the eyes of all. It only needs a few lilies to make the point, really a very restrained performance with nothing forced or 'over the top'. In the example on p33, two or three bulbs of Oriental 'Casa Blanca' grow in an earthenware container on a patio at the top of some steps. The scene, is given an extra dimension by the few lilies – height, colour, elegance. This is the magic of lilies. They transform their surroundings as few other flowering plants could begin to do.

Most kinds of lily are splendid in pots, much easier to grow than even daffodils, tulips or most commonly-used bulbs.   In some of the larger parks and gardens open to the public it is becoming a popular ploy to grow lilies in pots in the nursery areas and to introduce them into border schemes just when the flower buds are showing colour. Either the potful is carefully disengaged from its pot and the group planted up with the minimum of root disturbance, or the pots and lilies are simply sunk together into their designated blooming quarters. This is a well-established practice in North America where garden centres cater for the instant gardener with well-grown lilies in a selection of suitable types. The idea is worth copying in a small garden which needs to look its best at all times.

The Asiatics, the Trumpets and the Orientals are outstanding in pots. If you have limy soil then your best alternative with Orientals is to grow them in pots. There are sturdy dwarf Asiatics and Orientals especially bred for pot culture. The Pixie series of Asiatics, such as 'Golden Pixie' illustrated earlier in this chapter, are examples that are fully grown at around 30cm (12in). One of the commonest is 'Orange Pixie', but they are sold as mixed colours or named colour clones including Crimson, Orange, Buff, Butter, Peach, and 'Dawn Pixie'. Such kinds can be planted up and left to grow on in a cool greenhouse, a frame or in the open and then wheeled onto the patio as the flower buds fatten and are nearly ready to break. When the flowers have passed another lot of a slightly later cultivar, or a similar kind later planted, it can come top of the queue and do its turn. In this way it is easy to arrange a succession of lilies from the end of spring right through until late summer, starting with early Asiatics, moving through the popular trumpets and then to the Orientals, followed finally by *L. speciosum* and later trumpets such as *L. longiflorum*, *L. philippinense* and *L. formosanum* from freshly raised bulbs. The sturdier Asiatics will be the easiest to manage, and there are ranges of short-stemmed kinds particularly useful for patios, service and public utility areas.

Lilies will mix with almost any other containerised plants and can have smaller plants with them in their containers, perhaps trailing ones that will break the severe lines of the pot.

My own preference is for earthenware containers; plastic is utilitarian and fine for growing but looks less pleasing on display. Size depends on the type of lilies to be grown. You need substantial ones for the tall-growing trumpet lilies such as Pink Perfection, 'African Queen' or 'Royal Gold'. Their height makes them vulnerable to wind, a gust can cause havoc, and these impressive plants are perhaps more safely grown in half tubs, the weight of the compost should keep everything firmly anchored. Of course, the amount of feeding provided will ensure that the bulbs grow and increase well. I have seen containers of *L. regale* that have been grown for a decade in such a tub and although rather overcrowded at the end of this period all were healthy and flowering freely. The main chore to keep all well was the annual replacement of the top 10–15cm (4–6in) of compost.

DWARF PATIO LILIES

Asiatics such as 'Mont Blanc' or salmon-orange 'Harmony' are sturdy short-stemmed cultivars blooming at 60–75cm (24–30in). But there are even shorter-stemmed kinds, very useful for pots or for planting close to the front of any bed and for complementing taller border plants.

'Pixie' has a very pale cream flower with a greenish throat and white tips, the upward-facing heads open wide at perhaps 30cm (12in) high. There are a number of Pixie cultivars – orange and red ones being particularly popular. 'Golden Pixie' is a bright-coloured extrovert,

The dwarf 'Golden Pixie' is a compact Asiatic cultivar useful in the front of the border or in pots. Here it is happy in the border with *Eryngium giganteum* 'Miss Wilmott's Ghost' and hemerocallis

'Star Gazer' is the most widespread of all the Oriental lilies because of its tremendous success as a cut flower and pot plant, but here it looks magnificent in the border with fuchsia, anchusa and a host of other plants

which is easy to cultivate. Planting it with a more subtle but equally attention-grabbing plant, such as 'Miss Willmott's Ghost' (*Eryngium giganteum*), achieves a rather pleasing contrast of colour and flower type. The pretty thistle is biennial but produces huge quantities of seed so that it is no real hardship to hoe out the surplus seedlings leaving just sufficient to accompany next season's lilies.

There are now more than one series of dwarf trumpets being bred that will provide gardeners with very easily managed containerised trumpet lilies. One clone has for parents *L. longiflorum* and the world-beating 'Black Dragon'. While 'Black Dragon' may be 1.5–1.8m (5–6ft) high when settled, the new hybrid, 'Longidragon' has stems only 60–90cm (2–3ft) high but with glorious white trumpets with the traditional dark reverses of the parent. The American series, Alladin hybrids has a wide range of colours and was raised from the mating of the Easter lily, *L. longiflorum*, with various Asiatics. These would pass as large upward-

Joy' is pink with a crimson band down each petal and 'Mona Lisa', at 50–60cm (20–24in) a little taller, is pink and white. This last has made inroads into the European market and is most impressive with large outward-facing blooms that look splendid in pots and equally so in borders. The white and pink is highlighted with dark crimson spots in the centre of each petal. There is also a useful trio marketed as Little Rascals. These are 'Mr Sam', white and rich pink; 'Mr Rudd', white and gold; and 'Mr Ed', pure white. They grow to only around 30cm (12in) but have plenty of large outward-facing flowers.

ORIENTALS IN THE GARDEN

The main founder Oriental species, *L. auratum* and *L. speciosum*, are usually rather fleeting plants in all but a few gardens. The disappointment experienced by failure or only partial success with the species need not pass to the hybrid series. Most of those on the market are very, very much easier and more reliable. They do, however, like soil without lime and full of humus. Given these conditions few plants can be more awe-inspiring in the late summer and early autumn, the time of year that most of these come naturally into bloom.

The familiar 'Star Gazer' is often shunted into the garden after having being bought as a pot plant and enjoyed in blossom inside. With its upward-facing rich crimson flowers on stems 60–90cm (2–3ft) it is not difficult to associate with other border plants. One most effective combination is with silver-grey foliage. Consider a tight clump of *Anaphalis margaritacea* in front, preparing to cover itself with compact heads of small white everlasting flowers, and behind or to the side, perhaps *Brachyglottis* 'Sunshine', silver in foliage and golden in bloom. The popular dogwood, *Cornus alba* 'Elegantissima' with its bright variegated foliage makes a telling contrast of form and colour. However, Orientals are so glorious in bloom that care must be taken to avoid warring competitors. No dahlias and chrysanthemums!

facing Asiatics. They bloom in early and mid-summer with stems in the 60–90cm (2 3ft) range.

For decades commercial growers have been supplying florists with dwarf Orientals. Leading these is 'Star Gazer'. In the garden this cultivar will grow 60–90cm (2–3ft) high but pot grown ones are chemically treated to inhibit stature so that they can be marketed at little over 30cm (12in). Now, however, there is a range of proper genetic dwarfs. They are the result of a line of breeding that started with a *L. auratum* dwarf mutation many years ago. 'Little Girl' is a glowing soft pink with crimson spotting, 'Little

Complementary reds and rich green foliage also provide 'Star Gazer' with a suitable backdrop but perhaps the best answer is to rely heavily on ornamental grasses and ferns. They provide a cool restrained but pleasing accompaniment, quite different in colour, form and habit, yet somehow enhancing the atmosphere. Ferns especially bring with them the peace of eons before the first flowering plants arrived on the planet. Their intricate fronds exude a sense of stillness that complements the classy plant form of the Oriental lilies with sculptured leaves and extraordinary flowers each held magically into its own defined space. There are lots of ferns to choose from even if you restrict your choice to forms of the lady fern, *Athyrium filix-femina*, and the male fern, *Dryopteris filix-mas*. All wonderfully decorative plants and superb companions for lilies.

Some of the older Oriental cultivars take a lot of beating. One of the last to bloom is the appropriately named 'Journey's End', quite an extraordinary cultivar introduced in the late 1950s and still going strong. Many flowers are displayed in an elegant, semi-pendant poise, their rich crimson-pink colouring the whole wonderfully, and highlighted by the white filaments and rich chestnut stamens. In late summer and early autumn the 1.2–1.5m (4–5ft) stems can overreach rosemary, lavender, junipers or other neighbours and they delight with colour and scent. Hebes are usually in bloom at the same time, the purple-violet spikes complementing the lily's crimsons. Dutch growers market a splendid paler form also under the name 'Journey's End'.

You do not need huge numbers of these Orientals to make a crowd-stopping show in the garden border. 'Trance' is one of a series of free-flowering cultivars that can have a significant number of flowers on a stem. Its smiling warm pink shades are accentuated by the outward-facing disposition of the large blooms.

The Oriental 'Trance' looks very exotic in among such a fine mix of herbaceous foliage. It looks so distinct and exciting it could almost have come from another planet

40

By mid- to late summer many plants have finished flowering and their foliage provides a suitable backcloth for the appearance of this glamorous star.

Those that can afford to experiment with bulbs in the borders might like to try some of the unnamed kinds marketed under the label Devon Dawn, a strain bred by Derek Gardham and exceptionally strong in garden conditions. This strain was bred to resist the effects of virus which is the greatest danger to Orientals. It seems to be the most resistant yet achieved.

Of all Orientals, the most exceptional garden plant was achieved by the crossing of *L. speciosum rubrum* with *L. henryi*. The resulting hybrid, 'Black Beauty', has a constitution as hardy and resilient as a pig's snout. *L. henryi* must be given a great deal of credit for the constitution but the flowers favour *L. speciosum*. 'Black Beauty' makes very strong stems some 1.2–1.8m (4–6ft) high and as tough as bamboos. The strength is needed as a plant, when settled may produce over fifty blooms to a stem and some have been known to have in excess of a hundred and fifty! Such a plant needs a position where its display in late summer and early autumn will make its major impact and does not conflict with surrounding plants.

Bulbs of 'Black Beauty' are best planted in a humus-rich spot and left for two or three years to gain strength year by year and to build up into their huge displays. By this time the quantity of stems and blossom will be considerable and you have in effect a flowering shrub rather than a lily! It is best stationed between shrubs but without any near enough to encroach or stifle. The rich crimson of the flowers may look best displayed against a pale green background or one made light by a shrub's pale variegation.

LILIES FOR THE ROCK GARDEN

A rock garden or rock bed could be home for some of the smaller lily species. These might include *L. concolor* and *L. duchartrei*, together with the rarer and more exacting little ones that have a close relationship to the Nomocharis genus, such as *L. mackliniae*, *L. nanum*, *L. oxypetalum*, *L. sempervivoideum*, *L. amoenum*, *L. henricii* and *L. sherriffiae*, lovers of cool conditions and a diet of leaf mould and grit.

There are also smaller forms of American species such as *L. kelloggii* and *L. bolanderi* that would not look out of place in a rockery. These and the near Nomocharis types are rarely offered for sale but can sometimes be raised from seed (see p157) distributed by lily groups or societies and some commercial seedsmen.

L. pumilum and smaller forms of *L. bulbiferum*, or even *L. bulbiferum* itself could be

Midsummer borders are not short of colour with cultivars such as the pastel 'Peacock Creation', the red 'Mercedes', to the side, the tall, dark red 'Massa', behind, and golden 'Grand Cru' with its distinctive maroon centres, to the rear

accommodated by some larger rock gardens. The tiny *L. formosanum pricei* is readily available as plant or seed and will be only a few centimetres (inches) high when it opens its large, glistening white trumpet. It is a self-assured little plant, even if it looks just on the edge of comedy.

THE BOLD STROKE

Nothing succeeds like success, and lilies that begin to increase and start mass movements in beds and borders are very much welcomed. If our garden becomes a 'riot of colour' we delight in it, we can even help start the revolution by planting boldly in well-prepared soil.

Our borders, shown here in midsummer could probably have been better planned. I always seem to be in a hurry to find places for bulbs and a bare patch of soil is a temptation not resisted. But there is no denying the impact such groupings make. Shrubs impinging on the scene are a buddleia and in front a *Cornus kousa*. The bulbs were planted three of a kind and are shown in their second year.

Numbers impress, and a drift of lilies can be both exciting and enchanting. Some of the species and hybrids close to the species are among the most effective. Once settled they look right and will enlarge their territory year by year. In early summer the real lily pageant starts with *L. martagon* and its relatives. Here are lilies that positively look better in numbers. We try to grow them below trees and between shrubs. The trees are mainly robinias, which do not cast too severe a shade and with roots that are manageable. The shrubs are mainly viburnums, witch hazels, *Cotinus* and similar normally well-behaved characters.

L. martagon is not a mass-produced artifact each identical with the next. Really it is surprising that there is so much uniformity for a species with such a very wide distribution but clones do vary in height, in colour, in the number of flowers to a stem and to a lesser degree in flower size. The whites come spotted and unspotted, the coloured ones are usually fairly generously spotted but this feature is a variable. Interestingly the rate of bulb division varies considerably. In a drift it is the interplay of the varying heights and colours that adds considerably to the effect of the whole.

A few stems of white-flowered martagons gives extra life to the picture. Martagon groups can be kept unmixed successfully but I like to have hybrids near at hand. Small groups of the hybrids with *L. hansonii* planted near the martagons are effective, particularly the robust 'Marhan' – its soft orange makes a good contrast and of course it does bloom during the same period.

The American species and their hybrids are others that look well in groups and these excel in light woodland or on the edge of a copse. In the absence of woods or copses, they are best allowed a permanent site between shrubs. *L. pardalinum* and the Bellingham and Bullwood hybrids can be handled in a similar manner to *L. martagon*. At present we have groups under Scot's Pines and silver birches. The competition from the roots of the birches would be a little too energetic for some lilies but the Americans

seem to be up to the task. Suitable smaller associates are heathers and hellebores, an arrangement that will provide interest in the winter and early spring and also gives lilies some root shade along with a sense of community.

A QUESTION OF SCENT

One of the most frequent queries about new lilies is, 'Are they scented?' The average gardener expects lilies to be scented and is somewhat disappointed when they discover that most Asiatics have little or no perfume. The breeders have not bred the scent out, it was not there in the Asiatic species in the first place. Now, with the introduction in the breeding programme of new species such as *L. lankongense*, some scent is being added. Most trumpets and Orientals are heavily endowed, some

so much so that Dutch breeders are now selecting Oriental seedlings with less scent as market research has suggested that many people find the perfume too pervasive and strong for cut flowers or house plants. You can only satisfy some of the people some of the time!

A FINAL NOTE

Gardening is the opposite to an exact science. Some of the best effects can have been brought about by chance. The 'happy accident' is a recurrent theme. Sometimes we do make mistakes, lilies can be lost behind shrubs that have decided to grow apace or an under estimate of their height leads to six-footers at the front of the border. Kinds like the splendid trumpet 'Black Magic', pictured here among rue and a medley of other plants, can be a reasonable

The trumpet 'Black Magic' bewitches with dark buds opening to startling white trumpets and flooding the air with perfume

1.2m (4ft) the first year after planting but having got itself installed will probably be 1.5m or even 1.8m (5–6ft) in following years. These happenings are rarely tragedies, some weeks after flowering the plants can be lifted and repositioned.

When happy the more difficult species are best left alone. Most of the hybrids, however, are mobile bulbs, only too pleased to be lifted every few seasons and given more elbow room. The garden is a developing haven, it is a work of art in time. It can be developed: however perfect, new touches can be added here and there, fresh emphases made and new associations tried.

4

CULTIVATION

GENERAL REQUIREMENTS

The first and the last requirement for lilies is good drainage. The bulbs enjoy an open soil structure; they revel in humus but also relish a gritty component in their diet. Plants grow very fast through spring into summer; during this period they can make good use of copious draughts of water. Given this good start, they can then hold out against modest droughts although, as in nature, they are happiest with underground moisture in the absence of rainfall. In their wild homelands they may be without rain for months, but would be drinking the water derived from melting snows. In winter the bulbs will be unhappy to be standing long in stagnant water. Then, perhaps even more than at other times, happiness is sharp drainage.

Like clematises, lilies also like their heads in the sun and their toes in the shade. Beyond this, their specific needs or preferences are not onerous. Species such as *L. speciosum* and *L. auratum* regard lime as the arsenic of their world, a quick way to oblivion. Conversely, *L. candidum* likes rather than hates some lime but, in sole opposition to lily norms of behaviour, needs its bulbs planted just under the soil's surface, quite un-lily like. *L. martagon*, *L. monadelphum* and some others, once settled in their domain, may be happy to stay put for the next hundred years or so, and may extend their territory by seedling-led accession if given the opportunity. On the other hand, pretty little *L. pumilum* or *L. concolor* are often short-lived as individual bulbs. They can seed themselves to extinction, but this seed germinates freely and new plants are soon blooming.

In the well-tended, healthy soils of garden beds robust species such as *L. bulbiferum* and *L. dauricum* can be as generous of increase and bloom as the popular Asiatic hybrids such as *L.* 'Enchantment' (see p102) that they helped to breed. They need lifting and dividing every two or three seasons, before overcrowding brings into play the law of diminishing returns. Incidentally, I recently lifted a bulb of 'Enchantment' planted the previous year. The original bulb was now replaced by a cluster of eight sizable ones. Above these were other smaller bulbs, the result of the forming of small bulbs on the stems between the bulb and the soil

The famous Asiatic hybrid, 'Enchantment' (p102)

surface. There were thirty-two of these. On the current stems there were over a hundred bulbils in the leaf axils. Altogether, a population explosion.

LILIES AND LIME

Lilies as a whole are happy in neutral to slightly acid soils, but some grow with a limited amount of lime. The main classes are shown in the table below:

Happy with lime	Tolerant of some lime	Lime haters
L. amabile	*L. bolanderi*	*L. auratum*
L. candidum	*L. bulbiferum*	*L. bakeriana*
L. carniolicum	*L. canadense*	*L. japonicum*
L. chalcedonicum	editorum	*L. lancifolium*
L. concolor	*L. callosum*	*L. leichtlinii*
L. duchartrei	*L. cernuum*	*L. medeoloides*
L. hansonii	*L. davidii*	*L. neilgherrense*
L. henryi	*L. humboldtii*	*L. nepalense*
L. martagon	*L. lankongense*	*L. rubellum*
L. monadelphum	*L. leucantheum*	*L. speciosum*
L. pomponium	*L. longiflorum*	*L. wallichianum*
L. regale	*L. pardalinum*	Oriental hybrids
L. szovitsianum	*L. parryi*	
L. x *testaceum*	*L. primulinum*	
L. x 'Marhan'	*L. pyrenaicum*	
L. x *martagon*	*L. sulphureum*	
hybrids		
	Asiatic hybrids	
	Trumpet hybrids	

HUMUS AND MULCHES

Humus is beneficial in encouraging acidity, aerating the soil, aiding drainage and helping to maintain healthy soil organisms. It also acts as a sponge to retain moisture. As a surface mulch it can repress weeds, conserve moisture and help to insulate the soil from excessive temperature fluctuations.

Leaf mould and well-made compost are equally welcomed by lilies. Mulches of dead bracken, dead leaves and similar material can be useful around the year. Fresh fronds of bracken, cut and shredded before they unfurl, make a potash-rich cover. Shredded bark looks attractive and also insulates, suppresses weeds and

retains water while improving the soil structure. An 8–10cm (3–4in) thick mulch layer will last for around three years.

SUN AND SHADE

Lilies enjoy getting their heads in the sunshine, where insects are attracted by their colour and scent. However, quite a number – probably the majority – will be happy growing in light woodland, or the equivalent in modern gardens, under trees and shrubs where the bulbs will grow and enjoy dappled sunlight. In such sites trees and shrubs not only provide a backcloth for the splendid lily flowers, but roots working below will usually ensure that drainage is good by encouraging healthy soil structure and channelling surplus water upwards, to be lost through transpiration from the leaves.

Enough is, of course, a sufficiency. Lilies do not relish finding themselves below such impenetrable masses as provided by most conifers, although at some little distance they could benefit from the acidity promoted by fallen needles.

MOISTURE

In winter, many wild lilies are covered with snow and so are kept free from excessive wet. Spring rain and melting snow provide an abundance of moisture as roots move into top gear. In the garden, we need to minimise the effect of surplus winter water, and then maximise on spring and summer rains. Good soil structure and mulches help make the most of such rain. Waterbutts can be used to collect rainwater. Grown between shrubs, groups of lilies need not be in severe competition for water and will very rarely need watering as a matter of life or death. When watering, keep foliage, stems and flowers dry.

COLD AND HEAT

Lilies are remarkably resilient against both cold and heat. The bulbs are safely inured to the winter's cold, but occasionally can be severely damaged by a heavy late frost when they have fresh young growth well above the ground.

However, it has to be a very sharp, prolonged frost to cause a lot of damage. Grown between other plants, the bulbs are partially protected, but warnings of such severe frosts make it worthwhile giving extra protection to especially valued plants with a covering of straw, leaf or bark litter, or even sheets of newspaper or plastic sacks. Almost any thing will serve for the few hours needed to conserve heat and turn the frost aside.

Sun and heat rarely cause problems in temperate parts of the world. Trouble can be encountered if the rate of water transpiration from foliage is accelerated at a time when the ground has become almost desert-dry and the reservoir of soil water is very severely depleted. A thorough soaking of the ground will be required.

PLANTING LILIES IN THE GARDEN

Like all plants, lilies do not want to find themselves in the equivalent of a wind tunnel, but they do like air. At the risk of sounding repetitive – the importance of free drainage is difficult to exaggerate. Ideal soil is open, with plenty of soil air. A large humus content is highly desirable, good leaf mould is probably the best form. Dig the soil thoroughly and make sure it is well-drained, then plant in autumn or early spring. A late-summer or early-autumn planting allows the bulbs to get well rooted and established before the winter, the soil structure is allowed to arrange itself and drainage patterns can be formed.

Do not plant in late autumn if the soil is cold and sodden. Bulbs at this time are best potted up and kept overwinter, to be planted out at the end of winter. Bulbs planted in early spring will do well but, if compared to the same cultivars planted in autumn, are likely to be just a little less tall, a fraction less leafy and with flowers slightly smaller. As the lilies establish themselves, they will reach an optimum height and performance for the site and climate, and usually they will be far, far better in their second year than the first.

With the exception of *L. candidum*, bulbs should be planted deeply – if the bulb itself measures from base to nose one unit, there should never be less than two units of soil or compost above the planted bulb. A greater depth would not be harmful, and mulches can be added on top through the growing months.

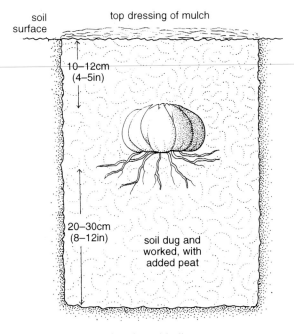

The planted bulb

With Asiatic hybrids, for example, 10–12cm (4–5in) of soil should be replaced above the top of the bulbs, and with larger trumpet bulbs this depth will be closer to 15–20cm (6–8in). Some *L. pardalinum* hybrids, allowed to grow for several years in our garden, seem to have moved closer to the surface, and are happy in a shallow spot. The bulbs measured 5cm (2in) from tip to base, but are only covered with 2–4cm (1–1½in) of soil.

Personally, I believe the oft-repeated advice to plant bulbs on a bed of sand is nonsense. In poorly drained soils it will act as a sump rather than improving drainage. It does not aid rooting, nor does it repel slugs. The only tiny benefit of sand would be that, when bulbs are lifted, they may come more cleanly delivered from the soil. Hardly worth the effort!

AFTERCARE

Discourage weeds, especially chickweed and similarly invasive green stuff which may foster slugs, by applying loose mulches of leaves, shredded bark or bracken through the winter. Mulches of shredded bark also encourage moisture retention and help keep soil temperatures equable, while well-rotted compost mulches provide food sources as well as eventually improving soil structure. Spent-mushroom compost also helps, but does contain relatively high amounts of lime.

I do not stake any lilies, but some may benefit from this if they grow in excessively windy spots or if a stem has been partially damaged. A stake can also protect those that are being kept for seed. If you wish to stake a lily it is best to position a short 'marking' cane before planting the bulb. Later a full-sized cane can be put in its place. Pushing a cane in beside a growing plant may send it clean through the bulb as stems do not necessarily grow straight up. Secure the stems to the canes using two or three ties rather than a single one which may become a stress point.

It is rarely necessary to water lily bulbs in the ground, but in times of drought a thorough soaking of the soil around important ones will be repaid by healthier growth and increase. Do not water the foliage, and do not splash either leaves or stems with soil or fertilisers. Feeding should not be required if bulbs are happy with what is provided naturally by the soil. Performance can be improved by light applications each season of a general fertiliser that is low in nitrogen and high in potash. Foliar feeding has a quick but rather fleeting effect. Lift crowded bulbs some 4–6 weeks after blooming, but proceed with caution: stems may arise erectly from the bulb but may deviate a little, or occasionally considerably, and so you may easily cause damage to the bulb. Tease bulbs apart, grade and replant them immediately. You can remove the old stem or reduce it to half height as a useful handle and supplementary label. Small bulbs not expected to bloom can either

Staking. When you plant the bulb insert a short stake next to it, this prevents accidental spearing of the bulb. When the plant grows to a size that needs support, replace the short stake with a large one. Use two or three ties to hold the plant rather than just one which may make a stress point

be given their space to grow with larger siblings or may be planted in a nursery row to fatten for a season.

POTTED LILIES

No bulb is easier to grow in pots than the lily – daffodils, tulips, hyacinths and crocuses are difficult in comparison!

The bigger the pot the easier it is to grow the bulbs. Three Asiatic hybrids can be housed in a two- or three-litre pot, but a larger one will give more room for roots and development of bulbs. Large, tall kinds, such as the trumpets *L.* Pink Perfection, *L.* 'African Queen' or *L. regale*, have big bulbs and a lot of superstructure when fully grown, and so require large containers for both rooting activity and stability. Nothing less than seven-litre pots should be considered for three bulbs of these kinds, as there must be room to place the bulbs on a bed of compost and then to cover their tops with at least another 10cm (4in).

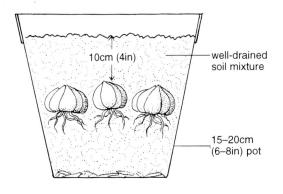

Potted bulbs

Half tubs and other large containers with drainage holes are ideal for larger groups of lilies. There is plenty of room to plant the bulbs deep down, they have ample rooting space and nourishment and will be absolutely stable when fully grown. The accompanying plants can add interest and contrast, as well as providing shade to the lower parts of the lilies.

COMPOST CHOICES

You can buy a commercial mix or compose one yourself. Of the commercial ones, ericaceous mixes are acidic – safe for all lilies. Unfortunately, most are peat-based, dry out quickly and can be difficult to wet again. Once dried out, it is best to stand the container in water until it is completely soaked, with the surface turning dark and moist – but this is not practical with half-tubs! You can spend a lot of time watering dry peat from above without penetrating more than perhaps a third of the way down.

Several commercial growers have started using equal parts of John Innes potting compost and an ericaceous one. We have used this or the recipe given below when growing commercially. The mix retained moisture well and encouraged healthy, extensive root growth. It was much easier to water, keep moist and healthy than pure, peat-based composts. All trumpet lilies and Asiatic hybrids were well served; Orientals were sometimes obliged to make do with this, but totally lime-free ericaceous composts were used for *L. speciosum* and very sensitive lilies.

For a lily planting compost, mix by volume the following materials:

1 part grit or washed sand
1 part fibrous peat (or equivalent) humus
1 part healthy loam or rotted turves

You could add extra food, such as small amounts of bone meal and sulphate of potash – 120 grams (4oz) bone meal and 30 grams (1oz) of sulphate of potash for a small barrow load. A balanced fertiliser can also be used; a slow-release fertiliser in granule form is most practical. If you wish to use a compound fertiliser, choose one designed for potatoes or tomatoes – high in potash and low in nitrogen.

Drainage is as important in containers as elsewhere. Pots are usually well drained, but make sure that half tubs and larger containers have drainage holes and keep them free of pests by covering them with discs of perforated metal

The figure labels: 10cm (4in), well-drained soil mixture, 15–20cm (6–8in) pot.

or fine-mesh plastic. An open, healthy soil structure ensures good drainage.

Put a layer of compost into your container, and place the bulbs in position, with their roots, if any, spread out. Allow 4–5cm (2in) between Asiatic bulbs and 15–18cm (5–6in) between trumpet lilies, if possible. Three bulbs up to 5cm (2in) in diameter can manage in a 2- or 3-litre pot, while five or six bulbs will need a 4- to 5-litre one. Unsurprisingly, large bulbs need larger pots. Trumpet lily bulbs can easily be 10–13cm (4–5in) in diameter, while lilies of the Pink Perfection strain can readily top 2m (6ft) when in bloom and certainly need a large, heavy container to stabilise the plant.

Bulbs can be potted in autumn or early spring and even as late as mid-spring. Keep the compost moist. This is relatively easy in the early stages, but not so easy when the plants are fully grown. Growth is rapid – bulbs potted in early spring under glass will bloom fourteen weeks later. It is almost impossible to overwater growing plants. In addition, you could give them a high-potash tomato fertiliser as liquid feed.

After flowering cut away the dead flower, leaving all foliage intact. Do not overlook the pots after the excitement of the flowers – the bulbs are best kept growing strongly for some weeks, and if you are busy it could be prudent to sink pots into the ground where they are kept cooler and moister than if they are left in the open.

Tip out the pots in late summer. Divide the bulbs and either repot or plant the bulbs in the garden. There are likely to be a number of smaller bulbs to be grown on. In larger containers and half-tubs you can grow bulbs on for a second season. Remove the top soil in late summer or autumn, perhaps as far as the top of the bulbs, replace it with fresh soil and then leave everything for another season.

Overwinter the bulbs in a cool greenhouse, a frame or car-port where the pots can be kept just moist without getting sodden. They are best in a slug-free environment and out of extreme cold.

PESTS AND DISEASES

Give your lilies the best possible environment: plenty of air and light, shade at the roots, a healthy, humus-rich, balanced and free-draining soil. Like the rest of creation, lilies have their own set of pests and diseases, some are serious, others are more easily rebuffed. Reading these sections of any gardening book is almost as off-putting as perusing a medical dictionary; but take heart, it always sounds worse than it is likely to be.

Viruses: Lily bulbs attacked by virus, the worst disease, display a number of symptoms, to a greater or lesser degree. Normally these include paler streaks in leaves and stems, distorted leaves, buds, flowers or stems and overall failing performance. The same virus may cause the precipitate decline of one lily while another species or cultivar lives with the disease with relative ease. Similarly, a plant with one virus may appear to manage without too much distress but, when attacked by an additional one, will collapse hopelessly. There is no real amateur cure for virus-infected bulbs – affected bulbs should be immediately destroyed before they infect other stock.

L. longiflorum and *L. formosanum* are particularly vulnerable to virus attack, as they show the symptoms quickly and markedly. They can be used to test the presence of virus in other stock by injecting them with material from doubtful cases.

Cucumber mosaic virus: This can cause very streaked foliage colour and distorted, brittle leaves and flowers. Leaves may become very pale and plants stunted. It is probably the most obvious and widespread virus, one that also infects many other garden plants such as tulips, dahlias and delphiniums.

Tulip breaking virus: This virus causes the broken colour that so excited Dutch tulip growers centuries ago. In lilies it causes mottling of the foliage, the lessening in intensity of darker flowers and sometimes the breaking of the colour.

Brown ring virus: This virus was discovered in L. 'Enchantment'. It causes the scales to be stunted and to be held more loosely. They are marked with brown rings and this tissue perishes. Plants become dwarfed and pale.

Lily symptomless virus: This difficult-to-spot, creeping disorder must be suspected if the plants look less lively, lacking the *joie de vivre* of their neighbours. They are on the slippery slope to extinction and, if you feel sure that you have discovered cases, they should be helped on their way without delay. Be careful to differentiate between plants that may not be flourishing as well as they might because of other reasons, such as overcrowding, competition from neighbouring plants, damage from rabbits or slugs, or distress from drought conditions.

Botrytis elliptica: This can attack the lily foliage, usually starting with the lower leaves which turn brown, shrivel and perish. Attacks are more likely in cramped growing conditions and when the atmosphere is moist and warm. Conversely it is less likely to get a foothold if the plants have plenty of air and foliage is dry and otherwise healthy. A dangerous source for botrytis can be *L. candidum* – with its overwintering rosette of leaves it provides a useful staging post for the disease spores. A systemic fungicide spray can be used as a preventative or to contain any attack. Burn infected leaves.

Basal rot: *Fusarium oxysporum f.sp narcissi* is the active agent causing basal rot in lilies and other bulbs. Living on bulb tissue in the soil, it can attack the bulb directly or more easily through already-damaged tissue. It normally attacks where the scales meet the base, turning tissue brown and continuing to rot inwards through the bulb to eventually destroy it. In store, bulbs can quickly spread the trouble through spores. Affected bulbs should be completely destroyed, and as a precaution you should lift nearby bulbs at the end of their growing season and dip them in a fungicide, following the manufacturer's instructions.

Blue mould on lily bulbs is normally a relatively harmless penicillium which will colonise damaged tissue. Cut such areas away and dip the bulb in fungicide.

Rabbits: Lilies are edible. In several parts of the world they are eaten by humans, and everywhere by rabbits. If you are plagued by these pests, enclose your lilies with cylinders of chicken wire, about 75cm (30in) high and buried 8–10cm (3–4in) deep and then turned outwards at right angles below the soil surface for a distance of 25–30cm (10–12in). If lilies are grown in association with other plants, for example annuals such as larkspur or love-in-the-mist, the wire can be disguised quickly.

Slugs: Slugs also like to eat lilies. They are most active and cause the greatest damage in early spring when the lilies are pushing stems up from their bulbs. These seem particularly attractive to slugs that either eat through them or munch sufficient to prevent the stem functioning properly. A programme of clean cultivation and the elimination of slug-friendly homes is called for. Slug traps and poison pellets used early in the year will prevent damage or bring it to the irreducible minimum.

Vine weevil: The larvae of the beetle (*Otiorhynchus sulcatus*) can make a nuisance of themselves, feeding on the roots and the bulb of potted lilies. They are fat, creamy-white grubs, up to a centimetre (½in) long, with brown heads and a slightly arched body, and unfortunately very resistant to insecticides. Good greenhouse hygiene is necessary – bulbs and compost should be examined carefully at the end of the growing season or if potted plants suddenly begin to collapse, so that grubs can be detected and dispatched. You can also kill the pest if it is rife in your bulbs by placing them in a polythene bag with a few mothballs for three weeks or so.

Lily beetle (*Lilioceris lilii*): Potentially the worst scourge of lilies, this is normally a pest of warmer areas. In Britain its present distribution is limited to the south of England. The Royal Horticultural Society publishes a leaflet about this pest and the entomologist at their Wisley Gardens is carefully monitoring the situation countrywide. In countries and areas free of the beetle it would make sense to take as much care with the distribution of lily plants and cut flowers to ensure that the pest is not spread further.

Both the handsome scarlet beetles and their larvae, which look like bird droppings, eat lily foliage. Both quickly demolish leaves and reduce plants to little more than a bare stem, with only a few tattered leaf remnants fluttering from the naked mast. Systemic insecticides or fortnightly contact applications of insecticides are required. This is not the time to argue the case for gardening regimes free of artificial chemicals – something with which I am normally in sympathy.

Larvae of the lily beetle

Eternal vigilance and regular checks of lilies at risk will alert you to the presence of the pest. You can collect both larvae and beetles and destroy them. Place a hand or container below the leaf from which you are picking the beetle so that it won't topple to the ground where it may be lost amongst the surrounding foliage despite its bright colour – if on its back it is not a brilliant scarlet.

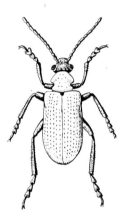

The lily beetle (x 5)

5

PROPAGATION

THE PROPAGATOR'S DREAM PLANT

For many gardeners the heart of their hobby is the propagation of plants. Here is mystery, wonder and excitement; art and science join forces, green fingers are flexed. And of all plants, the lily is perhaps the ultimate one for propagation: it can be increased successfully in so many worthwhile ways. Seed is freely produced and, if treated correctly, germinates with no trouble at all. Healthy bulbs increase by division. Many types produce small bulblets on the stem between the bulb and the soil surface. Some will naturally conjure up bulbils in the leaf axils all up the stems, others may be induced to do so. Scales can be broken from bulbs of all types and encouraged to give rise to one or more small bulblets along the fractured edge within a few weeks. Tissue may be taken from various parts of the plant, grown on rapidly under laboratory conditions, and split and resplit several times before the undifferentiated tissue pieces are encouraged to form plantlets with embryo bulbs, leaves and roots.

SEED VERSUS VEGETATIVE PROPAGATION

There is a distinct difference between plants raised from seed and those grown vegetatively. From seed, each plant is a distinct new individual with a unique DNA identity; vegetatively raised plants all have the same DNA identity as their parent because they are really still a part of that plant – cloned pieces all with exactly the same potential.

Plants of species raised from seed will vary, maybe by microscopic detail, sometimes quite surprisingly broadly, but all within the more or less strict specific limits governed by the species' genetic material. Hybrid seed normally gives rise to a range of obviously differing plants, although certain crosses repeated between two identified parents can, on occasion, produce a fairly uniform population, rather like the F2 hybrids used for bedding flowers and vegetable strains.

Advantages of using seed include:
● The new stock should be free of tissue-borne diseases such as viruses.
● Improved forms of species can be selected – perhaps hardier bulbs, better-formed flowers or more prolific bloomers.
● From hybrid seed distinct new individuals may be selected to be vegetatively propagated to form a new cultivar.

Advantages of vegetative propagation include:
● All the new plants will behave in the same way as the parents and give a uniform floral effect.
● Outstanding individuals, of either species or hybrids, can be reproduced exactly.
● Usually, but not always, it is possible to produce flowering plants more quickly than from seed.

SEED

A single seedpod may yield from one to over a hundred viable seeds. Most species and hybrids freely produce seed. There are hybrids and clones of species with greater or lesser degrees of sterility and there are rather more that tend not to set seed easily when self-pollinated.

Pods of early-flowering Asiatic hybrids, martagons and some trumpets can be harvested in the summer. For other, later trumpet types and the Oriental lilies you may have to cut the stems and allow seeds to finish ripening under cover.

Seedpods are ready for collecting when the tops crack open. The pods can be cut or snapped off. When ripe, the seeds are loose, tan coloured and can be shaken out onto a sheet of paper. The chaff of ovules that failed to make viable seed can be removed by gentle blowing or fanning. You can then sow or packet seed, taking care to label each lot before handling a fresh batch.

In late summer, when the weather turns wet and colder, seed ripening slows down or stops. Stems are then best cut half way up and hung upside down over a sheet of paper in an airy, dry place such as a conservatory, summerhouse or garage. As it ripens, seed begins to fall and soon all should be safely gathered in.

Fungus can destroy seed, especially in wet seasons and towards the end of the harvest time. Spores germinate on the pod or seed and send out creeping mycelium that invades the seed cells. The fungus moves rapidly from one seed to the next and, in a very short time, an entire podful is lost. Spray developing green seedpods with a systemic fungicide to prevent such disasters.

The gathered seed may be sown immediately or kept until very early spring. Store it dry and keep it cool, perhaps in the refrigerator, so it will not lose its viability by the end of the winter. The longer seed is kept after this period, the greater the likelihood of smaller numbers germinating.

ABOVE-GROUND IMMEDIATE GERMINATION (EPIGEAL IMMEDIATE)

Seed germinates in one of four ways (see p21); with above-ground immediate germination being the most common way. Seed germinates within a few weeks of sowing, each producing a narrow cotyledon leaf and later the first true spear-shaped one. Seed sown in the autumn reaches this stage at a time when it is becoming cooler and the light is failing. You may be left to nurse tiny young seedlings through the winter,

possibly in an unheated greenhouse. A fungicide spray will help you achieve this without loss, but many prefer to keep their seed for sowing at the end of the winter or the very beginning of spring, when the seedlings will have conditions all in their favour and can grow on without check. Germination rates can approach one hundred per cent.

UNDERGROUND GERMINATION (HYPOGEAL)

Those lilies that are hypogeal immediate germinators can be handled the same way as the epigeal immediate ones. They may, however, need to be given a cool period before sending up their first leaf.

The hypogeal delayed lilies can be sown immediately and allowed to get on by themselves, but it is possible to speed up germination. Hypogeal delayed seeds are triggered into action by changes in temperature levels. To start making little bulbs in the soil they require a period of twelve weeks at 18–21°C (65–70°F), followed by a minimum of six cool weeks, preferably just above freezing, at around 4°C (40°F), to jog them into leaf production. This means that we can work out a plan to get them underway:

● harvest and store dry seed
● dust or wet seed with fungicide prior to sowing
● sow seed in late autumn in moist vermiculite. Place in a polythene bag with air and keep at 18–21°C (65–70°F) for twelve weeks. Your living quarters or a place near a domestic boiler or radiator may provide the right temperatures.
● sort out the small bulbs, prick them off into trays or pots and cover them with 1cm (⅓in) of potting compost. Place outside, in a cool position for 6–7 weeks.
● in early spring, the small plants can be brought under cover or left outside. They are best grown on as strongly as possible at this stage as you will never have another chance to increase their size so quickly while saving a

complete year until their first flower.

L. martagon, which adopts this method of germination, may well have seed ripe in time to

L. martagon, which germinates underground, is wonderful for naturalising. The white *L. martagon album* makes a contrast to the pinky-mauve type (p63)

enjoy naturally the initial warm period through the rest of the summer and autumn, and the winter will then more than cover the required six cool weeks.

SEED SOWING

Seed needs air, moisture and warmth to germinate, as provided by a polythene bag with damp sterile matter such as expanded mica (vermiculite). Sow seed in a pot or tray of seed compost and allow the resulting seedlings to grow their first, or perhaps second, true leaf before pricking them out into small pots or trays. Alternatively if you sow them in a deep tray or pot,

they can be left several weeks or months longer until they are well grown. An open gritty compost with plenty of humus is best, for example a commercially produced ericaceous compost with additional washed sand or grit. We have successfully used 2 parts by volume of ericaceous compost with 1 part grit. The flat seed is spread over the soil surface so that none overlaps and is then lightly covered with 3mm (⅛in) of compost or grit.

After sowing, thoroughly moisten the pot or tray, preferably by standing it in clean water. Allow the surplus water to drain away for 5–10 minutes and then enclose the container in a polythene bag to keep the seed moist. Place the tray in a spot out of direct sunshine, at a temperature between 18–21°C (65–70°F). When green leaves appear above the surface, the polythene bag can be opened progressively, taking care not to let the compost dry out.

As seedlings grow, give them more air, water and some dilute feeding. Prick plants out into small pots and pot them on before they get root-bound.

RATES TO FLOWERING FROM SEED

	Under optimum conditions	Under average conditions
L. formosanum	within 1 season	2nd year
L. f. pricei	,,	,,
L. philippinense	,,	,,
L. concolor	2nd year	3rd year
L. pumilum	,,	,,
L. regale	,,	,,
Asiatic hybrids	,,	,,
Trumpet hybrids	,,	,,
Oriental hybrids	,,	,,
L. pardalinum	3rd year	4th–5th year
L. martagon	4th year	5th–7th year
L. hansonii	,,	,,

BULB DIVISION

The typical round lily bulb sends its flowering stem from its basal plate through the centre of the bulb. Around the bottom of the stem one or more embryonic growing points will emerge. In some lilies, new bulbs are produced from buds around the rim of the bulb's basal plate, which will develop into replacement bulbs for the following season. Each species or hybrid reproduces at its own rate – a very small bulb, a weak species, or a struggling bulb may produce just one new bulb; two new bulbs is more normal and, with really happy, robust bulbs, a three- to sixfold increase is possible.

When you lift bulbs at the end of summer, you will find the new bulbs still joined at the basal plate, but they can easily be cut or snapped off. If bulbs are left for two seasons before lifting, the original connecting tissue will have perished, and of course last season's bulbs will have produced their own successors.

The rhizomatous *L. pardalinum* and its relatives are best divided with a sharp knife so that each severed piece has at least one growing point, each with clusters of smaller, developing, white or pale cream scales, unlike the nicotine-coloured older ones. Rhizomatous bulbs need lifting with the same care a dedicated archaeologist might use to unearth some precious artefact as their scales are very brittle. I usually divide my rhizomatous bulbs almost immediately after flowering unless I intend to harvest seed. Stems are cut to a third of their length and provide useful handles for lifting the bulbs. At this time a new flush of roots is usually evident, just beginning to emerge from the base of scales. Early lifting will not damage these new roots which will grow rapidly once the divided pieces have been replanted and watered.

The types that benefit most from lifting and dividing regularly are the Asiatic hybrids and some of the species that were the founders of these races, such as *L. dauricum, L. bulbiferum* and *L. davidii*. These may be lifted in late summer, split and replanted in fresh spots or returned to their former positions, once these have been well dug over and envigorated with generous additions of humus.

The received wisdom about *L. martagon, L. hansonii* and their hybrids is that, having got bulbs growing nicely, it is best to leave them well alone. It is easy to see how such an attitude has developed: from seed it takes many years to achieve freely-blooming bulbs; bulbs purchased from dealers having perhaps spent quite a while in store before reaching the customers may 'not grow' above ground at all for a complete year although they will be forming a root system below and the following year will send up a stem. The gardener looks and thinks, 'At last. Now all's well, we had better let sleeping dogs lie and not rock the boat.'

To increase my own stock of better forms of *L. martagon*, I lift bulbs at the time seed is ripe, in late summer or early autumn, or a very few weeks after flowering if no seed is to be harvested. It is usually possible to tease apart or surgically split bulbs – some clones divide much more readily than others – and give them more room when replanting. They can be relied upon to bloom as normal. Inevitably some scales are dislodged but as these are left in the soil they may have produced handy little bulbs by next lifting time.

The same regime is applied to *L. hansonii* and the hybrids of these two species. Lifting is normally undertaken every two years but, if we are very eager, every year.

STEM BULBLETS

Bulblets may be formed on the underground part of the stem of stem-rooting kinds. The number and size depends on the species or cultivar and the strength of the individual bulb. The stem of a vigorous one can generate up to a dozen or more bulblets – perfectly formed small bulbs with scales and roots ready for independent life once the stem dies back. A few bulblets can be the size of a small walnut, most are more or less marble size, but they can be graded down to tiny ones with two or three wispy, minuscule scales. Even these very tiny bulblets can be potted up and, with care, be persuaded to fatten up.

The number of these bulblets to be harvested from the buried part of the stem is positively correlated to the amount and vigour of the

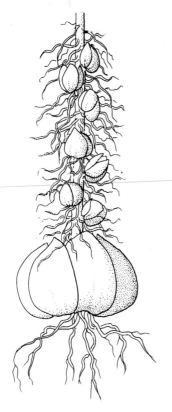

Bulblets forming on the part of the stem below ground at the end of the growing season

stem rooting. To increase the harvest by number and, even more significantly, by weight and volume, stem rooting needs to be encouraged. This can be done initially by providing an open, gritty, humus-rich soil and planting the bulbs with at least 10–15cm (4–6in) above their noses, kept moist but not over-wet. Stem-rooting activity can be dramatically increased by humus mulches from late spring onwards.

Outstanding bulblet producers are *L. lancifolium*, *L. henryi* and *L. regale*, together with hybrids having these lilies in their breeding. Others that may behave this way include *L. auratum*, *L. speciosum*, *L. davidii* and *L. longiflorum*. Stems of *L. dauricum* may meander a little having emerged from the bulb, and will produce bulblets along this length.

Species with stoloniferous stems, such as *L. duchartrei*, will form two or three bulbs along the wandering underground stem. If all goes well, these bulbs will repeat the process without any fussing so that in a very few years a colony can be established.

STEM BULBILS

The tiger lily, *L. lancifolium*, (*L. tigrinum*), is the leading exponent of the stem-bulbil method of increase. Small, dark buds appear in the leaf-axils; they swell to become purple-black mini-bulbs, sometimes starting to produce leaves and roots before they are fully ripe, and fall to the ground. While the majority of leaf-axils are happy to bear one bulbil, it is possible to find two or three in some. If left to their own devices they will eventually fall to the ground and pull themselves down into the soil. If you time your arrival before they are ready to fall you may be able to harvest as many as a hundred or so from a single stem!

Bulbils forming in leaf axils, as in *L. lancifolium*

Other species noted for similar tiger-lily behaviour include *L. bulbiferum*, in which some clones are clearly more adept and prolific than others. The lovely, rare, yellow trumpet *L. sulphureum* and the white *L. sargentiae* also produce bulbils, sometimes very prolifically. *L.*

The tiger lily, *L. lancifoilum* (*L. tigrinum*) (p82)

the production process may be easily maintained until the required number of plants is obtained.

An alternative method which I have used with many lilies that do not freely form bulbils also involves small bulbs as produced by scaling. When such plants have grown their thin, wiry stems these are carefully laid on the soil surface. The bulbs can then be loosened and the stems pinned down so that compost or soil is brought into full contact with them. The bending of the stem may help to change the metabolic balance. Whatever the reason – the stems usually bear a useful number of bulbils by midsummer, some already making roots.

LEAF BUDS

This is a method of lily propagation that I have only recently tried with varying degrees of success. Healthy leaves are taken from stems, each with a small heel. The heels are trimmed and the whole is first dipped in fungicide, and then one third tucked into a mix of grit and peat. Some lilies seem to be more likely than others to form small bulblets in this way – so far we have had more success with those taken in midsummer which were kept relatively cool.

SCALES

Propagating from scales is probably the favourite method – it is certainly the one that writers and television gardeners seem to enjoy exploiting. Another simple and prolific operation, there are variations in how it can be practised. As in all vegetative methods, the most important point to emphasise is that only plants apparently in unblemished health should be used for source material. Special care should be taken to avoid any that have virus symptoms and, if possible, only those should be used that are growing at some distance from potentially sick plants.

Scales can be taken at any time of year but they are probably best in mid- to late summer. This certainly applies to the Asiatic hybrids.

davidii may produce some bulbils of its own accord or can be induced to do so.

Hybrids of these species may give bulbils freely or can be persuaded to do so by cutting their flowering tops off before they get beyond being small buds. If bulbils are harvested and potted up before late summer a good proportion of reasonably sized ones can be got into such energetic growth as to bear one or more blooms the very next summer.

To achieve the greatest possible increase by bulbils for a particular type of lily, a semi-intensive regime can be started. Having made sure the chosen clone is one that can produce bulbils, we try to propagate as large a number of small bulbs as possible by harvesting bulbils and by raising small bulbs from scales. Under cool glass such small bulbs will produce wiry stems the following season and, if grown strongly, usually seem able to bear large numbers of bulbils, especially if any flowering buds or growing stems' tips are nipped off early. Once the summer crop of bulbils is harvested,

Bulbs from scales
a) Scales tucked into a mix of equal parts grit and peat and forming bulbils. Sealed bags of dampened vermiculite can also be used
b) Scale of *L. regale* 8 weeks after being detached
c) 'Enchantment' 8 weeks after being detached
d) *L. pardalinum* 8 weeks after being detached

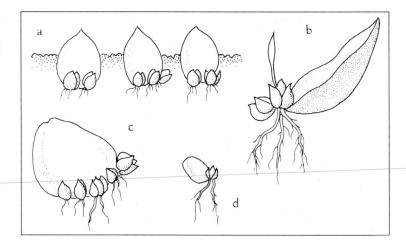

The aim is to take a few healthy scales from around the bulb – the outer ring may suffice. This is easiest once the bulb has been lifted from the soil, but many times I have scraped away the soil until the bulb is exposed to avoid disturbing it unnecessarily. I tend to do this so that half to two thirds of the circumference is seen and then it is possible to gently lever scales away and snap them close to the base. Two, three or four scales from one bulb may be sufficient and hardly cause any loss of vigour.

The detached scales are then labelled and allowed to soak in a systemic fungicide for 10–15 minutes before they are inserted in a tray of grit and peat or humus, or mixed into a handful of dampened, expanded mica (vermiculite) in a polythene bag. In bags, shake up the scales so they have contact with the material, enclose a label and seal the bag, with air inside. In trays, push the scales, base downwards, until only a third or less is visible above. Label the full tray, then water it, allow it to drain and then enclose it in polythene. Keep the scales warm, at around 18°C (65°F) and certainly not above 21°C (70°F), and check periodically. After about four weeks the fractured scale edges should be marked by one or more small bulblets. Once these have swollen to be obvious small bulbs, and perhaps are trying to grow a root or so, each one may be potted up as a unit. Alternatively, scales can be sliced lengthways so that each bulblet has its own scale

fragment and can be potted up. A dip in fungicide can forestall possible diseases. The young plants grow on quickly and can be nicely established before dying down for winter.

To maximise the number of bulblets obtained from scales, cut the scales across their centres, roughly parallel with their bases. The top halves will work exactly as if they were complete scales, with bulblets appearing along their cut edges, and the lower halves will also produce bulblets along the original bottom edge.

An alternative time for scaling would be early spring, which would allow a longer period to grow on the resulting bulblets. It is always tempting to take a few scales from a newly purchased bulb to start increase as quickly as possible. This also acts as an insurance against any untoward accident with the original bulb. A drastic scenario would be to select a bulb of the clone to be multiplied in early spring and to strip off all the scales down to the small centre, which could still be saved by treating it with fungicide and potting it up. As each of the larger scales may produce one to four reasonable bulblets and all others at least one, it should be possible to end the growing season with a population of several dozens from one original.

White midsummer lilies and roses make a familiar twosome in a cottage garden

6

THE LILY SPECIES

The lily, a plant of the northern hemisphere, is widespread and grows in a variety of habitats. Around eighty species are recognised by botanists, most of which are likely to be hardy in gardens in temperate regions. Species can be found growing from Siberia, North Korea and Japan down to the Mediterranean and, in India, quite close to the equator. Some of the lilies that prove less hardy in our gardens come from islands in the Pacific. From mountainous parts of Burma, Tibet and China come some species that almost blur the lines of demarcation between lilies and fritillaries and *Nomocharis*. These delightful plants are not likely to be found in showcases in the local garden centre – they are adapted to their homes and may remain tricky under cultivation until we have the technology to reproduce their natural conditions. Europe has a number of good species, North America has a major collection.

Lilies may grow in large populations or as scattered plants. They are found growing from sea-level to stations high up, perhaps 2600m (8500ft) high. One kind may be restricted to a certain kind of soil and not stray out of a narrow pH band – there are lilies that grow only on acid soils and others that are found on alkaline ones; many are happiest in the neutral middle.

A species may have a limited distribution, for example *L. regale* found only in one steep-sided Chinese valley, others can be wanderers like the champion globe-trotter *L. martagon* known from Siberia across to Poland and down to the Balkans. The latter varies in colour and size but, remarkably, the overall character of the plant remains very much the same and variation is limited. It is one species that is instantly recognisable, unlike a number of other wildings, such as some US species which tend to merge one into another. In the series of mountainous valleys in western America, species seem to have evolved in their isolated barricaded homes, being less well differentiated towards the more open ends of the valleys. In Taiwan, the trumpet lily *L. formosanum*, called after the island's former name, grows from sea-level to some 3600m (12,000ft). Populations of the lily living low down can be 1.8m (6ft) high with several flowers; those scratching a living high up are small plants of around 25–30cm (10–12in), usually with one bloom (*L. f. pricei*) and there are a range of intermediates.

MAIN GROUPINGS AND GARDEN WORTHINESS

No classification of living things can ever be perfect – nature is not tidy-minded in this manner. It is usual to follow a classification giving seven groups, some divided into sections. Each group contains species important to the gardener. Characteristics that are used to differentiate the relationships and groups are given in the order of their importance: type of seed germination, leaf arrangement, entire or jointed scales, heavy or light seed, bulb form and habit, perianth segments smooth or with raised points (papillae), nectary with or without hairs, turk's cap or trumpet-flower form, white or purple bulb, stem erect or stoloniform, obvious or absent/obscure leaf stalks, large or small stigma, stem-rooting or not, one or more stems per bulb.

The main species of each group are listed at the beginning. The order they are in indicates their relationships to each other.

LILY SPECIES AND GROUP RELATIONSHIPS (following Comber)

2 American

2a
humboldtii
ocellatum
columbianum
kelloggii
washingtonianum
rubescens
bolanderi

2b
pardalinum
vollmeri
nevadense
occidentale
maritimum
parvum
parryi
wigginsii

2c
superbum
michauxii
iridollae
michiganense
canademse
grayi

2d
philadelphicum
catesbaei

3 *candidum*

3a
candidum

3b
chalcedonicum
pomponium
carniolicum
pyrenaicum

3c
monadelphum
szvovitsianumum
ledebourii
kesselringianum
polyphyllum

3d
bulbiferum

1 *martagon*

martagon
hansonii
medeoloides
distichum
tsingtauense

7 *dauricum*

dauricum
maculatum

5 Asian

5b
callosum
cernuum
pumilum
amabile

concolor

5a
henryi

duchartrei
lankongemse
papilliferum
davidii
leichtlinii
lancofolium

5c
amoenum
arboricola
bakeranum
henricii
lophophorum
mackliniae
nanum
nepalense
ochraceum
oxypetalum
prumulinum
sempervivioideum
sheriffiae
souliei
taliense
wardii

6 Trumpet

6a
sargentiae
sulphureum
leucanthemum
regale

6b
longiflorum
neilgherrense
wallichianum
formosanum
philippinense

4 Oriental

speciosum

auratum

alexandrae
japonicum
nobilissimum

brownii
rubellum

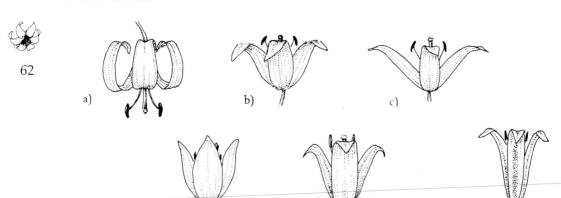

62

Flower shapes
a) Turk's cap, as *L. martagon*; b) bowl, as *L. bulbiferum*;
c) star, as *L. concolor*; d) cup, as *L. mackliniae*; e) open
trumpet, as Golden Splendour; f) trumpet, as *L. regale*

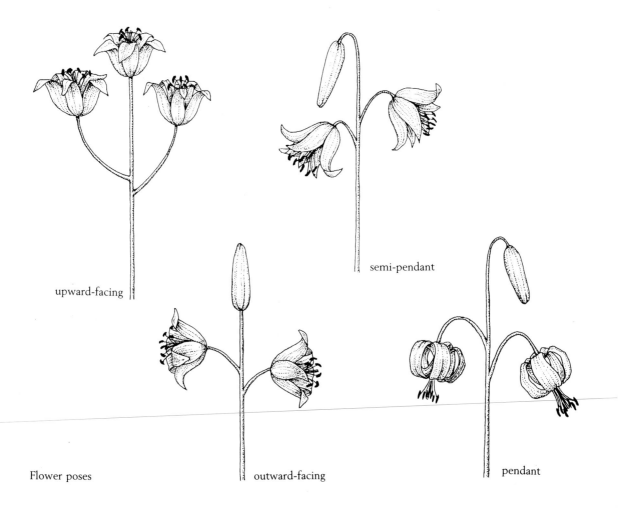

Flower poses

① *L. MARTAGON* AND RELATIVES

Characteristics of this lily group are: hypogeal delayed germination, whorled leaves, jointed bulb scales (except *L. hansonii*), heavy seed, smooth petals, erect stems, small flowers, fruit broad as long. Main species: *L. martagon, L. hansonii, L. distichum, L. medeoloides, L. tsingtauense.*

LILIUM MARTAGON
①
Lilium martagon L.

L. martagon, in the title role of this group, is plainly the star as far as gardeners are concerned. It has one of the longest histories of cultivation and is still highly valued, especially for its relatively early bloom and its trouble-free culture once established. Growing handsomely on a wide variety of soils and able to stand considerably more shade than most lilies, it makes a fine plant for light woodland or between shrubs.

The species grows in the Iberian peninsula, across the southern half of Europe, low into the Balkans, up into Poland, across to the Caucasus and across Russia to Siberia. The general format of the plant is remarkably standard, but in the most obvious characteristic, flower colour, there is a welcome amount of variation between pure white and very dark maroon. Flowers are usually speckled, sometimes heavily so. Different clones grow to their own optimum heights of 1–2m (3½–6½ft) with three or four whorls of leaves and one or perhaps two odd ones above the top whorl and below the bottom one. In early summer there may be up to fifty of the turk's-cap flowers on a stem, one to two dozen is the average. Usually coloured mauvey-pink and decorated with dark spots, the whites – with or without spots – are valued as they help to highlight the coloured ones. Dark maroon-burgundy lilies with a lacquer finish, usually grouped as *L.m. cattaniae,* seem at least as robust as the standard kind and are often taller.

Lovers of this old garden plant are happy to wait five years or longer to see bulbs raised from

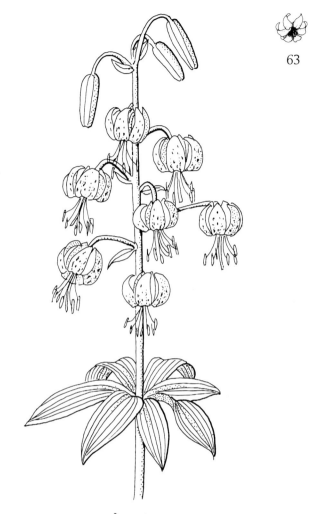

L. martagon

seed flower, hoping to select out particularly good colour forms. Splitting bulbs and scaling is certainly a quicker way of raising stock, but even then not a mass-production, overnight process – while most scales will produce a small bulb after a year, some only get down to work after a year's rest. (p95)

LILIUM HANSONII
①
Lilium hansonii Leichtlin

L. hansonii is a splendid, tough plant, rather more leafy than *L. martagon* and with even thicker textured, tangerine-gold flowers. These open at roughly the same time and look so thick as to have been made of orange peel – perhaps

63

64

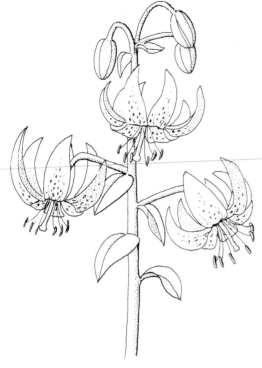

L. hansonii

marked with dark spots, may vary from tangerine to scarlet. Petals curl back, but not as much as in *L. martagon*. A native of Manchuria, Korea, and Japan, it is probably the trickiest of the martagons in the garden – plant it in light shade, with lots of humus, about 10–12cm (4–5in) deep.

L. distichum has a more restricted range in the same Far Eastern area. It is very rare in cultivation and seems to require similar growing conditions to *L. medeoloides*, although reportedly somewhat more robust. It can be a little taller. Horizontal or slightly downward-cast flowers have narrow petals reaching widely and then recurving. Colour is tangerine to pale red with a few spots.

L. tsingtauense is a slender plant usually up to about 50cm (18in) with outward- and upward-facing flowers with pointed, flat or slightly

it should have been called the 'marmalade lily'? The spotted petals recurve gently; they do not curl back to themselves to make cylinders as do those of *L. martagon*. It is happy in almost any drained soil including ones with free lime. Planted deeply it can make the most of its stem roots. The colour may fade in strong sun, so it will look most effective in partial shade. To get the best increase, lift the plants in late summer, split and replant them, while you can give the small fry on the rooting stem their own place.

(1)
L. MEDEOLOIDES, L. DISTICHUM, L. TSINGTAUENSE
Lilium medeoloides Gray, *L. distichum* Nakai, *L. tsingtauense* Eng.

The three remaining martagon-group species are slighter plants, unlikely to top 1m (3½ft), and each stem only sporting a single whorl of leaves. *L. medeoloides* is the smallest plant, usually under 60cm (2ft), with one to five nodding, orange flowers. The colour, usually

L. tsingtauense

recurving petals, rich orange with maroon spots, or occasionally yellow and unspotted. Well-drained, gritty soil with lots of leaf mould is the best home for all three lilies.

All three species have been in limited cultivation for some decades and are still being grown now in very small numbers. *L. tsingtauense* can be found in gardens in different parts of the world and seems to grow with relative ease.

L. tsingtauense, the only upward-facing martagon species

② AMERICAN GROUP

Group characteristics: hypogeal delayed germination (except *L. humboldtii*, *L. parryi*, *L. parvum*, *L. philadelphicum*), whorled leaves, jointed bulb scales (except 2a section), heavy seeds (except 2c), smooth petals, rhizomatous or semi-rhizomatous (not concentric erect), erect stems.

Main species: 2a: *L. humboldtii*, *L. occidentale*, *L. columbianum*, *L. kelloggii*, *L. washingtonia-* num, *L. rubescens*, *L. bolanderi*. 2b: *L. pardalinum*, *L. vollmeri (roezlii)*, *L. nevadense*, *L. occidentale*, *L. maritimum*, *L. parvum*, *L. parryi*, *L. wigginsii*. 2c: *L. superbum*, *L. michauxii*, *L. iridollae*, *L. michiganense*, *L. canadense*, *L. grayi*. 2d: *L. philadelphicum*, *L. catesbaei*.

These species have not proved particularly easy garden plants, although, where conditions suit them, many are very charming. *L. canadense* is one of the loveliest of lilies and has been grown on and off for centuries, unfortunately more often 'off' than 'on'. At least one species, *L. pardalinum*, is a first-rate, robust garden plant, and selected clones raised from seed may give us other garden-friendly forms in the future.

LILIUM BOLANDERI
② *Lilium bolanderi* S Watson

A dainty lily from southern Oregon and northmost California, it has made intermittent forays into European gardens for the past hundred years, but has never stopped long. The stems may carry from one to ten very dainty flowers, horizontal or gently tilted downwards, dainty enough to suggest the common name 'thimble lily'. The little bells with spreading, unreflexed petals are plum-bloomed orange or wine red outside and paler inside and boldly spotted golden towards the base. Leaves in whorls and scattered above, give a blue cast by the glaucous finish. A moist, gritty, peaty soil suit it best during growth. 30cm–1m (1–3½ft).

LILIUM COLUMBIANUM
② *Lilium columbianum* Hanson ex Baker

Widely distributed from British Columbia down to Oregon and California where it may be found from sea level up to a height of around 1500m (5000ft), this species usually grows in moist meadows or woodland. Small rounded bulbs produce stems with pale green leaves in whorls and scattered upper leaves below a pyramid of nodding turk's-cap flowers. Small but plentiful – ranging from six to over fifty – the flowers are hung out as widely-spaced lanterns of rich orange, paler yellow or

66

near-red with maroon dots. Grown in European gardens at different times without great difficulty in well-drained, acid soil, it has not been as long lived as some other types. Grows easily from seed which is more available than that of many kinds. Keep from excessive wet outside active growing period. 60cm–1.5m (2–5ft).

LILIUM HUMBOLDTII
(2a) Lilium humboldtii Roezl & Leichtlin

This is one of the outstanding species of this section, more robust than most and might be thought the North American rival to the Asiatic tiger lily, a many-flowered lily generously maroon-spotted and of pendant turk's-cap form. Stems may have a dozen flowers, with some taller plants' flowers carrying many more, sometimes as many as eighty. Even before flowers are produced the plants look splendid with distinguished whorls of foliage – maybe of some twenty leaves up to 12cm (5in) long. The flowers are largish, 7–8cm (3in) across, a shining orange with dramatic maroon-purple spots, some outlined in yellow. A variable species in all its parts, but always noteworthy. Large bulbs tend to grow from their sides giving a leaning, somewhat lop-sided appearance – an unusual but not unknown feature amongst lily bulbs. 1–1.5m (3½–5ft).

L. ocellatum was long listed as a variety of this species and may be an easier plant to grow. L. humboldtii is not the most difficult of American species, although collected or newly planted bulbs may slowly produce a system of basal roots the first year, only venturing above ground the second year. Like many American species, it needs dry conditions from midsummer until the end of autumn, with first-class drainage through the winter.

LILIUM KELLOGGII
(2a) Lilium kelloggii Purdy

If L. humboldtii is thought of as the American equivalent of the Asian L. lancifolium, then L. kelloggii might pass as the New World stand-in for the Old World L. martagon. The erect stems are adorned by correct-whorled foliage below a

pyramid head of one or two dozen, scented, nodding turk's caps. Similar in colour to L. martagon, the flower buds open near white and become mauve before dying off a dull purple. Most forms have a central yellow stripe to the petals and are peppered with tiny dots. The pinky mauve is best held in semi-shade. It is to this species that breeders have looked for the introduction of pink into American group hybrids. It is a scarce lily and in cultivation will need perfect drainage as well as moisture during the growing period up until blooming followed by about three months of drought. 1–1.2m (3½–4ft).

L. ocellatum

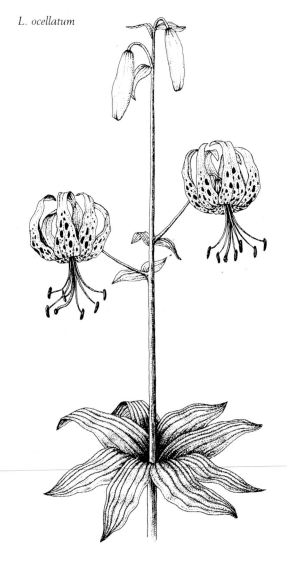

LILIUM OCELLATUM
(2a)
Lilium ocellatum Kellogg

Once listed as a form of *L. humboldtii*, this lily is found to the south and west of that species' distribution. The flowers have crests, particularly noticeable at the petal bases, and are a shining orange, well ornamented with maroon spots ringed by crimson – the same colour as the petal tips. Also unlike *L. humboldtii*, it has jointed bulb scales, root-producing stems and is generally an easier plant to grow. Floriferous, sometimes with over three dozen flowers to a stem, it is likely to grow best in places that mimic the conditions of a moist woodland edge, but with reasonable drainage.

LILIUM RUBESCENS
(2a)
Lilium rubescens S Watson

This beautiful, upward-facing lily opens ivory-white, soon becoming pinky-mauve – some forms are already an attractive pink when opening – before taking on the sombre purple of old age. There is usually some light dotting, occasionally a more extensive peppering. This lily is fairly closely related to *L. washingtonianum* but, apart from its upright pose, it also differs in having very much smaller bulbs and smaller flowers with petals 4–5cm (1½–2in) long. The stems can carry thirty, and occasionally over a hundred, blooms. Usually the flowers are flatish stars and some gently recurve. In nature the species grows in open woodland in southern Oregon and north-west California, in soils with perfect drainage. 1–1.2m (3½–4ft).

LILIUM WASHINGTONIANUM
(2a)
Lilium washingtonianum Kellogg

This variable species, has horizontally held, trumpet- or funnel-shaped flowers, with long-ish oblong petals, bluntly rounded at their ends and only flaring out at the tips to show off their colour. Usually white with purple spots, the trumpets may or may not be stained purple at the base, and there are forms such as *L.p. purpurascens* in which the white blooms move

quite quickly to a lilac pink and end a dark purple. With a dozen or more flowers to a stem, individuals are displaying all colour stages. Bulbs of *L. w. purpurascens* seem to grow more easily than those of the type, which is not to say it is an easy plant. All need gritty, well-drained soil with good quantities of leaf mould or humus, but most important is the desire of these 'dryland lilies' for a dry period from flowering until the beginning of winter, followed by a few frost-free months before getting into active growth again. 1–1.2m (3½–4ft).

LILIUM MARITIMUM
(2b)
Lilium maritimum Kellogg

A smallish species found along the Pacific coast, this lily is not an easy one in cultivation. The small bulbs will require a humus-rich soil with perfect drainage and the young, early foliage may need protecting from frost. The stems usually have scattered leaves and an orange-red, bell-shaped few chubby flowers with golden, purple-spotted throats, held horizontally. 45cm–1m (1½–3½ft).

LILIUM NEVADENSE
(2b)
Lilium nevadense Eastwood

This species should probably be more correctly known as one allocated to *L. kelleyanum* Lemmon. Similar to a smaller *L. pardalinum*, in nature it lives a solitary life unlike its bolder, clump-forming relative. The leaves may be scattered or standing in whorls. It has been successfully involved in hybridising.

LILIUM OCCIDENTALE
(2b)
Lilium occidentale Purdy

Very, very rarely, this lily can be found growing along the coast of southern Oregon and northern California, usually on well-drained hummocks in boggy areas. As with other species in such habitats, it is under considerable threat in the wild and could soon be added to the list of defeated, one-time wild plants. In some gardens it has been grown with some success, with up to twenty dark red hanging flowers, spotted or splashed with orange towards the green centre.

The narrow foliage is carried both in whorls and scattered. 60cm–1.5m (2–5ft).

68

(2b)

LILIUM PARDALINUM
Lilium pardalinum Kellogg

The panther lily, *L. pardalinum*, is the standard bearer for the group. Its strongly rhizomatous bulbs make a mat not far under the soil surface and from here it sends up stems erect as bamboo canes. Healthy whorls of foliage are displayed below the tall heads of nine to ten pendant flowers, hanging on longish pedicles. The strongly recurved petals are a brilliant dark red at the tips, giving way to a tangerine-gold centre, heavily marked with dark spots. Widespread in the Pacific states, its distinctive features are more obvious on the printed page than in the wild.

L.p.giganteum is a splendid, strong garden plant, now thought to be a hybrid of the species with one of the outriders. Its stems are thick, strong and very upright, the wide-whorled foliage classy. The heads carry several similar flowers, perhaps slightly larger than the standard, and the pose is also similar, nodding or more or less outward facing. This is probably the easiest of the American species to grow outside its natural habitat – a long-lasting garden plant with very little need for fussing.

(2b)

LILIUM PARRYI
Lilium parryi S Watson

This distinctive and lovely species has clear, rich lemon-yellow, trumpet-shaped flowers with between one and fifteen blooms per stem in the wild, while under cultivation special stems may carry a crowded cylinder of fifty or more – one stem was exhibited with over eighty! The long, light green leaves are as narrow as grasses; the scented flowers are held horizontally or very slightly downwards, their trumpet shape not compromised by the light recurving of the tips. The glossy, brilliant, deep lemon-gold flowers are very lightly peppered with brown and highlighted by the boldly presented, orange-brown anthers. Originally growing in large numbers in California and Arizona, it was so attractive to pickers and growers that it is now relatively rare. Its preferred sites are mountain stream-sides, in deep, well-drained soil with abundant moisture well below the bulbs in the growing period, and safely tucked under blankets of snow through up to six months of winter.

L. parvum

(2b)

LILIUM PARVUM
Lilium parvum Kellogg

This little alpine species grows from 1500–3000m (5000–10,000ft) up the Sierra Nevada of California to the Cascade Mountains of South Oregon, on stream-banks and meadows watered by glacial melt, in a mix of granite sand and humus. Handled as an alpine plant, the small bulb is not one of the more difficult species – it has been grown at different times in Europe for well over a century although never in large numbers. At present there are several colour forms in British gardens. Although a plant of the hills, its wiry stems can grow to 60cm–1.20m (2–4ft) and occasionally up to 2m (6ft). The upward- or outward-facing, cone-shaped blooms are normally orange, sometimes yellow, pink or red, usually spotted dark maroon. The petals are only slightly recurved. This lily grows relatively easily in most humus-rich soils, in an open, airy site – wet and close, moist atmospheres are likely to lead to bud and flower rot.

L. vollmeri

LILIUM VOLLMERI
(2b) *Lilium vollmeri* Eastwood

Formerly known as *L. roezlii*, this is a *L. pardalinum*-type plant, as close to *L. occidentale* as any species. Found in nature in very wet soils of very high humus content, it does not necessarily require these conditions in cultivation; good drainage is important, as well as the standard requirements of humus, moisture and drainage. The hanging flowers have strongly recurved, orange petals, with maroon-black spots in the centre, with one to three, occasionally half a dozen or even more flowers per stem. The narrow leaves point upwards and are crowded in a scattered formation up the stems, although small whorls occur. 45cm–1.5m (1½–5ft).

LILIUM WIGGINSII
(2b) *Lilium wigginsii* Beane & Vollmer

From the mountains of the Californian and Oregon borders, this is a classy plant with rich green leaves and stems, and lemon or gold nodding, perfumed turk's-cap or bell-shaped flowers peppered with pinpoints of purple. The foliage is more or less clustered to the stem, pointing upwards. Bulbs should enjoy moist, humus-rich, cool conditions and be kept dry through the winter. 30–45cm (1–1½ft) or more.

LILIUM CANADENSE
(2c) *Lilium canadense* L.

The dream species of every fancier, this lovely lily has been known in cultivation since the early 1600s yet is still a plant only for the fortunate few. Widely distributed from Quebec across to Nova Scotia and down to western Virginia, Pennsylvania and Alabama, it is now much scarcer than even one or two decades ago. It usually chooses places near water, by streams, with plenty of moisture for the roots through the hot summers, yet with good drainage for the bulb itself. In the winter it is likely to be snow-covered. Not the sort of conditions it is easy to recreate in most gardens! However, it also often grows in woodland edges – a condition that we might choose for it in our gardens. The stems are very erect, with whorls of healthy, green leaves topped by a few scattered ones. The pendant flowers are held on long pedicles, somewhat more upright than an angle of forty-five from the stem, giving each

70

Much admired, graceful *L. canadense*

 LILIUM GRAYI
Lilium grayi S Watson

This lily is a distinctive, rather slighter relative of *L. canadense*, a rarer plant and certainly no easier in cultivation. Light woodland or similar conditions with a humus-packed soil would seem to be the order of the day. It grows with some success in a number of British gardens. The stoloniferous bulbs are rather sparsely equipped with plump scales in the spreading rhizome, from where the slender stems arise, carrying perhaps one to about half a dozen bell-shaped blooms, not more than 5cm (2in) across. These long bells hang, but are swung away from the more strictly vertical pose of *L. canadense*. The flower colour varies, usually a rich crimson-red giving way to an orange or golden, maroon-spotted throat. The plentiful, narrow leaves are normally arranged in packed whorls. 60cm–1.5m (2–5ft).

L. grayi sometimes swings its bell-flowers wider

bloom its own airspace. Narrow, hanging buds open petals that curve gently out to the horizontal yet maintain a slender, unopened base, from half a dozen to twenty or more blooms to a stem, in garden forms usually coloured a clear yellow with generous dark spotting, in nature coloured from lemon to dark orange-red. The populations from drier, lower areas are likely to be red and have been distinguished botanically as *L.c. editorum*. Its nearest relatives are *L. grayi*, with bells held more horizontally, and *L. superbum* and *L. michiganense* from neighbouring territories, with more strongly recurved petals – very attractive, but more ordinary if one dare to suggest this about any lily! The bulbs of this species have the most well-developed, stoloniferous method of growth. 1.2–2m (4–6½ft).

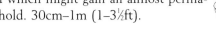

LILIUM IRIDOLLAE
Lilium iridollae M G Henry

(2c)

This very rare little species from southern American states grows shallowly in humus-rich, boggy areas. It has very small bulbs, perhaps only 2cm (¾in) across, and one or a few nodding, turk's-cap flowers of rich gold. It adopts the Madonna lily's habit of producing a rosette of slender leaves after blooming which will overwinter. If seed should ever be available, the resulting plants could prove very tricky to keep. 45cm–1.2m (1½–4ft).

LILIUM MICHAUXII
Lilium michauxii Poiret (Lamarck)

(2c)

Sometimes listed incorrectly as *L. carolinianum*, this stoloniferous bulb is similar to *L. canadense*, but in overall appearance closer to *L. superbum* and found mainly to the south of that species' distribution. It is less easy in cultivation – it will need excellent drainage, an acid, humus-rich soil and enough of it above the

to try and which might gain an almost permanent foothold. 30cm–1m (1–3½ft).

LILIUM MICHIGANENSE
Lilium michiganense Farwell

(2c)

A widespread species of the *L. canadense* – *L. superbum* complex. The flowers are held on typical, long, rather erect, pedicles that only turn at their apex to allow for fully-pendant flowers with a narrow base and boldly recurving petals. One to a dozen blooms top the whorls of foliage. Happy, strong bulbs may produce stems with significantly more blossom. The flowers are usually a very rich orange-red, heavily spotted maroon on the lower third, with a green base; there are some yellow variants. This stoloniferous bulb requires similar soil conditions to *L. canadense*; in the wild it is a plant of meadows and prairies, not of woodland. 1.2–1.8m (4–6ft).

LILIUM SUPERBUM
Lilium superbum L.

(2c)

This – appropriately named – species has been known in cultivation from at least 1738. It has a larger bulb than most of the other species of

L. michauxii

bulbs to make good use of the stem roots. The stems carry one to four or five nodding, scented, turk's caps of rich tangerine with pale golden throat. A lily that it would be interesting

L. superbum

72

the group, with the rhizomes underpinning a strong stoloniferous habit. Healthy whorls of large leaves suggest a robust plant. The large, hanging blooms remind one of the *L. canadense* grace, by their pose and the restrained, slender base but differs in its petals which recurve considerably. The petal tips are crimson, while below the colour is a rich orange-red, heavily dotted or splashed with maroon towards the flower centre. The protruding anthers are a rich red. This is the standard livery, there are plenty of variants, some an unsullied yellow-gold. This is certainly a lily to try in a deep, lime-free soil, between shrubs or in light woodland conditions. Once settled, it is not one of the more difficult Americans. 1.2m (4ft) or more.

(*left*) *L. catesbaei* and (*right*) *L. philadelphicum*

LILIUM CATESBAEI
(2d)
Lilium catesbaei Walter

This lily looks as if it was made up from a child's construction set! It is a tiny, rare wild plant, almost unknown in cultivation. Its bulbs are very small, a loose cluster of a few narrow scales that somehow manage to produce a slender upright stem with plenty of narrow leaves arranged alternately and held rather uprightly. Usually, the flowering stems are happy with one relatively large, wide-open bloom, staring upwards rather like a diminutive *L. bulbiferum* or *L. dauricum*. The gold or tangerine petals are freckled with maroon, especially towards the centre, with the tips a rich red. It is a difficult plant for cultivation, probably best under cool glass, where its overwintering leaves can be kept healthy. It requires an acid soil. 30–60cm (1–2ft).

LILIUM PHILADELPHICUM
(2d)
Lilium philadelphicum L.

The buds of this lily open like a firework with six splashes of colour floating in space apparently without support – or almost so, as the shanks of the petals are long and very, very narrow. The blooms of this small, slender plant are upward looking, with one or two wide-open flowers of bright orange-red, with a golden throat marked with dark dots. There is considerable variation in flower colour, size and amount of dotting. Unlike *L. catesbaei*, it has leaves in whorls, with some scattered ones above. It differs also in having small, properly bulb-shaped bulbs, composed of waisted scales and operating as a stoloniferous type, but only just. New bulbs are produced tightly alongside the old one. It grows in drier areas in the wild; in cultivation it could be tried in a gritty mix with plenty of leaf mould, but would probably need overwinter protection. As with some of the more difficult and unusual of these American species, seed is sometimes available, bulbs more rarely so as it seems difficult to keep in cultivation. 60cm–1m (2–3ft).

L. philadelphicum

(3) L. CANDIDUM GROUP

Group characteristics: epigeal germination (except *L. bulbiferum*, *L. polyphyllum*, *L. monadelphum*), delayed, heavy seeds, scattered leaves, many entire bulb scales, erect stems, almost complete lack of stem roots (except *L. bulbiferum*), erect bulbs, turk's-cap flowers (except *L. candidum* and *L. bulbiferum*).

I have taken the liberty of subdividing the group into four: 3a characterised by winter rosette of leaves, open, outward-facing flowers; 3b characterised by turk's-cap, pendant flowers, rather narrow foliage; 3c characterised by large, wide, pendant flowers, broader foliage than 3b; 3d characterised by large, upward-facing flowers, strong stem rooting, formation of bulbils in leaf-axils (some clones).

Main species: 3a: *L. candidum*. 3b: *L. chalcedonicum*, *L. pomponium*, *L. carniolicum*, *L. pyrenaicum*. 3c: *L. monadelphum*, *L. szovitsianum*, *L. ledebourii*, *L. kesselringianum*, *L. polyphyllum*. 3d: *L. bulbiferum*.

LILIUM CANDIDUM
(3a)
Lilium candidum L.

The Madonna lily has a long association with human culture. Its culinary use apparently predates its early use as a decorative plant as featured on frescos and vases of the Minoan civilisation around 1500BC. Religious connotations preceded its elevation as a Christian

74

The Madonna lily, *L. candidum*

symbol for Renaissance artists. A name followed by the initial L denotes the botanist with priority claim for the naming and describing of the species, the real founder of modern nomenclature, Linnaeus. Immediately we know that any L species will have been known to cultivation from the middle of the 1700s.

This lily is a one-off species in several respects. Culturally it is alone in needing to be very shallowly planted, its bulb nose almost level with the soil surface. It also enjoys rather than hates lime. After the flowering stem has done its job, the bulbs produce rosettes of leaves by late summer which remain throughout the winter. They certainly mark their stations but can sometimes harbour fungus spores over winter. It is a species best grown in isolation to try to forestall its propensity to fall

prey to any virus around and waste away, act as a virus carrier, or become a culture bed for botrytis disease. Still today the best clumps of Madonna lilies are found in cottage gardens devoid of any other lilies.

In health it can be very lovely in the early summer, with tall stems holding from three to a dozen or more large, open, white flowers facing outwards. There are a number of clones marketed, some chary of setting seed. However, some good wild, seed-bearing forms have been used to propagate the species and more virus-free stock has been raised by cloning screened tissue. Serious growers of lilies will enjoy the sight of this species in other peoples' gardens or, if they have the room, will grow it in severe isolation to prevent spread of disease. Such a position should have well-drained soil and be open to sunlight and air. It can be grown between shrubs, but the best clumps I have seen have been more or less in the open and without any of the root shading sometimes advocated. (p95)

LILIUM CARNIOLICUM

(3b)   *Lilium carniolicum* Bernardi & Koch

While displaying similarities to *L. chalcedonicum* and *L. pyrenaicum*, this lily is somewhat variable and distinct from these other plants. It is botanically closest to *L. pyrenaicum* and *L. ponticum*, and has been placed as a subspecies of *L. pyrenaicum* along with *L. ponticum* by Brian Matthews. It is not so muffled up with foliage as *L. pyreniacum* and is also less leafy than *L. chalcedonicum* and has none of its leaves pressed towards the stem. The leaves are somewhat larger, marked below and at the margin with hairs that are absent in *L. chalcedonicum*. The thick-textured, turk's-cap flowers are a rusty red, not highly polished. This lily is a mountain plant from the Balkans. The subspecies *L.c. albanicum* has hairless leaves and is usually an even slighter plant with yellow or old-gold flowers, although reds have been found. *L. jankae* is an eastern form of the species, a yellow-flowered type with purple spots, taller at around 75cm (2½ft) and usually with more flowers. They all enjoy soil with lime. 45cm–1m (1½–3½ft).

(3b)
LILIUM CHALCEDONICUM
Lilium chalcedonicum L.

L. chalcedonicum may well have been grown in gardens for over 200 years – now it is almost a rarity, having had to battle with modern hybrids. It is a pleasing plant, with very brilliant, thick-textured, turk's-cap flowers in narrow pyramids. In the type they are polished and unspotted, while a spotted, more vigorous kind called *L.c. maculatum* has been grown in gardens. The species has a somewhat unusual appearance as the stems are well furnished with leaves with those that belong to the bottom half pointing outwards while above the half-way mark the smaller leaves tend to be upright, almost clasping the stem. 1–1.5m (3½–5ft).

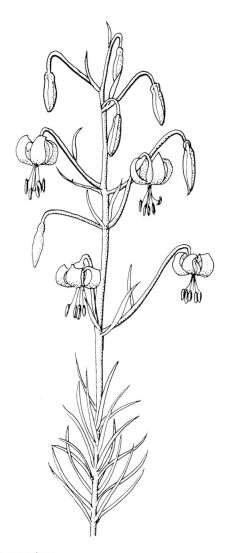

L. pomponium

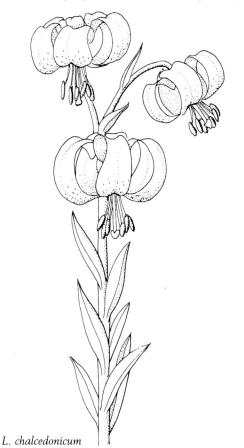

L. chalcedonicum

(3b)
LILIUM POMPONIUM
Lilium pomponium L.

Native in the mountain ranges of southern France and northern Italy, the Maritime Alps, this perky lily can be a real delight. In the wild the small bulbs produce two or three tightly-curled-up, deep orange-red turk's caps. Its mountain homes are normally on limestone; in the garden it is happy with or without lime – perhaps indicating a preference for an alkaline soil. In cultivation, away from grazing animals, it may produce half to a dozen blooms, looking very pretty. Best in a really warm spot, it is not necessarily a long-lived lily; however, it seeds freely, easily achieving a bloom in the third year. 30–60cm (1–2ft).

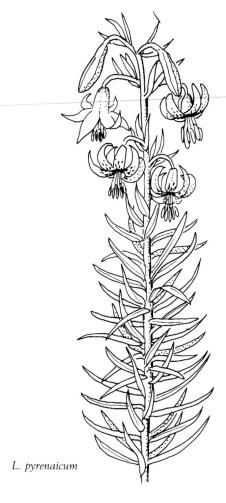

L. pyrenaicum

LILIUM PYRENAICUM
(3b) *Lilium pyrenaicum* Gouan

This splendid lily has tended to suffer a poor press for the disagreeable smell of its flowers. Yet you normally have to get very close and be very sensitive to note this at all. It is, however, one of the easiest of all lily species to grow and the earliest to bloom. It grows rapidly and the very well-dressed, leafy stems hang out buds, opening the first ones by the end of spring, with rich lemon-gold, turk's-cap flowers heavily dotted by early summer. The sturdy stems have

lots of outward-pointing, narrow, bright green leaves. Newly planted bulbs that have been out of the ground some while may sulk for a season but, once settled, the bulbs are likely to form expanding clumps and have been known to naturalise in hedgerows in Devon and in parts of Scotland. The bulbs grow happily in widely differing soils, both with and without lime. The standard flower colour is a slightly acidic yellow, but there are forms more warmly coloured, including full orange-reds. 60cm–1m (2–3½ft).

LILIUM KESSELRINGIANUM
(3c) *Lilium kesselringianum* Mischenko

This is a rare lily from the Caucasus, looking like a much slimmer version of *L. monadelphum*, with paler flowers of narrower petals, cream or palest yellow with a light spattering of tiny, dark dots. Established plants can grow to 60cm–1.2m (2–4ft).

LILIUM LEDEBOURII
(3c) *Lilium ledebourii* Boissier

This rare species from Iran and the Caucasus looks a little like *L. pyrenaicum*, with plenty of narrow leaves rather upwardly proffered and a few nodding, white turk's caps, each with a cluster of small dots around a green centre. Pleasantly scented, it is again in cultivation after considerable gaps since its first description well over a hundred years ago. 1m (3½ft).

LILIUM MONADELPHUM
(3c) *Lilium monadelphum* Bieberstein

One of the most handsome of lilies, *L. szovitsianum* is botanically submerged, but in this book we have separated the two. The large bulbs of many narrow scales may sulk for a year when first planted before producing growth above ground. The stems are well supplied with scattered, narrow, slightly hairy leaves of about 12 x 2.5cm (5 x 1in). The flower heads may number three or four blooms but can have as many as thirty hanging, wide open, large and impressive flowers, with petals 9cm (3½in) long when flattened out. The recurving petals are dotted with pin-prick red spots towards the centre. This lily is one of the earliest to bloom, out by early summer when you may be surprised by its pleasing scent. Once established, it is one of the easiest to cultivate on any reasonable soil, with or without lime. Seed easily germinates as hypogeal delayed, although plants are slow to reach flowering size. The name refers to the unusual feature of the stamens being fused at their base by the ovary, unique in the genus. The degree of this fusion varies and is sometimes absent as in the *L. szovitsianum* populations. 80cm–1.5m (2½–5ft).

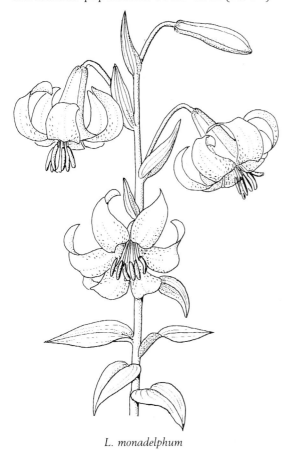

L. monadelphum

LILIUM POLYPHYLLUM
(3c) *Lilium polyphyllum* Don

This is an attractive lily from the Himalayas, but not one that has made a strong presence in the garden having appeared at scattered intervals but then dying out again. If strong clones could be built up it would be a desirable kind

with stems from 1.2–1.5m (4–5ft) and capable of more and normally carrying a load of a dozen hanging blooms and, again, able to double this. The flowers are half trumpets that open and tend to curve back. They are ivory in bud, and outside when open, creamy inside and mauve-flushed or lined longitudinally. It would probably like being kept relatively dry in the winter.

LILIUM PONTICUM
(3c) *Lilium ponticum* Koch

This is a relative of *L. monadelphum*, a smaller flowered plant, stout in growth but inferior in garden worthiness. Hanging flowers of primrose with heavily stained maroon black centres, one to seven per stem. 1–1.40m (3–4½ft).

LILIUM SZOVITSIANUM
(3c) *Lilium szovitsianum* Fischer & Ave-Lallemant

This lily is a variant of *L. monadelphum*, normally found in the Caucasus in the southern part of the distribution of the total species. The stamens of this plant have anthers of orange-brown pollen that contrasts well with the yellow flowers; in the *L. monadelphum* type the pollen is a matching yellow. Its handsome wide bells can have petals 10–12cm (4–5in) long when straightened, and the broad heads are equally impressive with a single flower as with a new seedling bulb, or the score or more of a redoubtable veteran. It is one of the best naturalising bulbs, splendid as an edge-of-woodland plant or between shrubs. If left undisturbed, seed may fall and germinate. To be more sure, harvest and sow seed under controlled conditions. Even then it may take up to five years to get bulbs large enough to bloom.

LILIUM BULBIFERUM
(3d) *Lilium bulbiferum* L.

It is to this European species that we owe much of the genetic input for the Asiatic hybrids. Once a treasured garden plant, it has for the past hundred years been in competition with its hybrid offspring. Nevertheless a good character plant, also as the far more commonly grown *L.b. croceum* variant, it sports tangerine-orange

78

L. bulbiferum croceum

flowers with petal tips and bases. Once numerous in the wild, across from the Pyrenees through the Alps to Czechoslovakia and Hungary, its brilliant orangey-red flowers made it the target of collectors.

The name 'bulbiferum' is justified by the bulbils that can appear in leaf axils. Not every clone, nor even the same plant in different seasons, will necessarily produce bulbils, but most inherit the ability to do so on occasion. The stout plants usually have plenty of scattered shiny foliage. The top of the stem and the leaves may have white, fluffy hairs; the leaves can be as long as 15cm (6in). Cup-shaped, wide flowers stare upwards, on the lesser stems singly or only two or three but on more major ones up to four dozen! The pointed petal tips and the base are clearly very much richer in colour than the body shade; the flower centre can be conspicuously splashed with chocolate-maroon and marked by raised spots. In all normal soils bulbs grow strongly – lime they can take or leave. They are good feeders, the basal roots being generously helped out by stem-rooting systems. 30cm–1m (1–3½ft).

④ ORIENTAL GROUP

Group characteristics: hypogeal, delayed seed germination (except a *L. brownii* form and rarely *L. speciosum*), erect stems, stem rooting, scattered leaves, distinct leaf stalks, erect bulbs, white bulbs (except some *L. speciosum*), entire scales, trumpet flowers (except *L. auratum* and

L. speciosum). I have subdivided the group into four: 4a characterised by strongly recurving petals and very distinct leaf stalks; 4b characterised by large, flat, open flowers; 4c characterised by more or less trumpet-shaped flowers and short leaf stalks; 4d characterised by trumpet-shaped flowers, horizontal flower pose and relatively broad leaves.

Main species: 4a: *L. speciosum*. 4b: *L. auratum*. 4c: *L. alexandrae, L. japonicum, L. nobilissimum*. 4d: *L. brownii, L. rubellum*.

④ₐ LILIUM SPECIOSUM
Lilium speciosum Thunberg

Pressed to choose just one lily for beauty many fanciers would not hesitate to nominate this lovely Japanese species. Its gloriously scented flowers are but part of its allure – the whole character of the plant speaks quality. Slender, wiry stems have classy, healthy, wide leaves, held at jaunty angles by long leaf stalks. The semi-pendant flowers are held by long pedicles so that there is air around them. The whole flower head of some three to dozen blooms is displayed in a graceful, uncrowded manner – something that can still be said of outstanding stems with as many as fifty blooms! Two hundred years ago Thunberg chose the name speciosum for the species, meaning 'handsome', 'brilliant' or 'good looking', an appropriate one.

This is one of the later-flowering lilies,

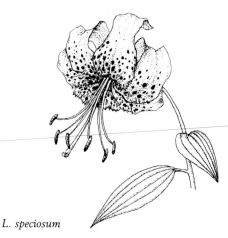

L. speciosum

flowering in early autumn rather than late summer. In milder climates it will grow well outside in lime-free, humus-rich soils – it is one of the most avid lime-haters. Grow virus-free bulbs in isolation, far from other lilies that may be carrying infection. It is a good pot or container plant, especially in cooler areas where it can be grown in lime-free soil. Selections have been made and marketed as *L. s. album*, pure white; *L. s. roseum*, white and suffused crimson-pink; *L. s. rubrum*, with petals almost wholly crimson. 'Uchida' is a particularly strong good form, named after the Japanese nurseryman who spent many years selecting only the strongest and best.

LILIUM AURATUM
(4b) *Lilium auratum* Lindley

This wonderful lily was introduced from Japan in the 1860s, a sensation when first seen in Europe and America, and a wonder ever since, although not always a guaranteed success. At its glorious best it has many wide-open, outward-facing flowers, 25–30cm (10–12in) across, flooding the air with perfume, starting in late summer and continuing for weeks into mid-autumn.

In the wild it grows in Japan in poor soils – volcanic ash – giving instant drainage. In winter the bulbs are covered with snow and therefore kept really quite dry. In the growing period there is plentiful rain, but in bloom they expect weeks of sunshine. Early cultivators often made the mistake of overfeeding the bulbs and causing their premature death. Virus, botrytis and the inadvertent application of lime can also destroy it.

L. auratum has easily the largest flowers of the genus, forming widespread stars with little reflexing of the petals. Basically white, each petal has a conspicuous central stripe of yellow, justifying its popular name 'golden-ray lily'. While some flowers are all snow-white, most have some crimson dotting; in some there is a definite crimson-pink suffusion and the red pigment can supplant the golden ray in some forms, leaving only a golden base. Particularly large-flowered forms have been marketed under the name *L.a. platyphyllum*, plants that are characterised also by larger leaves and only modest dotting in the very big flowers.

Plant the sizeable bulbs topped by 10–12cm (3–4in) of gritty soil with lots of leaf mould. Although the stem roots are important, extra-deep planting does not encourage rooting as well as the addition of leaf mould mulches with washed sand or grit as the plants grow.

LILIUM ALEXANDRAE
(4c) *Lilium alexandrae* Wallace

A rare plant from some of the smaller southern Japanese islands, and a close relative of *L. nobillisimum* from neighbouring islands, both have made fleeting appearances in European gardens. Somewhat tender, they require greenhouse protection, especially from excessive winter wet. The flowers, held horizontally – wider trumpets than *L. nobilissimum* and possibly less numerous – are normally white with a greenish base, sometimes flushed pink. The pollen is brown.

LILIUM JAPONICUM
(4c) *Lilium japonicum* Thunberg

Like most lilies in this subgroup, this species does better in New Zealand, parts of Australia, Oregon and similar spots. It has been grown successfully in Europe in well-drained, humus-rich soil, with plenty of moisture during the growing period, and dryness in the 'dormant' months. In the wild, it is snow-covered through the long winter. It is a strong stem rooter. The slender, wiry stems are only modestly clothed with dark narrow leaves. One to six long buds open to form funnel-shaped flowers with reflexing petal tips. The petals are 15cm (6in) long and present fragrant, soft rosy-pink blooms. There are paler forms, some just blush white. 45cm–1m (1½–3½ft).

LILIUM NOBILISSIMUM
(4c) *Lilium nobilissimum* Makino

A rare lily from the southern Japanese islands, likely to do better in milder areas or in greenhouses. In summer the sturdy stems with short-stalked, dark leaves have one to six green-marked buds, opening as large, startlingly white, open trumpets. The strongly scented flowers are boldly proffered, very clearly above the horizontal, and the dramatic dark anthers display yellow pollen. 45–60cm (1½–2ft).

LILIUM BROWNII
(4d)
Lilium brownii Brown

The success of the trumpet species *L. regale* and the deservedly popular hybrids has tended to overshadow the qualities of other species that might be garden-worthy, such as *L. brownii.* This large-flowered, unscented lily has purplish buds and wide-open trumpets looking very dramatic with its large, dark anthers.

The type as described has not been found growing wild and as a self-sterile plant must be assumed to be a single clone, but *L. b. viridulum* of Central China is similar, with a greenish rather than purplish stem, with smaller leaves towards the top of the stem and with heavily-perfumed blooms. Most forms open pale yellow inside and turn quickly to white, while the outside bud is less dark. In the lower range of *L. brownii* distribution, the form *L. b. australe* takes over, a rather taller and stronger plant. *L. b. viridulum*, which one ought perhaps to think of as the type, may grow to 65cm–1.2m (30in–4ft) while *L. b. australe* may reach twice that height. This species requires more work than *L. regale* and the white trumpet hybrids, and is unlikely to regain its former popularity until more robust, easy clones have been developed.

LILIUM RUBELLUM
(4d)
Lilium rubellum Baker

This classy, small lily originates from mainland Japan, where it grows between shrubs and in grassland in mountains from 750–1800m (2500–6000ft) high. It is rather like a dwarfer *L. japonicum*, with considerably wider, scattered or alternate leaves, measuring up to 10 x 3cm (4 x 1¼in). Its flowers are wide-opened trumpets or bowls of lovely pink, usually with maroon dots in the centres, and with some

paler blush-pink forms. This is one of the earliest lilies to bloom – once started it moves steadily to produce one to six, horizontally-held, scented flowers by the end of spring or early summer. The round, rather narrow-scaled bulbs grow best in an acid soil with plenty of grit and leaf mould with an open structure. Once happy it may grow on for decades – especially if not endangered by virus or botrytis from neighbouring lilies. Cool, light woodland with some shade would be an ideal home. 30–75cm (1–2½ft).

(5)   ASIAN GROUP

Gathered together in this group are some rather disparate species, including the joker of the pack, *L. henryi*, such well-known kinds as the tiger lily, *L. lancifolium*, and all those species with an identity problem, the ones that seem to have borrowed something of the *nomocharis* or fritillaria genera.

Group characteristics: epigeal-immediate seed germination, scattered leaves, entire bulb scales, light seeds, turk's-cap flowers, white concentric bulbs, more or less stoloniferous stem, stem roots, small stigma.

The group is officially subdivided into three, but it would seem to make more sense to allow four and to hive off *L. henryi* into a subgroup of its own. This species differs from the rest of the Asian group as its bulbs are coloured, its seed heavy, and the seed germinates in a delayed-epigeal manner.

Subgroup characteristics: 5a: pronounced turk's-cap flower form, large bulbs (except *L. duchartrei, L. lankongense, L. papilliferum*), stems markedly stoloniferous in *L. duchartrei* and *L. leichtlinii*, rather less so in *L. davidii, L. lankongense* and *L. papilliferum.* (*L. henryi* and *L. lancifolium* have erect stems.) 5b: small bulbs, prolific seeders. 5c: stems not stoloniferous.

Main species: 5a: *L. henryi, L. davidii, L.*

duchartrei, L. lankongense, L. lancifolium, L. leichtlinii, L. papilliferum. 5b: *L. amabile, L. callosum, L. cernuum, L. concolor, L. pumilum.* 5c: *L. amoenum, L. arboricola, L. bakeranum, L. henricii, L. lophophorum, L. mackliniae, L. nanum, L. nepalense, L. ochraceum, L. oxypetalum, L. primulinum, L. sempervivoideum, L. sherriffiae, L. souliei, L. taliense, L. wardii.*

LILIUM DAVIDII
(5a) Lilium davidii Duchartre

In this splendid species erect, dark stems support a pyramid of orange-red flowers, held nodding from long, horizontal pedicles, their curled-back petals decorated with raised black or dark-purple spots. Stems may have 20–40 flowers. The anthers are orange-scarlet. The whole plant may be thought of as a more refined tiger lily, with more polished flowers and the stems carrying a lot of narrow, dark

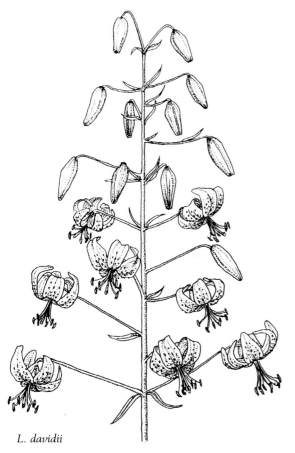

L. davidii

foliage which arches from the stem and becomes steadily shorter as it ascends. Usually there is a tiny tuft of silky-white hairs at each leaf-axil and where flower pedicles join the stem.

This lily grows well in humus-rich, well-drained soils. When exposed to air, the scales of the plump, white bulbs colour up so that bought ones will be pinky-mauve. The stems arise straightforwardly erect, but may deviate a little before rising to the surface. This rooting part of the stem can engender useful numbers of small bulbs.

One of the most distinguished variants is *L. d. willmottiae* which has a very much more pronounced stoloniferous stem, often putting in an appearance above ground well over 30cm (12in) from where the bulb was planted. The leaf axils are usually without the little fluffy tufts of the type. It differs also by having a sloping stem and an inflorescence arching under the weight of its flowers, sometimes over a hundred per stem. You would be prudent to give it some artificial support. Bulbs can sometimes die, but there are usually plenty of smaller ones waiting to take their turn. *L. davidii* is one of the more beneficial influences on the breeding of the Asiatic hybrids and could still be used to good effect.

LILIUM DUCHARTREI
(5a) Lilium duchartrei Franchet

This lily is a species from the mountain ranges of western China usually found 2400–3500m (8000–12000ft) high where it grows in thickets, forest edges and alpine meadows. It appears to enjoy well-drained, moist slopes where it can form useful colonies. In gardens it has not always proved easy, but sometimes grows with surprising abandon. Our plants have always been quite content with flowering stems around 30–45cm (12–18in) with one or two flowers, but it has the ability to reach 1.2m (4ft) with perhaps six nodding, martagon-like flowers in early summer. They are marble-white, prettily dotted and splashed with violet-purple. The yellow anthers quickly peel open to

82

reveal nicely contrasting tangerine pollen. As the flowers age their white gives way to reddish purple. A colony can look very effective as the stems are slender and graceful.

This species is the leading exponent of stoloniferous stem procreation. Just bury the neat, white bulbs in a labelled point A and retire. The bulb will start into growth and send slender stems through the soil, perhaps 30cm (12in) away but often considerably further before reaching point B and turning up to produce a stem. An open leaf mould, well laced with grit and a little healthy loam should suit, and it would appear not to object to some lime. In this small heaven it can quite quickly establish a flourishing colony in two or three seasons. Ours have been most successful in semi-shaded cooler spots. There is a disadvantage to this method of increase – if a bulb gets virus, the whole colony can go down.

LILIUM HENRYI
(5a)
Lilium henryi Baker

This is a pivotal species in terms of the wild lily, and it has proved equally centrally poised in hybridising work. *L. henryi* is distinct and would seem at least as distant from its relatives as the species *L. dauricum* which reigns in virtual isolation in its own group 7. It is thought that *L. hansonii* is the closest we now have to the identikit picture of an original founding plant for the genus. This prototype is thought to have had small, yellow or orange flowers with thick petals and lightly-sketched nectary furrows. It is drawn as a strong, upright plant with leaves in whorls, the stem growing from an erect bulb and having some stem roots. *L. henryi* does not match these specifications as closely as *L. hansonii*, as it has scattered leaves and the nectary furrow is very clearly marked. Nevertheless it would seem to be a surviving lily that established its credo early on and to have stuck to it with the minimum of deviation for many centuries.

This lily has large bulbs with strong, arching, purplish stems and bold, scattered, rich-green leaves, touched purple at the leaf axils. Most of the leaves are long and relatively broad, perhaps 15 x 3cm (6 x 1¼in), but for a short length below the flower head there is an abrupt change to more numerous, short, wide leaves. Apart from *L. wardii* which shows this inclination to a lesser extent, this foliage dichotomy is unique amongst lilies of this group.

The large flowers appear in mid- and late summer, nodding from longish, horizontal pedicles. The scentless, tangerine blossoms are characterised by the considerable number and intricacy of the fleshy, raised points, *papillae*, the strongly recurved petals, the darker central spotting and the green nectary furrows leading back into the hearts of the blooms. Thick, tough-textured flowers seem right for a tough plant. It will grow almost anywhere, less well in very acid soils, and will flourish in gardens with few or no other lilies. It is probably better with some lime in the rootrun, and is a stem rooter. The bulbs can stand some abuse, but are perhaps best lodged between shrubs where the roots get some shade and the stems have support and perhaps also a little shade to help retain the orange colouring which may bleach in strong sunlight. It is strongly resistant to virus – another important factor for the use of this species in hybridisation.

LILIUM LANCIFOLIUM
(5a)
Lilium lancifolium Thunberg

For many this may well be the first Asian species they grow. It is a splendid garden plant. Almost too strong and easy to increase, it can be infected with virus without losing much of its vigour and, unfortunately, in this way acts as a source of infection for more precious kinds so should be grown as far from other lilies as possible. It makes a handsome stand with strong dark stems well clothed with narrow, dark, arching foliage and a usual height of 1.5–1.8m (5–6ft). It produces a pyramid arrangement of hanging turk's-cap flowers in rich orange and red shades with bold spotting in purple-black, and may bear between eight and three dozen. It blooms from late summer into early autumn.

L. lancifolium

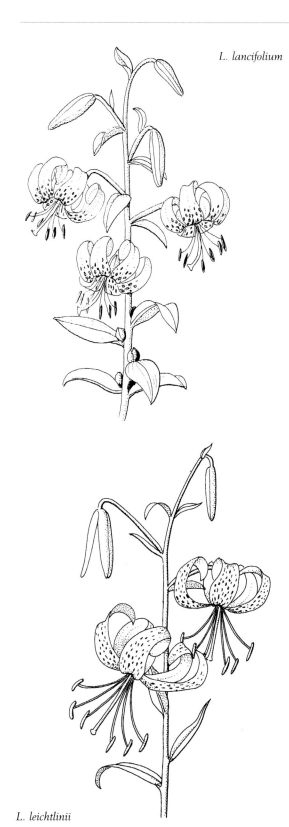

The usual garden form is a triploid, but the wild ones are normally diploid. However, the species has such a long history of cultivation as a fodder plant that it is difficult to be sure of really wild populations. There are yellow forms under the name *L. l. flaviflorum*, effective with rich gold strikingly spotted flowers.

The species is one of the founders of the Asiatic hybrids some of which inherit the bulbil-producing capacity that makes this such an easy plant to propagate. One stem can produce over a hundred bulb bulbils in the leaf axils; when ripe these fall to the ground towards the end of the autumn and pull themselves into the soil with strong rooting action.

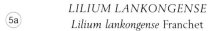

LILIUM LANKONGENSE
Lilium lankongense Franchet

This lily is closely related to *L. duchartrei* – originally it was confused with it. *L. lankongense* comes from the same part of the world, from a more restricted area to the south. It is distinguished by growing habit and flowering form. The bulbs make only a token gesture towards stoloniferous stem growth. Slender, wiry stems support 6–15 nodding blooms in mid- to late summer, typical turk's caps, the petals curling back with pointed tips, unlike the blunt-ended petals of *L. duchartrei*. The flowers are a very pleasing pink with purple-maroon spots, darkening with age. Cool, lime-free spots with moist rootruns similar to those enjoyed by *L. duchartrei* are best. Seed germinates freely and the young plants grow quickly. Dr North used this species successfully to raise his most welcome series of hybrids; other breeders are following his lead. 60cm–1.20m (2–4ft).

LILIUM LEICHTLINII
Lilium leichtlinii Hooker

This is a yellow form of the much more widespread red *L. leichtlinii maximowiczii*, Really, the red kind should be sitting at the top of the table, not only is it the more numerous but it is the stronger plant, however, *L. leichtlinii* is very pleasing with erect dark stems and narrow leaves and with fully-pendant flowers of wide

L. leichtlinii

84

turk's-cap form, normally a very bright golden-yellow with a sprinkle of dark spots. *L. maximowiczii* is a rich orange-red with the same scatter of spots. The stems of both are polished and without the bulbils of *L. lancifolium*. They are attractive plants and useful in breeding. 1–1.6m (3–5ft).

LILIUM PAPILLIFERUM
(5a) *Lilium papilliferum* Franchet

A rare species from rocky, desolate, high mountain haunts in north-western Yunnan this lily is also rare in cultivation. It looks like an alpine martagon with very dark maroon, tightly recurved, little, hanging blooms with pointed petals. The tiny bulbs, not more than 2.5cm (1in) broad, produce wandering stems that eventually make slender, upright stems with many narrow leaves, especially lower down. Coming from a mountain habitat, this species is fairly drought resistant. It grows in limy or slightly acid soils. 30–60cm (1–2ft).

LILIUM AMABILE
(5b) *Lilium amabile* Palibin

This attractive lily from Korea has not proved too difficult to grow in reasonably drained soils. About six hanging, rich-red turk's caps open in midsummer. Numerous, scattered leaves, each up to 10cm (4in) long and 1cm (½in) wide, gently arch away from the wiry stem but it has a leafless base. The flowers are quite wide, with petals 5–6cm long, and are gracefully displayed on longish pedicles and have conspicuous, dark-chocolate anthers. Normally rich scarlet, the petals may be paler, and there is a yellow counterpart, *L. a. luteum*. It differs from the remainder of the Asian group, apart from *L. henryi*, in having heavy seed. 75cm–1m (2½–3½ft).

LILIUM CALLOSUM
(5b) *Lilium callosum* Siebold & Zuccarini

Another dainty, small-flowered lily from Korea, China, Manchuria, Japan and Taiwan, this species is close to the much better known *L. pumilum*, although it is usually taller and blooms later, in mid- and late summer. Dainty, yet slightly bolder than *L. pumilum*, its slender leaves are broader and longer, and its flowers slightly larger. It has the same rather short pedicles so that the flower head of five or six flowers makes a narrow, dull orange-red raceme, darker on the outside, with some understated dark dots towards the centres. It is scarce in gardens but could be happy in a warm, open spot. It is a stem rooter.

LILIUM CERNUUM
(5b) *Lilium cernuum* Komarov

From Korea, Manchuria and northwards, this is another species from the small-flowered *L. pumilum* complex. It has the slender, erect stems typical of small bulbs, and narrow, grassy leaves, not more than 5mm (¼in) wide but up to 18cm (7in) long. The base of the stem is usually bare of foliage and the flower head is well clear of leaves. However, where foliage is present, it is crowded. Curled-up, nodding flowers appear early to midsummer, pleasantly scented and coloured a lilacy martagon-pink, dotted dark purple. Opening pale, they darken with age so that one head may be sporting various shades. This pleasing little, stem-rooting lily is happy in a drained soil, with or without lime. Like most of this group, it is not reliably long-lived, yet seed is freely produced and grows well, blooming in the third year. Grow it in an airy site and keep an eye on it, to avoid crippling botrytis. 30–75cm (1–2½ft).

LILIUM CONCOLOR
(5b) *Lilium concolor* Salisbury

I admit a special fondness for this jaunty little species. It saucily flouts normal Asiatic manners and looks upwards in bloom with wide stars of narrow petals painted a brilliant scarlet unsullied by spots, a frank 'look who's here'-type flower. Neat leaves are more or less alternately displayed, somewhat sparsely low down. The bulbs are small, round arrangements of a few clasped scales, altogether not much bigger than marbles. They want first-class drainage with plenty of humus in the hope of keeping them another year. Harvest seed pods to ensure a succession – it germinates very freely and plants will soon bloom. 30–75cm (1–2½ft).

L. concolor

LILIUM PUMILUM
(5b) *Lilium pumilum* De Candolle

This is still sometimes listed as *L. tenuifolium*, a name it held for many years. It is a delightful plant – small-flowered but prolific and quickly rushing into bloom from seed. It is perhaps too ready to do this and may exhaust itself, but it usually provides plenty of viable seed before departing this life.

The bulbs are small and round with a few tightly clasped scales. Wiry stems reach up to display from one to a score of tightly curled turk's-cap flowers staring straight downwards from their narrow pyramid arrangement and overlooking the plentiful narrow grassy leaves

that tend to curl around the stems. Standard flower colour is a brilliant vermilion, made more effective with its high gloss finish, but there are golden and intermediate forms.

It is best not to consider this a long-lived plant, but the bulbs can be helped to a longer life by thwarting their seeding potential. As seed produces flowering bulbs in a couple of seasons it is no hardship to maintain a stock. One could grow it in the border, in the rock garden, the scree or as an early-flowering pot plant. Normally around 30–60cm (1–2ft) but much taller forms have been found.

LILIUM AMOENUM
(5c) *Lilium amoenum* Wilson

One of the rarely cultivated lilies on the borderline of the genus where it meets the *nomocharis*, this is a plant for alpine-house conditions. It will have one to three hanging, wide, rich rosy or mauve-pink cups with recurving petal tips. The leaves are narrow, although broader than those of *L. sempervivoideum* which is probably its closest relative. 30cm (1ft).

LILIUM ARBORICOLA
(5c) *Lilium arboricola* Stearn

This oddity was discovered by Kingdom-Ward in northern Burma, where it made its home in the trees – a rare epiphyte, growing in the humus-rich detritus collected in the crooks of tree branches. It has apple-green, recurving petals. While it is never likely to be long in cultivation, if ever, it would be interesting if the pollen could be used to hybridise some other species of this group – a range of green or green-tinted lilies could be appealing.

LILIUM BAKERIANUM
(5c) *Lilium bakerianum* Collett & Hemsley

A few instances are recorded of the successful cultivation of this lily species under airy greenhouse conditions, but success has normally been short-lived. Its natural home is the upper reaches of Burma and western China. Large, nodding or semi-pendant, wide trumpet-

86

shaped ivory flowers are suffused green outside and spotted with maroon inside, sometimes quite heavily. When seed is available, adventurous fanciers with mild climates might try bulbs outside. It is a plant with wandering, stoloniferous stems.

LILIUM HENRICII
Lilium henricii Franchet

(5c)

This delightful little plant has an advanced case of schizophrenia – its flowers are similar in appearance to those of the equally enchanting *Nomocharis aperta*, especially in bloom, and it certainly has the grace of the *Nomocharis*, wide-open bells swinging away from a rigid, pendant pose. Looking at the overall cut of her jig however, it falls this side of the *Lilium/Nomocharis* divide, its slender stem being neatly furnished with narrow, shining leaves. There may be three to six white or blush-pink flowers per stem, with a little basal splash of maroon. It has only rarely been grown in cool gardens in drained soils rich in leaf mould. 60–90cm (2–3ft).

LILIUM LOPHOPHORUM
Lilium lophophorum

(5c)

This newly introduced species from northwest Yunnan, where it grows in high meadows, is a dwarf plant with upright leaves similar to those of some tulips – cylindrical and masking the short stem. Its normally single large, rich-yellow flower has long, twisted petals pointing shyly downwards almost as if attempting to make itself look smaller. This is a plant for moist, peaty, cool soils with good drainage. 15–20cm (6–8in).

LILIUM MACKLINIAE
Lilium mackliniae Sealy

(5c)

This lily is a choice and very distinct species, one that every fancier would like to see flourishing in the garden. It does grow well for some, but it is vulnerable to virus which quickly leaches away its vigour. Grown in isolation from other lilies, it may flourish in cool humus-endowed semi-shade. Here stems may have one

to six hanging bells with petals only opening gently at the mouth, the buds open slowly to a longish bell shape, then develop to a flanged cup, a rich lilac-mauve outside, with the pigment concentrated by the stalk and paling to the petal tips, and a white blushing pale-pink inside. Altogether it is a quality plant. 20–75cm (8in–2½ft).

L. mackliniae

LILIUM NANUM
Lilium nanum Klotzsch & Garcke

(5c)

Welcome back! This little plant has been classified as a fritillary and more recently has spent considerable time as a *nomocharis*, but now it has returned to its earliest attribution, the lily genus, where surely it is bound to stay. A small plant, it has narrow, grassy leaves scattered on the stem below the single, large, drooping bud that opens to display a wide bowl of pale lilac, freckled maroon and darker at the base. Some flowers are a rich, dark amalgam of purple and dark tan, and there are also soft-yellow forms (*L. n. flavidum*). 15–40cm (6–15in).

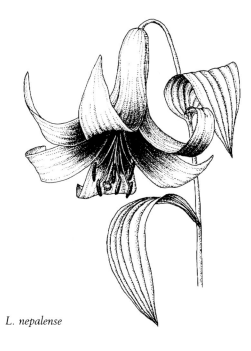

L. nepalense

LILIUM NEPALENSE
(5c) Lilium nepalense D Don

This is a real character actor. Bulbs send out stoloniferous stems that after 30 75cm (1–2½ft) turn upwards erectly with strong, slender canes with relatively few scattered, broad leaves and large, hanging, wide-mouthed lime-green bells, heavily stained on the inside in a dramatic deep-burgundy or mahogany from the centre for half or two-thirds of each petal. The petals are 15cm (6in) long so the flowers look spectacular. Two or three can be borne on a stem. Under glass the bulbs can be in bloom any time from late spring until midsummer. Except in favoured areas, it is a plant for the cool greenhouse where it will need growing in a border or large container to allow space for the stoloniferous stems to wander 20–60cm (8–24in) before breaking the surface. Along its

buried part, the stem should produce a useful crop of bulblets. Some grit, some loam and an abundance of leaf mould are the soil requirements.

LILIUM OCHRACEUM
(5c) Lilium ochraceum Franchet

The lilies *L. nepalense*, *L. primulinum* and *L. ochraceum* are closely related, and some botanists might consider them as different parts of one variable species. The smaller-flowered *L. ochraceum* with its strongly recurving petals seems to represent one extreme. Its Yunnan habitats are drier than those of the other species and it is somewhat more amenable in cultivation. The present consensus is that this plant should be considered a variety of *L. primulinum*.

LILIUM OXYPETALUM
(5c) Lilium oxypetalum Baker

Another ex-*nomocharis*, this bright yellow lily is distinct from *N. nanum flavidum* by virtue of its much broader, shorter leaves and its habit of carrying more than one drooping head. The *L. o. insigne* form has narrower leaves and pinky-mauve and limey-yellow flowers that darken with age. Together with *L. nanum*, this is probably one of the most amenable of the *nomocharis*-type plants in the garden. They all like humus-rich soil that remains moist without getting sodden. Normally they would be best in cool semi-shade. 15–25cm (6–10in).

LILIUM PRIMULINUM
(5c) Lilium primulinum Baker

Like *L. nepalense* this lily has an orchid-like beauty, its greenish-yellow and dark-maroon pigments being rarely found together except in orchids. The texture too has something of the near-plastic firmness of orchids. A number of relatively small features differentiate this species from *L. nepalense* – it does appear to have no or very restricted use for stoloniferous-stem growth, its nectary is usually green not maroon and anther filaments are also not flushed with purple.

The flower described by Baker working at Kew in 1892 was an all-yellow one, a relatively rare manifestation in the species, the more widespread form being *L. p. burmanicum* with typical mahogany-purple throat and generally a taller plant than *L. nepalense*, perhaps reaching 1.3–2m (4–6ft) with two to six or seven hanging flowers with slightly more recurving petals than typical for *L. nepalense*. Its petals may measure anything from 5–15cm (2–6in). It is a stately plant with distinguished foliage, the largest leaves measuring 15 x 4cm (6 x 1½in). *L. p. ochraceum* is much smaller, with more turk's-cap-shaped blooms. You could try it in sheltered spots in warm areas; in almost all parts of Britain it will need a cool greenhouse.

LILIUM SEMPERVIVOIDEUM
Lilium sempervivoideum Leveille

(5c)

The stems of this tiny plant from Yunnan may have a lot of narrow, grassy leaves but will usually only boast one or two nodding, wide, white, cup-shaped flowers with tiny purple dots. Probably never in cultivation. 15cm (6in).

LILIUM SHERRIFFIAE
Lilium sherriffiae Stearn

(5c)

This rarely cultivated, fascinating little lily also looks over the generic fence at the *nomocharis* and *fritillaria* species. The one or two hanging bells are darker on the outside, an amalgam of purple and brown, and yellowish inside, usually quite clearly chequered in the fritillary manner, so by colour and pattern imitating the neighbouring genus. Probably not at present in cultivation. 30–60cm (1–2ft).

LILIUM SOULIEI
Lilium souliei Franchet

(5c)

This little lily could be forgiven for being dizzy – it has moved from the *fritillaria* to the *nomocharis* genus after a brief sojourn amongst the lilies and is now back home where it will surely stay for, although it is on the edge of the genus, its total character is more lily-orientated than any other. In Tibet this lily grows high up in moist meadows and rocky places, sometimes on the edges of woodland. The small bulbs produce stems with scattered, rather upward-reaching leaves, normally carrying a single, cup-shaped flower held horizontally. Its colour varies from dark maroon, plumy to purple-brown with some green suffusion at the base. It has been collected a number of times in the past few decades but has yet to take up permanent residence in our gardens. 20–40cm (8–16in).

LILIUM TALIENSE
Lilium taliense Franchet

(5c)

This species, together with *L. duchartrei* and *L. wardii*, forms a closely-related triumvirate, guarding the *martagon* pretension of this sub-group. They have the *martagon*-shape, colours

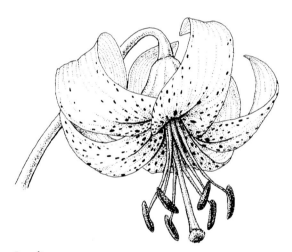

L. taliense

and flower pose. *L. taliense* is akin to *L. duchartrei* in its white flowers but these are generously spotted purple. It looks a plant with more backbone than the other two species, dark stems carrying up to a dozen nodding blooms on pedicles extended horizontally. The purple pigment of the peppered dots is used for the nectary channel and may lightly suffuse the petals of some clones. This species has not proved long-lived in cultivation, but is worth trying from any seed that may become available from China in the hope that more amenable clones can be selected. It grows on soils both sides of neutral, and some clones have half-heartedly stoloniferous stems. Above ground the stems are furnished with plenty of long, grassy, arching leaves. 1.2–1.8m (4–6ft).

LILIUM WARDII
(5c)
Lilium wardii Stern

The name of this lily commemorates the explorer and plant collector Kingdom-Ward who first found it in 1924. It has been successfully grown in a few gardens, but is rare unless a succession is established from the plentifully borne seed. Young seedlings grow quickly to maturity. As many as forty nodding, turk's-cap flowers are arranged on dark, horizontal or ascending pedicles, longer than those of *L. taliense* and so producing a more graceful effect. Flowers are a rosy shade with a hint of mauve, spotted crimson-purple over two-thirds of the petals. Purple anthers soon split to reveal orange pollen. Most clones have stoloniferous stems travelling some 30cm (1ft) or so before producing a 1–1.5m (3½–5ft) stem, displaying dark leaves, wider than those of *L. taliense* and with much more clearly defined veins. The underground stem will produce several bulblets. This species has been brought into the Asiatic breeding programme of one or two breeders – and with good effect.

(6)
TRUMPET GROUP

We arrive now at what the casual gardener tends to think of as the real lilies – large trumpets, mainly white and strongly scented. The botanists approach the group and start dividing them. Coomber splits them into two groups, using a variety of criteria. A florist would also divide them into two – those that are pure white and the others. The gardener is likely to make his classification in cultural terms – those that can be grown outside in the garden successfully and those that need a greenhouse. Gardeners would think it an important group if it had only one species, *L. regale*; cut-flower

growers would value it as highly for the sake of *L. longiflorum*; but there is a little more to it than these two, very important kinds.

Group characteristics: epigeal-immediate germination, stalkless, scattered leaves, entire bulb scales, light seeds (except *L. regale*, *L. longiflorum*, *L. neilgherrense*), trumpet-shaped flowers, erect bulbs, large stigmas, stems with roots. The group is split into two: 6a characterised by dark purple or brown bulbs; 6b characterised by white bulbs and large flowers with narrow, trumpet tubes.

Main species: 6a: *L. sargentiae*, *L. sulphureum*, *L. leucanthemum*, *L. regale*. 6b: *L. longiflorum*, *L. neilgherrense*, *L. wallichianum* *L. formosanum*, *L. philippinense*.

LILIUM LEUCANTHEMUM
(6a)
Lilium leucanthemum Baker

The original type-species introduced by Henry in 1889 has long gone. Farrer found the form *L. l. centifolium* in a couple of cottage gardens in China and this is the form that has remained in cultivation. From seed it gives a scatter of forms, some like the original Henry plant – it looks as if varietal names mean very little in this case. Basically a strong plant with substantial leaves as large as 25cm x nearly 2cm (10 x ¾in), it has proper, large, trumpets, held slightly below the horizontal, a shiny white with primrose-yellow throats, buds flushed green and maroon. It can carry over a dozen such large flowers. The species is lovely but lacks the extraordinary, street-wise robustness of *L. regale*. It was one of the founder species of the American trumpet hybrids such as 'Black Dragon', and could still be used to raise fresh strains. 2–3m (6½–10ft).

LILIUM REGALE
(6a)
Lilium regale Wilson

If only one lily were to be grown this would have to be it! It is quite splendid. I shall quote Ernest Wilson, writing about his discovery of this paragon.

90

'There in narrow, semi-arid valleys, down which thunder torrents, and encompassed by mountains composed of mud-shales and granites, whose peaks are clothed with snow eternal, the Regal Lily has its home. In summer the heat is terrific, in winter the cold is intense, and at all seasons these valleys are subject to sudden and violent wind storms against which neither man nor beast can make headway. There, in June, by the wayside, in rock-crevices by the torrent's edge, and high up on the mountainside and precipice, this lily in full bloom greets the weary wayfarer. Not in twos or threes but in hundreds, in thousands, aye, in tens of thousands . . . For a brief season this lonely, semi-desert region is transformed by this lily into a veritable fairy-land.' It still grows there but in lesser numbers. After discovery in 1903, bulbs bloomed in cultivation two years later and since then this has been the leading garden trumpet lily. It has proved so amenable to cultivation that most gardeners ignore other, more difficult species. *L. regale* can admit one possible weakness: if it gets into early growth, leaves and shoots can be killed by a very hard, late frost. However, this is very rarely likely except in unusually vulnerable gardens. Surrounding shrubs and plants can help protect growth. Long-term sites ought to be well drained and dry rather than wet. Seed germinates freely and young plants will carry single blooms in their second year. Larger bulbs will give six to thirty big, heavily perfumed flowers. The type has large, promising buds coloured purple, pinky-brown; there is also a pure-white version,*L. r. album*, with green-tinted buds and pure-white flowers save for the standard golden throat. This must be one lily which should be tried by the newcomer – it can hold its own against the hybrids. (p95)

LILIUM SARGENTIAE
(6a)
Lilium sargentiae Wilson

Another rare species in cultivation, this lily comes into bloom after *L. regale*, in mid- to late summer. It is again a majestic flower with large, polished trumpets of shining white with a golden throat, sometimes the purple-brown buds give a pink cast to the inner surfaces. Its purple anthers with brown pollen clearly mark it apart from *L. regale*'s yellow anthers with richer, golden-yellow pollen, and the leaves are broader than the narrow ones of *L. regale*. It produces stem bulbils which make bulb increase easy. It is unfortunately prone to botrytis and virus and, of course, virus will be present in bulbils of infected plants. Seed grows well to give clean stock – at least to start with. The *imperale* and Imperial hybrid series are still in cultivation, derivations from the mating of *L. sargentiae* with *L. regale*.

LILIUM SULPHUREUM
(6a)
Lilium sulphureum Baker

Undoubtedly one of the glories of the genus, but alas once it has left its native northern Burma and western China, it tends to fall victim to virus. Every so often a small, fresh influx helps to keep alive the tantalising prospect of a group of these lilies flourishing in the garden, the envy of all other lily growers. It will grow 1.2–2.4m (4–8ft) outside but much taller under glass. The stems are very well furnished with dark green leaves, twice as broad as those of *L. regale*, and with fat, dark bulbils in many axils, being one of the most prolific in this respect. More than a dozen blooms grow on a strong stem, large, trumpet-shaped flowers nicely opened at the mouth with recurved petal tips. The petals can be 25cm (10in) long, so the blooms are certainly impressive. They are scented and a glowing, soft yellow, normally much richer towards the centre. This lily is a strong stem-rooter and should grow in an open, humus-rich soil. The species has been used to produce golden-trumpet hybrid series, and is again being so employed. The aim usually is to reproduce the majesty and colour, while combining it with better resistance to virus.

LILIUM FORMOSANUM
(6b)
Lilium formosanum Wallace

This lily was named after its island home, before it became recognised as Taiwan. At lower altitudes it may produce 1–2m (3–6ft) high stems with narrow-trumpet flowers, widely expanded at the mouth. The buds are usually wine-red and green, the flowers glistening white, rather like fine china. These larger plants are normally classed as fairly tender by those growing in a climate like Britain, although we have had some reasonable success outside with some. It is of course excessively prone to virus.

The well-known form from higher altitudes is the dwarf *L. f. pricei*, which only grows 20–60cm (8in–2ft) high, but is hardier. Its single bloom looks almost comical. I do not know of it being used in breeding, but one could envisage a series of pleasing, dwarf, coloured lilies well suited to small, modern gardens and pot culture. There is a selection offered as *L. f.* 'Little Snow White' which is described as hardy, lined with wine-red in bud, with pure-white trumpets on stems 15–22cm (6–9in) high. The species seeds prolifically and can be brought to bloom within the year.

The diminutive *L. formosanum pricei*

LILIUM LONGIFLORUM
(6b) *Lilium longiflorum* Thunberg

This is the Easter lily that has been, and still is, extensively exploited as a cut flower – it is frequently used in church decor and for funeral tributes. This association with funerals is unfortunate and tends to blight many people's attitude to white-trumpet lilies. More committed lily lovers have forgotten such prejudice. Grown by the hectare in mild-enough climates, it is thought of primarily as a greenhouse plant elsewhere, like all those of the 6b subgroup. Maybe there are climatic changes here – certainly we have grown this species successfully outside in our non-Florida-like West Midlands climate for several years. The scattered, broad leaves are up to 18cm (7in) long and 2.5cm (1in) wide. Pale-green, large buds open to produce long-shafted, scented blooms curving outwards for their upper half or third. The petals maintain close contact with each other for the lower half, and the large anthers with golden pollen finish the picture.

LILIUM NEILGHERRENSE
(6b) *Lilium neilgherrense* Wight

This rare lily is the one growing closest to the equator. Originally from India, where it is found – all too rarely now – in the southern mountains at altitudes of 1800–2600m (6000–8500ft), it would be a tragedy if this was finally eradicated by continued collection – if this has not already happened. It should be found growing in rocky spots or in scrub by streams. It would be quite tall, the stems carrying one or two very large trumpet flowers, 25–30cm (10–12in) long, so difficult to miss. The stems wander for 30–60cm (1–2ft) from the bulb before turning upright. Bulblets are produced on the stem below ground and bulbils above. The white of the flowers is unsullied except for the suffusion of yellow in the throat and a creamy cast to the buds. 1m (3½ft).

LILIUM PHILIPPINENSE
6b *Lilium philippinense* Baker

This lily comes from the mountains of the Philippines and may have to be grown as a greenhouse plant, although it can be surprisingly hardy. We have had it outside for some seasons in the West Midlands. It is not often for sale as a bulb, but seed grows freely and plants can bloom within one growing season, certainly they can be brought into bloom under cool glass in two years. Slender stems hide behind much grassy, narrow foliage. Its very long, narrow trumpets are all grace, held horizontally and shining white except for green or purple suffusions on the outside of the base of the outer petals. It is in competition with *L. wallichianum* for the prize as the longest, most slender of trumpets. 1m (3½ft).

LILIUM WALLICHIANUM
6b *Lilium wallichianum* Schultes

From the Himalayas, this is a graceful white lily with extraordinarily slender trumpets, the tubes very gently widening from where it joins the leaf stalk to the mouth where the petal tips are curved outwards and just a touch backwards. They may have a light pencilling of mauvey-purple-green on the buds, but the overall dazzling white, all satiny smooth, is only made the cooler by the suggestion of green outside and in the confined depths of the centre of the trumpet. It has small bulbs, like *L. formosanum* rather than *L. neilgherrense*, which suddenly send up stoloniferous stems a considerable distance away weeks or months after all the other species have started, unless hemmed in by the sides of a large pot. The foliage is longer than that of most species and very narrow, and the flowers only appear in the autumn, making it one of the latest to bloom. Grown outside it can be so late that the blooms are frosted before they open, so it may be best enjoyed under cool glass. It is worth the effort – the slender trumpets are pure magic. Lots of bulblets are produced on the wandering stem, especially if grown in almost-pure leaf mould. 1m (3½ft).

DAURICUM GROUP
Group characteristics: hypogeal-immediate germination, scattered leaves, no leaf stalks, jointed bulb scales, papillose petals, hairy nectaries, erect flowers, concentric bulbs, stoloniferous stems, stem-rooting.

Species: 7: *L. dauricum, L. maculatum.*

LILIUM DAURICUM
7 *Lilium dauricum* Ker-Gawler

This bold, handsome plant grows widely in north-east Asia, for example in Mongolia and Korea. *L. dauricum* is a plant full of guts, perhaps it could be thought of as a stronger Asian equivalent of Europe's *L. bulbiferum*. Stout, strong stems wander away from the bulb to produce a rooted stem base on which bulblets are borne. Scattered, shining-green leaves, 10–15cm (4–6in) long and 2.5cm (1in) wide, are boldly displayed in an arching manner below the head of 1–12 upward-facing, large bowl-shaped flowers. The flaming-scarlet flowers with conspicuous brown spotting appear in early summer. In many clones the petals are narrow at their golden base, so that daylight can be seen between, but overlap generously in the main parts. There are forms with the petals overlapping right down to the base of the ovary. At one extreme of the colour range there is an all-yellow form, *L. d. luteum*. This is one of the founder species of the modern lily hybrids that are gathered together under the name 'Asiatic hybrids' (see p101). Seed germinates quickly and plants grow strongly. 30–75cm (1–2½ft).

LILIUM MACULATUM
7 *Lilium maculatum* Thunberg

After a chequered history, this name has been reinstated for the plant previously grown and known as *L. wilsonii* Leichtlin. Japanese botanists have found this to be a good species, with perhaps three main forms of which the form described here is the former *L. wilsonii* and the most important. The species as a whole is close to *L. dauricum*, a case could be made for amalgamation. The now surplus name, *L. wilso-*

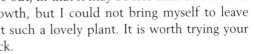

nii, was used to honour G. F. Wilson whose garden is now famous as the Royal Horticultural Society's gardens at Wisley. This strong-growing, upright lily has large, wide flowers in salmon-orange shades with a prominent stripe of gold from the centre of each petal down to the base and large dark dots. The petal tips are recurving and the edges are sometimes slightly fringed – an unusual feature for a lily. Yellow forms are known.

BEST GARDEN SPECIES

These lilies are chosen as outstanding, distinct kinds, both beautiful and highly reliable. They should be easy, permanent plants in most gardens once settled in. *L. canadense* is the odd one out, in that it may be less than extrovert in growth, but I could not bring myself to leave out such a lovely plant. It is worth trying your luck.

L. bulbiferum
L. canadense
L. dauricum
L. hansonii
L. henryi
L. lancifolium

L. martagon
L. pardalinum
L. regale
L. szovitsianum
    (monadelphum)

7

HYBRID LILIES

Lilies have always been admired, although they have not always enjoyed the same soaring popularity as today. Once they were the rich man's plaything, when intrepid explorers and collectors sent back bulbs and seeds from Asia to Europe and America. These proved to be wonderful, new, exciting plants but often capricious, and many of the precious lilies lasted only a few years. The lily achieved its reputation for beauty and difficulty in these years between the end of the nineteenth century and the outbreak of the First World War.

One new species did more than any other to refute this bad publicity: *L. regale*. Huge numbers were grown and prices tumbled to a low that all could afford. This trumpet-lily was introduced in the first decade of the century, having been unknown before this.

EASY-CARE LILIES

The lily revolution really got underway in the 1950s, when the work of Jan de Graaff in Oregon began to make a huge impact on the gardening public. All the best forms of species and hybrids were brought together, and a large-scale programme of hybridisation got under way. Phalanxes of new hybrids were introduced and proved to be so much more spectacular in growth and reliability as well as looks that they became irresistible. Globally, the main breeding work has been with the Asiatic hybrids, especially with those that have upward-facing flowers. Rapid propagation, quick and easy culture combined with attractive colours and flower forms that ensured easy packing and distribution, guaranteed success, making it the ideal cut flower. Many millions are sold annually in most European countries, in America, Australasia and all over the world, in florist's shops and all sorts of stores. Even those with only a modest interest in gardening have bought packets of bulbs or carried home pots of lilies in growth. The lily is proving the ideal plant for modern homes and gardens. This explosion of interest would not have taken place if the plants had remained as relatively idiosyncratic as the original species. Breeding programmes have cancelled out many of the inhibitions and problems with the wild plants and now we enjoy one of the easiest of plants.

Once you have tried a few Asiatic hybrids and found out how easily they grow in pots or in the garden, it is a short step to becoming an *aficionado* keen to try new kinds and types and also 'to spread the word'. The diversity allows you to specialise, perhaps rejoicing in the almost overwhelming Orientals, or finding the long-lived, naturalising martagon types just the thing to bring magic to your garden. Some growers become so fascinated in the wild kinds that hybrids are almost forbidden, but this is the exception – most growers are like me, enthralled by the whole genus.

NATURAL CYCLES

Hybrid lilies are offered as cultivars and as mixed strains. Thus you can buy a cloned cultivar such as 'Enchantment', with all the bulbs producing identical plants, or bulbs of a strain such as Citronella which is a 'grex', a number of clones of the same or very similar parentage with many characteristics in common, but not producing identical flowers. Commercial growers and dealers are happy to increase both classes of products and to market them. Nomenclature rules, which are accepted

L. martagon forms

L. Bullwood hybrid (IV)
(L. pardalinum giganteum
× pink Henry Bolander hybrid)

L. regale album

L. candidum

L. 'Marhan' (II)
(L. martagon album × L. hansonii)

world-wide and used in this book, state that cultivar names should be enclosed in single quotemarks, names of a grex or a strain should be free of these, but start with a capital letter.

The wild lily increases mainly by seed, and this is a realistic way for gardeners to increase their stocks. I believe that almost everyone might benefit from raising their own plants from seed. Of course you may want to purchase new cultivars, but you might get the most interest and beauty from the genus by relying on seed-raised plants. Chapter 8 explains some of the opportunities and techniques available.

Some cultivars have been in cultivation for well over fifty years and are still worth growing, but perhaps we should think of lilies as plants that go through a natural cycle, to be replaced after some years. Growers of species know that some kinds are naturally short-lived, and they always have replacement seedlings coming along. The hybrids are unlikely to die out in this manner, but we could help to keep all well by arranging a turnover. We can then keep our outstanding kinds and also constantly upgrade the collection or change its balance. You need not be put off either if you only have a relatively small garden – some of the most successful breeders have had little space.

CLASSIFICATION OF LILIES

The horticultural classification as detailed below was a sensible and brave attempt to maintain some order when lilies began to be more widely bred some decades ago. Fundamentally, it is based on the derivation of the hybrids, the dominant species of the parentage deciding the division to which the new hybrid is assigned. This has served us well, but with the increasing diversity of the parentage of new lilies and the very definite breakdown of the former breeding barriers, partial or complete, between the different divisions, the classification of new cultivars is becoming more and more arbitrary. We are entering a multi-racial lily world and a fresh look at classification is becoming urgent.

Such a new classification may have to depend entirely on the phenotype – the sum of visually observed characters – rather than the genotype – genetic garniture – characteristics. Appearance and character is all. No classification is going to be perfect, it cannot be anything but arbitrary, yet it would help everyone if it gave some clue as to the look of the plant and flower. Some of the factors might be: flower shape, flower size, flower pose, foliage form; secondary factors might start with colourings.

THE MAIN CLASSES OF LILIES

In the popularity stakes, the clear winners are the Asiatic hybrids, followed by the trumpets and then, coming up close, the Orientals. These cover only three of the nine divisions of garden lilies – eight for kinds of hybrid origin and the ninth for all species and their natural forms. A fairly recent tinkering with the classification has arranged the four classes of division VI solely on the basis of flower shape.

'Casa Blanca', the successful Oriental hybrid (p131)

At the present time the classification does bring some semblance of order, but some revision will become necessary as the numbers of inter-division hybrids increases. The complexity of some new hybrids might give Solomon a

(*above*) 'Prominence' is one of the numerous upward-facing Asiatic hybrids (Div Ia)

(*right*) 'Barbara North', a downward-facing Asiatic hybrid, has *L. lankongense* as one parent, a species that bequeaths its graceful poise

THE HORTICULTURAL CLASSIFICATION OF LILIES

Division	Description	Example
I	Hybrids derived from such species or hybrid groups as:	*L. amabile*, *L. bulbiferum*, *L. cernuum*, *L. concolor*, *L. davidii*, *L. lancifolium*, *L. leichtlinii*, *L. pumilum*, *L. x maculatum* *L. x hollandicum*
I (a)	Upright-facing flower(s), single, one or several in an umbel or raceme (often compressed)	'Enchantment', 'Apollo', 'Prominence', 'Yellow Blaze'
I (b)	Outward-facing flowers	'Fire King', 'King Pete', 'Corsage'
I (c)	Downward-facing flowers	Citronella, 'Pegasus', 'Barbara North'
II	Hybrids of *Martagon*-type, with parentage owing most to a *L. martagon* form and/or *L. hansonii*	'Marhan', Backhouse Hybrids, 'Sutton Court'
III	Hybrids derived from *L. candidum*, *L. chalcedonicum*, *L. monadelphum* and other European species (not *L. martagon*-types)	x testaceum, 'Limerick', 'Uprising'
IV	Hybrids of American species	'Shuksan', 'Robin', Bellingham Hybrids
V	Hybrids derived from *L. longiflorum* and *L. formosanum*	'Longistar', 'Longidragon', 'Casa Rosa'
VI	Hybrid trumpet lilies and Aurelian hybrids derived from Asiatic species such as *L. henryi*, but not those from *L. auratum*, *L. speciosum*, *L. japonicum* and *L. rubellum*	*L. henryi*
VI (a)	Those with trumpet-shaped flowers	'Black Dragon', Pink Perfection, 'Damson'
VI (b)	Those with bowl-shaped flowers	Heart's Desire, 'First Love', 'Lady Anne'
VI (c)	Those with flat flowers	'Bright Star', Golden Sunburst, 'White Henryi'
VI (d)	Those with distinctly recurved flowers	'Lady Bowes Lyon'
VII	Hybrids of Far-Eastern species such as:	*L. auratum, japonicum, rubellum, speciosum*, including any of these hybrids with *L. henryi*
VII (a)	Those with trumpet-shaped flowers	'Angelo', 'Joy', Mr Sam
VII (b)	Those with bowl-shaped flowers	'Casa Blanca', Devon Dawn, 'Trance'
VII (c)	Those with flat flowers	'Star Gazer', 'Pink Beauty', Imperial Crimson
VII (d)	Those with recurving flowers	'Sans Souci', 'Journey's End', 'Black Beauty'
VIII	Hybrids not provided for in any other division	
IX	All species, their varieties and forms	

headache. Meanwhile, catalogues and lily fanciers tend to use names rather than numbers for the different divisions; so we have:

Asiatic hybrids (Div I)
Martagons (Div II)
Candidum or
 European hybrids (Div III)
American species hybrids (Div IV)
Longiflorum hybrids (Div V)
Trumpets & Aurelians (Div VI)
Orientals (Div VII)

ASIATIC HYBRIDS (Div I)

The beginnings of lily breeding may have been Japanese gardeners collecting and treasuring natural hybrids, in times long past. The Japanese islands are home to a selection of species – and to a very long tradition of horticultural expertise and love of flowers. It seems probable that kinds found growing wild in Korea and China will have been introduced into Japan very early. A series of plants under the name *L. maculatum* apparently with much *L. dauricum* blood arrived in Europe in the last century and were then subjected to hybridisation with the European *L. bulbiferum*. These and other similar series were offered under the names, *L. x hollandicum*, *L. x umbellatum*, *L. x thunbergii* and *L. x elegans*.

In various parts of the world, in the 1920s and 1930s, these early hybrids were crossbred with the species *L. davidii* together with its form *L. d. willmottiae* and of course *L. lancifolium* and its yellow form, *L. l. flaviflorum*. Most of these early hybrids have long disappeared, yet a few such as 'Fire King' have survived; this one is still grown commercially. In various proportions its breeding involved *L. dauricum*, *L. davidii* and *L. d. willmottiae*, *L. bulbiferum croceum* and the original mix *L. x maculatum*.

The Stenographer series were bred in the 1920s and 1930s by Miss Preston in Ottowa from *L. davidii willmottiae* crossed with *L. dauricum* seedlings. The series was of orange-red kinds like 'Grace Marshall' which features in the background pedigree of such important

cultivars as 'Connecticut King'. Another similar series was bred by Dr Patterson at the University of Saskatchewan in the 1940s.

An early American hybrid was given the ugly name 'Umtig', suggested by the parentage *L. tigrinum* (now *lancifolium*) x *L. umbellatum*. It was this plant mated with a lemon *maculatum* clone, 'Alice Wilson', that Jan de Graaff used as the foundation of his Mid-Century hybrids which were very successfully marketed from the 1950s and began the renewed interest of amateur gardeners in hybrid lilies. Some of these hybrids were in their turn crossed with *L. davidii* and with the gutsy *L. amabile luteum* to give yellows such as 'Destiny' which is still listed commercially. The Harlequin strain is reported as bred by de Graaff by mating *L. cernuum* with Mid-Century kinds. These were marketed as a mixed range with blush-pink, rosy, cream, yellow, orange and red represented. They do have rather narrower foliage but are more vigorous than some subsequent *L. cernuum* crosses. Most faced outwards and some are still marketed and grown today, more than forty years after their introduction, a fair testimony to their vigour.

Mainly following the work of Judith McRae in the USA, *L. concolor* has entered the increasing complicated genetic stew. Many of the hybrids have a lot of the vivid perkiness of *L. concolor*. Judith McRae has also helped to bring *L. pumilum* into play, now excitingly part of the make-up of tetraploids such as 'Fire Alarm'. Ed McRae has made huge contributions across the whole lily genus: amongst the Asiatics, he is looking to the polyploids to give increased strength and disease resistance. Also in America, Len Marshall is involving other species such as *L. callosum* and *L. wardii*.

Dr North in Scotland, working then at the Scottish Horticultural Research Institute at Invergowrie, Scotland, managed to use the species *L. lankongense* with *L. davidii* and a number of Asiatic hybrids to breed a series with graceful pyramids of hanging flowers. These are much prized by lily fanciers, though some report them as rather fleeting plants.

UPWARD-FACING ASIATICS (Div Ia)

Unless otherwise stated, all the following bloom in early to midsummer.

100

'Alpenglow'

'Alpenglow' Rather tight cones of pointed, blush and darker dog-rose-pink flowers. A sturdy-stemmed, early flower that appeals to most. 60–75cm (2–2½ft). (above and p105)

'Apollo' This is a sturdy, strong plant with lightly pink-flushed, ivory buds opening to very wide, saucer-shaped, white flowers with slight central touches of green, wide, overlapping petals and orange stamens. The crowded, but tidy heads resemble upward-facing moons – so why 'Apollo', the sun-god, perhaps because he was patron of music and poetry? 70cm (28in).

'Atlantic' A good, distinct, white flower with evenly-formed, pure petals, except for the ring of a few dark beauty spots in the centre, and a touch of green from the shafts of the petals. The anthers are a good dark-orange contrast. 90cm (3ft).

'Avignon' 1984 (Unnamed seedling x 'Eurovision') The flowers are an Indian-orange with deeper red midrib and slightly reflexed tips. The nectary area is violet-red, the pollen dark rusty-red. The flowers measure 15cm (6in) across, with petals 8 x 5cm (3 x 2in). 1m (3½ft).

'Ballade' Wide, starry, salmon-orange flowers, with the small bowl centre lightly dotted, arranged in a pyramid head. 75cm (2½ft).

'Bright Beauty' A splendid, sturdy plant with a crowded pyramid of large, apricot and golden-orange flowers with maroon-dotted throats. 90cm–1.20m (3–4ft).

'Brushstroke' 1985 (Unnamed white 1a x (('Connecticut King' x (*L. dauricum* x *L. leichtlinii max-imowiczii* 'Unicolor'))) Large, cream stars of long, recurving petals, becoming white, maroon-dotted throat. The distinctive feature is the central, rich, dark plum-burgundy brushmark, break-

ing to several points away from the centre. The anthers are rich-orange. A really eye-catching plant with 5–15 well-spaced flowers, in good heads growing to a splendid 1.5–1.8m (5–6ft).

'Byam's Ruby' ('Brenda Watts' x 'Cabeli') The seed parent is one of the orange Stenographer series and the pollen parent from 'Vermilion Brilliant' x 'Wallacei' from the *hollandicum – maculatum* family. It is a very deep burgundy-red. 90cm (3ft).

'Canasta' 1984 ('Grand Prix' x 'Pirate') Nicely-spaced, dark-glowing, red-polished flowers of open bowl form with gently re-curving petals, lightly peppered with tiny spots in centre. The flower pose is outward to upright, a pleasing attitude. The dark foliage and stems promote a healthy appearance. 90cm (3ft).

'Carla Luppi' 1983 (('Amber Gold' x 'Kinsen') x ('Amber Gold' x 'Kinsen') – 'Kinsen' was from 'Destiny' x (*L. lancifolium* x *L* x *maculatum*)) Neat pyramid heads of very wide, very open, refreshing, lemon-yellow flowers with a few dark beauty spots in the centre, good, contrasting, orange stamens and clean, green stems and foliage. 90cm (3ft).

'Charisma' 1976 (Mid-century hybrid x (*L. davidii willmottiae* x 'Mahogany')) A short-stemmed, brilliant-orange flower with golden-yellow central flash. 30cm (1ft).

'Cherished' 1989 (Unknown parents) Distinctive, with dark rosy-pink buds and petal reverses. The very wide stars are a mid-lilac-pink that has a slightly creamy-flushed base where there are a few

L. 'Massa'

L. 'Menton'

L. 'Mercedes'

L. 'Roma'

L. 'Apollo'

L. 'Connecticut King'

L. 'Luxor'

L. 'Enchantment'

L. seedling

L. 'Sterling Star'

L. 'Grand Cru'

L. 'Red Carpet'

small, dark spots. Many blooms that can measure 15–18cm (5–6in) across, flowering in early summer. 90cm (3ft).

'Cherry Smash' 1988 ('Dunkirk' x 'Charisma') Bred by L. Marshall, this lily is in bloom when others are just thinking about forming buds, from late spring to early summer. Sturdy, upright stems with rich foliage and dark, upward-pointing buds, opening to wide stars of unspotted cherry-red. 90cm (3ft).

'Cocktail' 1985 (Pink seedling x 'Connecticut King') Mixed shades of buffy-cream, gold and rose-pink; with a scatter of purple chocolate spots in the centre. 75–90cm (2½–3ft).

'Concorde' 1976 (Selection from Sundrop grex) A smooth-petalled, wide-open, lemon flower, with recurved petal tips, a touch of green in the throat which is generously peppered with dark, chocolate-red spots. The Sundrop grex was bred from a Connecticut hybrid crossed with *L. dauricum*. 'Concorde' is a strong-stemmed kind. 90cm (3ft).

'Connecticut King' 1967 This has proved the most successful commercial yellow lily in the face of much serious competition. The breeding background brings together much of the main influences through the mid-century and the Stenographer hybrids, and relies heavily on the beneficial influence of the yellow *L. lancifolium flaviflorum*. Growing strongly, with leafy stems all shining bright-green, and wide, packed heads of tough, unspotted, yellow flowers, 12–15cm (5–6in) across. Rich gold merges into a wide halo of deeper gold fading to a yellow throat around the green nectary area. 90cm (3ft). (pp101, 145)

'Corina' 1978 ('Cinnabar' x (*L.*

davidii x 'Radosnaya')) Evenly-shaped, wide-petalled, uniformly pinky-red flowers with some dark brown spots towards the centre. 90cm–1.20m (3–4ft).

'Cote d'Azur' 1984 (Unknown Parents) Uniform, deep rosy-red, lightly spotted, wide-petalled, open flowers in well-packed flower heads on strong stems. 45–60cm (1½–2ft).

'Destiny' 1950 (*L. amabile luteum* x 'Valencia') Famous mid-century hybrid with wide bowls of lemon-gold, spotted chocolate. The bulbs have very narrow scales. 75–90cm (2½–3ft).

Devon Gems 1985 A strain from Derek Gardham with red, orange and yellow flowers in early summer, strongly growing. 90cm (3ft).

Devon Pastels 1985 D. Gardham's strain of hardy plants in many soft shades of red, pink, tangerine, yellow and cream, early summer flowering. 90cm (3ft).

'Dreamland' 1984 (Unknown parents) This L. Woodriff cultivar is a free-flowering, wide bowl-shaped, golden lily with a warm apricot infusion in the petal centres, overlaid by a few dark spots. 90cm (3ft).

'Electric' 1985 ('Prince Charming' x 'Ladykiller') An unusual lily with widespread orange, lilac and pink petals, with a wide, near-white band on at least two-thirds of the petal margins. The petal tips and margins can be flushed pink. The centre of each flower has a shower of maroon spots. 75cm (2½ft).

'Enchantment' This flower, introduced in 1947, the standard-bearer for the mid-century hybrids that were energetically marketed in the 1950s, has proved a huge

success as a cut flower. It is perhaps the one lily that most gardeners can name. Periodically stocks have been cleaned of virus and prove it again to be a remarkable plant with plenty of fresh, green foliage and strong, green stems with crowded heads of starry, vivid orange spotted blooms. Some critics suggest that the flowers are packed a little too tight and that the vibrant colour is difficult to associate in the garden. Would that all our problems were so small! 75cm–1.2m (2½–4ft). (p101)

'Eurovision' 1984 (Red seedling x 'Pirate') A vigorous plant with smooth, even, rich-orange flowers with a deeper throat, it has dark brown spots over half of each petal on around nine flowers per stem. 1.2m (4ft).

'Festival' Distinctive lily with good-sized, pointed, wide flowers with red-tipped and -edged petals that give a bronzey cast to the central yellow which is handsomely painted with dramatic dark spots. Deep chocolate buds and reverses. It blooms midsummer and then produces a heavy crop of stem bulbils, almost rivalling *L. lancifolium* in its profligacy. It has strong dark stems and dark green pointed leaves. 90cm–1.2m (3–4ft).

'Firecracker' 1975 ('Harmony' x 'Byam's Ruby') This is a smallish, rich orange-red flower, produced in large numbers on a wide pyramid-head. 1–1.2m (3½–4ft).

'Grand Cru' A dramatic personality, it has dark leaves and strong stems that hold many spaced, large, golden flowers with broad petals, distinguished by their very strongly painted, dark mahogany-maroon, rounded splash of colour in the centre of each petal towards the base. 75–90cm (2½–3ft). (p101)

'Gran Paradiso' A full-blooded, rich red flower with orange throat on pyramid-shaped flower heads, it has been used as cut flower. A triploid and a useful breeder with tetraploids. 90cm (3ft).

'Harmony' A mid-century hybrid with wide bowls of broad, pale tangerine petals with few dark spots, sitting as broad heads on strong, short stems. 60–75cm (2–2½ft).

'Harmony'

'Heartspell' 1986 ('Juliana' x 'Firecracker') One of a series of flowers difficult to describe as their flowers are a melted mix of pink, crushed strawberry and peach with a touch of gold in the centre towards the base of each petal. Dark maroon, almost black spots are evenly spread over the lower third or half of the petals. Well-arranged heads. 90cm (3ft).

'Impact' 1988 ('Connecticut King' x (*L. leichtlinii maximowiczii* 'Unicolor' x 'Golden Wonder') F2) Another of the brushmark-types, this is a starry, soft tangerine flower with contrasting, boldly painted, red brushmarks and below a few similarly coloured

spots. The brushmarks spread across the width of the petal or leave just a narrow margin at the edge; a small, much darker area in the centre of the mark adds to the drama. 90cm–1.20m (3–4ft).

'Jetfire' 1981 (*hollandicum* type x 'Connecticut King') This showy lily has spotless, wide flowers with recurved, flaming orange petals that are shining gold in the centre. The three outer petals are narrower than the broad inner ones. The leaves are numerous and rather narrow. 75–90cm (2½–3ft).

'Joanna' 1981 (*L. wilsonii flavum* x 'Connecticut King') A strong plant with dark foliage and two dozen or more bright yellow flowers in large heads. Each petal has a deeper zone in the centre and is spotted chocolate above a green base. The anthers are a dark orange-brown. 1.2–1.5m (4–5ft).

'Ladykiller' 1974 (*L. lancifolium* seedling x 'Harmony') Rich orange-red flowers, spotted dark maroon-red; in midsummer. 90cm (3ft).

'Latoya' 1985 ((seedling x 'Sterling Star') x (('Showboat' x 'Sterling Star') x ('Connecticut Star' x 'Sunrise'))) Uniform, dark pink-red, durable flowers of starry form without dotting. 90cm (3ft).

'Liberation' A pronounced pyramid of many starry, shining pink flowers with a lilac-mauve undertone, relatively broad, green foliage and sturdy stems. 75–90cm (2½–3ft). (p105)

'Lime Ice' A strong plant with bright green foliage. Mid-yellow flowers with suggestions of limey-green and more pronounced, green nectary throat. 1.2m (4ft).

'Luxor' A strong-growing, quickly increasing bulb with stout stems

well clothed with broad, polished, mid-green leaves and well-arranged flower heads with 10–25 large blooms of broadly overlapping, rich gold petals, with a much deeper shade in the centre – almost a pale tangerine. One of the best in this colour range. 1–1.5m (3–5ft). (p101)

'Malta' Sturdy, spotless, rich pinky-lavender flowers, arranged as smooth stars, 12–15cm (5–6in) across and durable. This lily flowers early and sets seed freely. 60–90cm (2–3ft).

'Marilyn Monroe' A fine, strong, all yellow-gold lily with thick-textured, good-sized flowers in well-spaced heads. 90cm–1.2m (3–4ft).

'Massa' A tall lily with many deep red, open flowers. Massive stems with 12–25 blooms, wide-petalled and of a very rich shade. Bulbils are easily provoked and may flower within twelve months. 1.5–1.8m (5–6ft). (below and p101)

'Massa'

'Medaillon' 1978 This is an established lily with pleasing, very wide-petalled saucer-flowers of an

appealing, soft creamy-yellow merging into a smallish area of stronger yellow towards the centre, with a small number of deep brown spots. The stems are sturdy and the foliage is a dark, rich green. It is not one of the taller kinds and so is easy to place towards the front of any bed. 60cm (2ft).

'Menton' 1993 ('Avignon' x seedling) A strong lily with good broad foliage, stout stems and well-disposed, large flowers opening in succession for weeks. The broad, overlapping, widespread petals are an even, pale salmon with very few dark spots. Good increaser. 90cm–1.20m (3–4ft). (p.105)

'Mercedes' 1986 (Unknown parents) This lily boasts strong, wiry, dark stems, pointed, narrowish, dark leaves and boldly arranged, brilliant flowers of very pointed,

(*left*) 'Mercedes'; (*below left*) 'Medallion'; (*below right*) 'Mont Blanc'

starry outline, the tips a very deep red which gives way to a rich orange-red with dark spots. Like a larger edition of 'Pirate'. It may produce many bulbils. 90cm–1.2m (3–4ft). (left and p101)

'Mont Blanc' A 'Yellow Blaze' seedling, with some of its splendid vigour, although rather dwarfer and earlier into bloom, this lily was introduced at the end of the 1970s and is still going strong as garden plant and cut flower. A sturdy, good plant with wide-open, rounded, ivory-white flowers, lightly dotted in the centre. It combines well with geraniums and annuals such as love-in-the-mist or cornflower – blue flowers accentuate the soft colour of the satiny flowers. 60–75cm (2–2½ft).

'Moonflower' A 'Connecticut King' seedling, introduced 1979. Soft-glowing, creamy-yellow flowers with rich, deep golden blotch dotted dark brown. 75–90cm (2½–3ft).

ASIATIC HYBRIDS *(shown at 1/3 life size)*

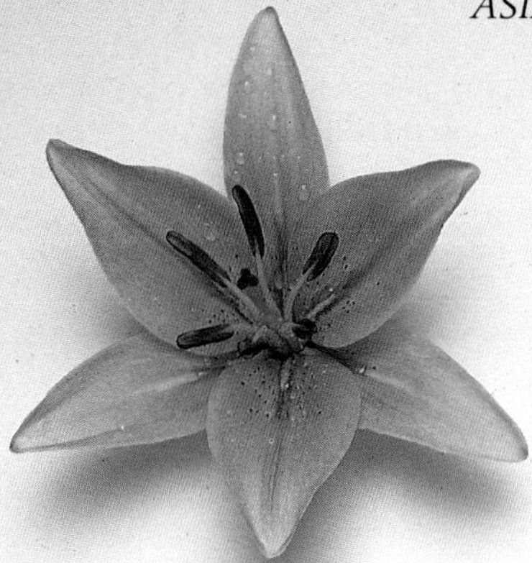

L. 'Peacock Creation' (Ia)
mature flower

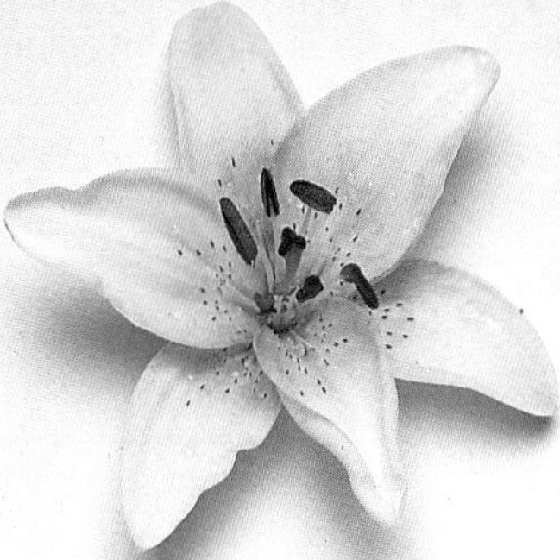

L. 'Alpenglow' (Ia)

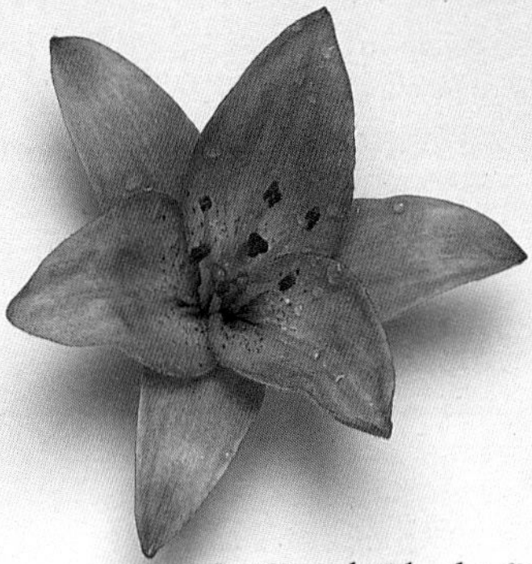

L. 'Peach Blush' (Ia)
mature flower

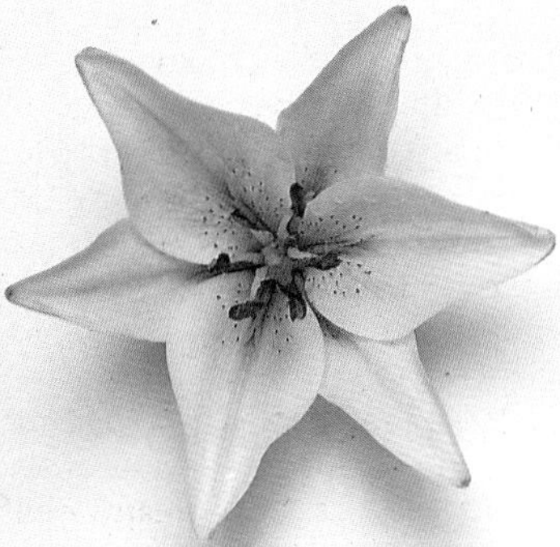

L. 'Peacock Creation' (Ia)
newly opened

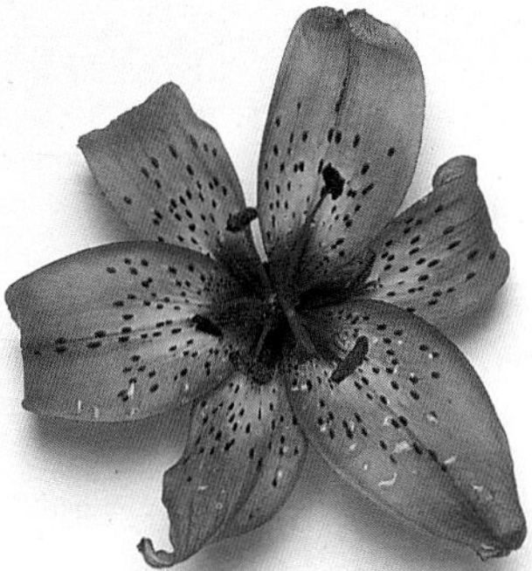

L. 'Lorelli' (Ia)

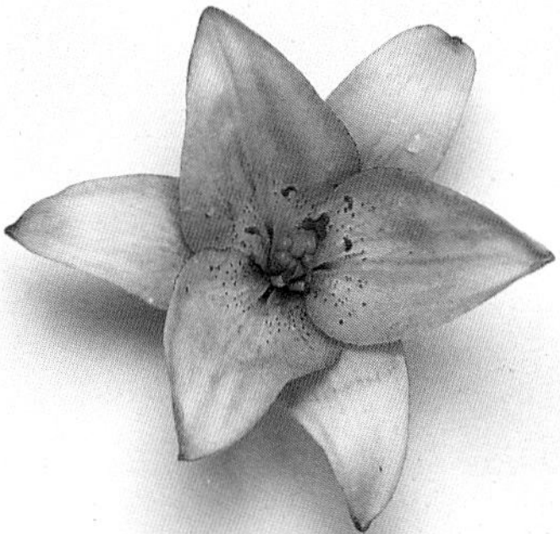

L. 'Peach Blush' (Ia)
newly opened

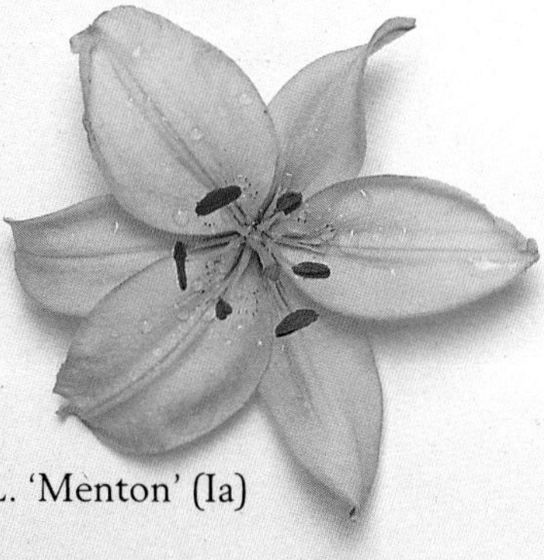

L. 'Menton' (Ia)

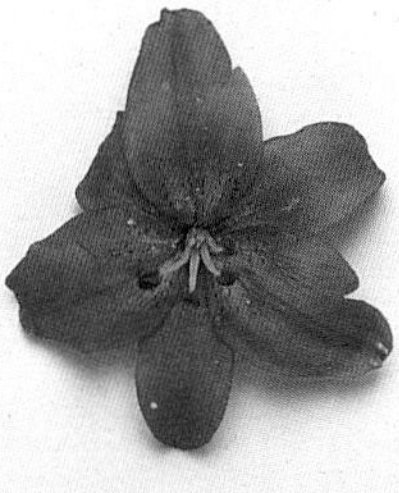

L. 'Liberation' (Ia)

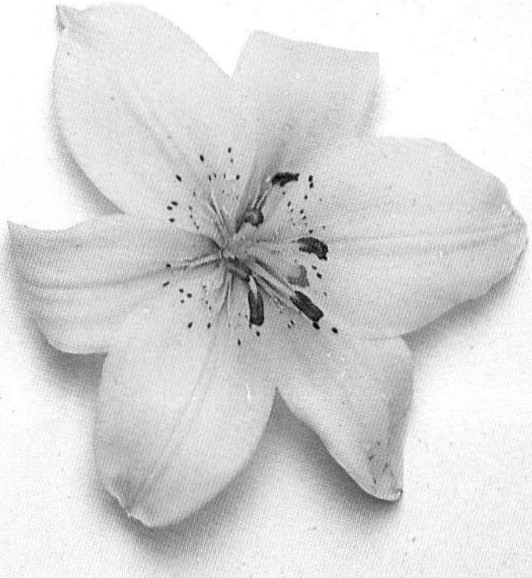

L. 'Roma' (Ia)

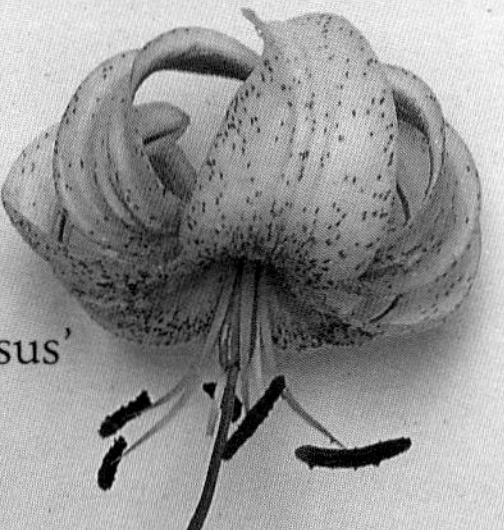

L. 'Pegasus'
(Ic)

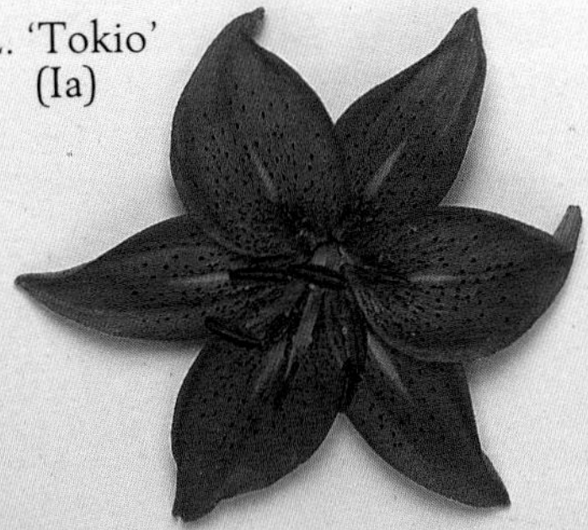

L. 'Tokio'
(Ia)

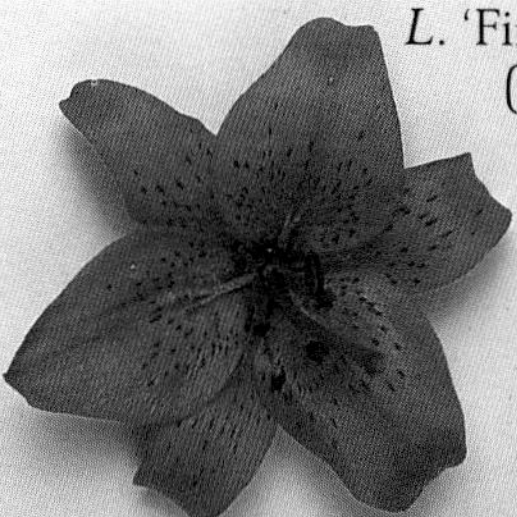

L. 'Fire King'
(Ib)

106

'Nivea' A many-headed, medium-sized flower giving an overall salmony-orange effect, this busy, industrious bulb is a frothy bloomer. 90–1.2m (3–4ft).

'Orange Aristo' (*hollandicum* kind x 'Tabasco') A rather old-fashioned type, this lily is almost a bedding plant with glowing tangerine flowers with a stronger-coloured blotch and dark, rusty-red spots. 60cm (2ft).

'Orange Pixie' (('Harmony' x 'Sunspot') x Charisma) A lily with bright orange-red, pointed, starry flowers with chocolate-maroon pepper-spots. Its very short stems make it a useful pot plant, although the flowers are relatively large for the plant size. 30–40cm (12–15in).

'Orange Triumph' Of the old *maculatum-umbellatum-hollandicum* brigade, but one of the best of these with around a dozen sizeable, wide-petalled flowers of glowing mid-orange, spotted dark maroon-purple. 1.2m (4ft).

'Orchid Beauty' Quite a charmer with petals gently but definitely recurved, somewhat limey-yellow with orange-red nectary and central shading and some beauty spots. A floriferous good plant. About 60cm (2ft).

'Pandora' One of Dr North's Asiatic hybrids with no trace of *L. lankongense*. A short-stemmed, many-headed, rich orange lily that is useful for its very early season. 50–60cm (20–24in).

'Peach Blush' ('Cinnabar' x (('Lemon Queen' x 'Destiny') x 'Edith Cecilia') F2 x ('Hallmark' x *dauricum*) Sturdy-stemmed, with polished, outward-pointing leaves and very well-spaced heads of large flowers. The colour varies from peachy-salmon to a paler, buffy pink, depending on the age

of the flowers. In some lilies such a range of shades can be disconcerting, in this it is charming. 60cm–1m (2–3½ft). (p105)

'Peacock Creation' 1990. (Unknown parents) Strong bulb and plant that puts on quite a performance – peacock seems right! It has very crowded heads of pointed or wide-funnel form flowers; they do not have room to open too wide. It makes an interesting and showy mass in mid-summer. 90cm–1.2m (3–4ft). (p105)

'Phoebus' 1976 (A North hybrid of 'Connecticut Lass' x 'Destiny') A good, all golden-yellow, unspotted, mid-season flower. Produces bulbils. 75–90cm (2½–3ft).

'Pirate' 1971 ('Paprika' x (('Lemon Queen' x 'Mega') x 'Edith Cecilia') A sprightly plant with dark wiry stems and dark pointed leaves. Medium-sized flowers are in vivid shades of red and deep orange and dotted. Very pointed petals and starry outline, but perhaps the most noticeable feature is the high lacquer finish. 75–90cm (2½–3ft).

'Presto' A many-flowered tight but neat, pyramidal head of blazing scarlet crimson flowers, without spots and very early. Very strong plant, increasing quickly. 1.2m (4ft).

'Rangoon' (*L. lancifolium flaviflorum* x *wilsonii*) x 'Redstart') One of Derek Fox's early hybrids, a bright orange-red with darker centre and dark spots. Large wide flowers. 1.2m (4ft).

'Red Carpet' An early opening *umbellatum*-type cultivar with wide deep bowls of broad overlapping petals. The form is almost goblet-shaped but the petals curve outwards. A good number of rich dark scarlet-red blooms in

a compacted raceme, very early in the season. 75cm (2½ft). (p101)

'Roma' 1989 (Unknown parents) Creamy-white, wide-petalled flowers make a good head above healthy dark foliage on strong stems. Can be induced to give large crops of large bulbils. 1.2m (4ft). (p105)

'Roman Candle' 1988 ('Pirate' x (*L. concolor* x *L. pumilum*)) One of a relatively new series exploiting the genetic potential of *L. concolor*. In this splendid example, steel-strong black stems hold a tremendously long, very floriferous column of vivid stars of fiery orange-red. It explodes into blossom early in the season, with spring just over. The very dark stems and foliage are the ideal background for the floral effort, which is likely to be of two dozen or more flowers per stem.

'Rosefire' An extrovert mix of colour on flowers that are large on the *L. dauricum* pattern with light to be seen through the narrow petal shafts. Broad petals are basically a shining orange-red with a central zone around the throat that is a glowing golden-yellow and the base the darkest of the three tones, a rich orange. 90cm (3ft).

'Sans Pareil' One of the tricolor kinds, this is very showy and the colour mix may be too much for some. Rich, bright lavender-pink petal tips, almost half the petal length, around a warm yellow centre with a dark maroon-pink-splashed base. 90cm (3ft).

'Sargent Kelley' 1985 ('Pirate' x seedling) A bowl-shaped flower of

Seedlings at present under trial by the author. The first number refers to the sequence of selection and the second to the year of selection

SEEDLING ASIATIC HYBRIDS, *Division Ia, upward facing and Division Ib, outward facing*
(shown at ¹/₂ life size)

No. 1/94 (Ia)

No. 22/94 (Ib)

No. 1/93 (Ia)

No. 9/94 (Ib)

No. 7/93 (Ia)

No. 2/94 (Ia)

Unnumbered

No. 12/94 (Ib)

No. 4/94 (Ib)

No. 7/94 (Ia)

No. 5/94 (Ia)

No. 23/94 (Ia)

rich deep glowing red, uniform in colour, with petals opening out and gently recurving. A few small pepper spots in centre. A strong plant that is a fertile breeder with pollen gametes of both diploid and tetraploid values. 90cm (3ft).

'Silly Girl' 1983 (1a purple seedling x 'Prince Charming') A bright tricolored flower – a lilac-toned pink with a triangular patch of creamy-yellow next to a deep maroon-pink base, two thirds of the petal is flecked with showy maroon spots. Rather narrow foliage on wiry stems. 60–90cm (2–3ft).

'Simeon' 1984 ('Prune' x 'Sterling Star') Green buds turn to amber and then split open to form wide bowls with recurving petal tips. Inside, the pale colouring is a soft buff which could have been worked up on a palette using pink and palest orange. A sprinkling of small maroon spots in the centre bowl. Extended head with plenty of bloom. 75–90cm (2½–3ft).

'Sirocco' 1984 (L. x hollandicum x 'Papillon') Light pinky-yellow with darker throats with a few spots. Buds and reverses strong peach. The flowers are 15cm (6in) wide and not recurved. 1.2m (4ft).

'Snowstar' 1985 ('Sterling Star' x seedling) Might well have been called 'Snowdrift' as it covers itself with wide heads of pure white flowers making wide-petalled stars. An improved 'Sterling Star'? Buds are a limey-green, stamens are tangerine and the foliage a good green, wider leaves than 'Sterling Star' and virtually without that one's freckling. Good stems. 75cm–1.2m (2½–4ft).

'Sterling Star' 1973 (('Lemon Queen' x 'Mega') x ('Edith Cecilia') x 'Croesus') Has had a fine career as a cut flower and garden plant. Bulbs offered for sale now should be ones that have been grown on from tissue culture to clean the cultivar from virus. Wiry dark stems and narrow dark foliage below well-spaced, wide stars of white, attractively and evenly spotted in the lower half or two thirds of each petal. 75–90cm (2½–3ft). (below and p101)

'Sterling Star'

'Sun Ray' 1965 ('Connecticut Lass' x 'Keystone') The same parentage as 'Connecticut King' and from the same stable. It is difficult to suggest which of the two flowers is the more successful in the garden. Both have a distinguished record as market flowers. 'Sun Ray' is an exceptionally robust, quickly increasing garden plant with typical shining mid-green foliage and stout green stems holding good heads of many deep golden blooms, two or three dozen on main stems. Unlike 'Connecticut King' there is a light sprinkling of brown spots and flowers turn somewhat more outwards. 90cm (3ft).

'Syndicate' 1985 ('Passat' x 'John Dix') Widespread pointed flowers of rich salmony-peach-pink which gives way to a yellow throat notable for its well-defined dark maroon spots. Pleasingly arranged ascending heads, strong dark stems and foliage. 75–90cm (2½–3ft).

'Tamara' A pretty flower of mixed colours, red petal tips give way to cream and amber shades in the centre with grey-brown dotting. 60–90cm (2–3ft).

'Tender' 1990 (Unknown parents) Stout stems with bright green, quite broad foliage. Relatively large flowers are generously produced in an umbel-like compressed raceme, a pale unspotted dog-rose pink. 90cm–1.2m (3–4ft).

'Tokio' Vivid, wide open, very flat flowers in basically two colours – a rich orange with the centre a glowing gold. 60–75cm (2–2½ft). (p105)

'Tropicana' 1976 (Of unknown parents, a Woodriff hybrid) Still a most pleasing, starry-flowered dwarf lily of appealing soft shades. Pointed petals are pinky-red, giving way to a mid-yellow centre and finishing with darkly painted nectary furrows that form a red star in the base. Lots of bloom. 60cm (2ft).

'Tweedle-dee' 1978 A selection from the Rosewarne Experimental Station in Cornwall, from their dwarf Pisky grex. Wide open, flat flower with broad, rich yellow petals with a richer throat, much decorated with largish brown freckles. A striking kind. 50cm (20in).

'Unique' 1987 ('Pirate' x ?) Sharply pointed stars of shaded pink, rich at the tips and in the centre where there are a few dark dots. The main sections of the petals are white shaded lilac-pink. Many-headed and long-lasting. 1–1.2m (3–4ft).

'**Vesper**' This is a clone chosen out of the original Vesper strain. Altogether a very cool and classy lily, with broad, open, pure white, spotless, flowers of oval-pointed petals recurving gently from a green nectary base. Flowers have a hint of cream in the centre. They are gracefully arranged in a neat pyramid head. It is the dark stems and leaves that give the plant that extra edge. 90cm (3ft).

'**Wattle Bird**' 1978 (Seedling x 'Connecticut King') Another good, unspotted yellow flower with a deeper blotch in the centre of the wide petals. 90cm (3ft).

'**White Happiness**' 1979 Ivory-white flowers with dark maroon spots and rusty-red anthers.

'**White Prince**' 1979 An unspotted flower of generous proportions, opening ivory-cream but soon turning to white. 75–90cm (2½–3ft).

'**Yellow Blaze**' 1965 ('Nutmegger' x *wilsonii flatus*) This 'oldie' earns its place by being such an easy, strong plant and producing good crops of bright flowers in late summer. The strong green stems are well furnished with healthy, shining mid-green foliage. The clean, rich yellow flowers are wide despite the marked curl of the petal tips. There is a small green nectary base and chocolate spots are freely distributed. The narrow petal shanks form air holes in the centre of the flower, making this plant more distinctive. 90cm–1.2m (3–4ft).

OUTWARD-FACING ASIATICS (Div Ib)

'**Apricot Supreme**' 1987 ('Thunderbolt' x 'Tetra Rachel Pappo') Epoch-marking flower bred by Le Vern Freimann, a tetraploid, whose seed parent is a distinguished Aurelian from Division VI and whose pollen parent is an Oriental. It is difficult to justify the classification except that the rich apricot flowers look Asiatic. They are held pendant from the horizontal, and are large, nicely dotted and well held in pyramid heads. It is both a fertile breeder and strong plant. 90cm–1.2m (3–4ft).

'**Brandywine**' 1953 ('Brenda Watts' x yellow *hollandicum*) A brooding, dark orange flower with red spots, wide open, rather flat, with recurving petal tips. A short cylinder of flowers is carried on sturdy stems. 90cm (3ft).

'**Bullseye**' 1986 ('Connecticut Lemonglow' x ('Connecticut King' x (*L. dauricum* x *L. leichtlinii maximowiczii* 'Unicolor')) F2) A showy lily with good-sized, lemon-yellow blooms of outward-spreading, broad petals curving backwards at the tips. The brush-mark plum-red of the petal centres produces a circle, around a pale yellow base. It has strong stems and foliage, giving a polished, overall picture. 60–90cm (2–3ft).

'**Cheyenne**' A strongly drawn character with almost black stems and very dark, healthy foliage below considerable column pyramids of deep chestnut-crimson-red flowers that open from promising dark buds, perhaps two dozen to a stem. Early flowering and long-lasting. 90cm–1.2m (3–4ft).

'**Corsage**' 1961 One of the kinds with no pollen, it has a good number of smallish, pale pink flowers, centred cream, with a peppering of small maroon spots. The buds are pale yellow-and-pink when they open and these colours are kept on the reverses of curled-back petals. 90cm (3ft).

'**Exception**' 1978 (*L. cernuum* hybrid x (*L. cernuum* hybrid x *L. davidii*)) Like 'Corsage' it has no pollen and a rather similar colouring – reddish-pink and ivory with grey spots, but a larger flower. The filaments in this flower tend to be flattened into make-believe, small petals. 90cm (3ft).

'**Fire King**' 1930s ((*L.* x *hollandicum* x *L.* x *maculatum*) x ('Crovi-dii x *L. davidii willmottiae*)) A remarkable plant to have held its place so long, the crowded head of flowers glistens a deep vermilion with a scattering of purple spots. The petals are broad and overlapping, their tips recurving, the foliage is palish green with the many leaves graded to become smaller as they go up the stem. 90cm–1.2m (3–4ft). (p105)

'**Geni**' Of the outward-facing lilies this is virtually alone in offering rich lavender-pink flowers in good numbers on black stems. The wide-open flowers with recurving petal tips are enhanced with a light sprinkle of dark specks confined to a ring around the centre. 90cm (3ft).

'**King Pete**' 1975 ('Panamint' x 'Connecticut King') A bold and distinctive kind with large, broad-petalled flowers of creamy-yellow, generously overpainted tangerine-gold towards the centre. The generous sprinkling of purple spots is an important element of the design. The nectary base is green. Well-spaced flowers are carried on strong stems. 90cm (3ft).

'**Moulin Rouge**' 1978 (Unknown parents) Medium-sized, thick

No. 16/94 (Ic)

No. 7/93 (Ic)

No. 22/94 (Ic)

No. 16/94 (Ic)

No. 7/93 (Ic)

No. 22/94 (Ic)

No. 6/93 (Ib)

Unnumbered (Ib)

Unnumbered (Ib)

No. 24/94 (Ib)

No. 15/94 (Ib)

No. 46/94 (Ib)

flowers of rich orange-red that does not quite swamp the intermittent orange veining and blotching, with dark chocolate spots. 90cm–1.2m (3–4ft).

'Nicole' This is a classy cultivar with narrow, dark foliage and almost-black stems carrying a pyramid of ivory buds that open to display shining, white blooms almost flat in the centre, with gently recurving petal tips. Behind the protruding rusty-orange anthers the central third of each petal is neatly marked with a series of dots and dashes drawn from the centre outwards. These lines and spots are a very dark maroon. The flowers are slightly perfumed. 1.2m (4ft).

'Paprika' 1958 ('Fireflame' x red *hollandicum*) Midsummer flowers of dark burnt-mahogany-red in close heads. 60–90cm (2–3ft).

'Peach Melba' A pleasing plant with strong, wiry stems perhaps carrying one or two dozen refined precisely placed blooms in an extended flower head, coloured peachy-pink – or is crushed-strawberries closer? – with creamy centres and a light scatter of spots around the richly painted, dark

rose nectary furrows and base. 90cm (3ft).

'Pink Tiger' 1976 (*L. lancifolium* hybrid x 'Discovery') Flowers are vibrant, rich scarlet with a light purple cast and with chestnut-red spots. 90cm (3ft).

'Prins Constantijn' 1970 (*L. leichtlinii maximowiczii* x Citronella) Orange-red flowers with recurving petals, well spotted with dark red, sit in large numbers on pyramid heads. 90cm–1.2m (3–4ft).

'Redstart' 1960 (*L.* x *hollandicum* x *L. lancifolium* (triploid)) Dark chestnut-red, heavily freckled, flowers with recurving petal tips, still a useful, wide-petalled flower and good plant. 90cm (3ft).

'Red Velvet' Smooth, rich, glowing red flowers of thick texture, well-formed and -placed. Very hardy, strong plant, a triploid. 1.2–1.5m (4–5ft).

'Rockstar' Delightful, starry lily, clearly showing *L. concolor* influence. The flowers are an even, warm, deep salmon or pinky-tangerine on neat, triangular flower heads, each one held on

wiry, dark, upward-facing stalks that are slightly tilted outwards. One of the first lilies to open. 75–90cm (2½–3ft).

'Sarah Marshall' A remarkable *L. wardii* hybrid (breeder Len Marshall), it sports an elongated pyramid of wide-open, pointed flowers in rich pinky-red and strong stems. A strong plant, it does not drop pollen. 90cm (3ft).

'Showtime' 1988 (*L. hollandicum* x (*L. pumilum* x *hollandicum*)) This lily looks as if it were bursting with health, with its very strong stout stems and lots of shining leaves below well-spaced, large shining, gold flowers with sometimes a suggestion of red. They are thick textured and without spots. A splendid, early garden lily. 60–90cm (2–3ft).

'Summit' One of Len Marshall's *L. callosum flaviflorum* hybrids, these lilies make very strong plants with narrow foliage and stems. The triangular heads have many starry, recurving, palish-yellow blooms, flowering later than most, opening in mid- and late summer. A drought-resistant, hardy plant. 1.5m (5ft).

DOWNWARD-FACING ASIATICS (Div Ic)

'Amber Gold' 1964 One of the Fiesta hybrids owing much to the background influence of *L. amabile*, *L. dauricum* and *L. davidii*, this lily is amber-coloured with a good sprinkling of maroon spots and has extended florescences on very dark stems. 1–1.2m (3½–4ft).

'Big Max' 1988 (('Connecticut King' x 'Hallmark') x (*L. leichtlinii*

Seedlings at present under trial by the author. They are labelled by sequence and year of selection

max. 'Unicolor' x white Pastel hybrid)) Like a number of these downward-facing Asiatics, this one blooms about three weeks later than the main flush. Its crowded, well-arranged heads of reflexed blooms declare its *L. leichtlinii maximowiczii* parentage. It is a robust plant with dozens of tangerine, lightly spotted flowers in midsummer. 1.2–1.5m (4–5ft).

'Cabriole' An elegant kind with gracefully recurved turk's-cap flowers in soft, warm peach

shades without any spots and with much protruding, dark anthers, held on extended, dark pedicles. 60–90cm (2–3ft).

Citronella strain 1958 After all these years this is still a series of plants well worth growing, a selection from the Fiesta hybrids. The specifications allow some variation from rich amber-gold to lemon, invariably decorated with little black spots and always completely pendant, although the size of the flowers can vary. The large-flowered clones have fewer than

112

the dozens of blooms that decorate the candelabra of the smaller ones in midsummer. 1.2–1.5m (4–5ft).

'Connecticut Yankee' 1959 (*L. lancifolium flaviflorum* x 'Gold Urn') Large, unspotted, tangerine flowers in large numbers, well-spaced. 1.2m (4ft).

'Discovery' 1962 (('Lemon Queen' x 'Mega') x 'Edith Cecilia') A very attractive flower with the same parents as 'Sterling Star' and 'Pirate'. The large, recurving flowers are of mixed shades, with the petal tips dark reddish-pink grading to a mauve-rose and then to near-white centre, lightly suffused pink and maroon-spotted. Long, dark pedicles hold the flowers gracefully in their own airspace. 90cm (3ft).

'Fireworks' ('Matchless' x (*L. concolor* x *L. pumilum*)) 'Matchless' is an orange-red from 'Enchantment' x 'Connecticut Lemonglow'. With this interesting pedigree one would expect a vibrant orange-red with an extended raceme of many small flowers, and the guess would be right. Perhaps one would not visualise such a rampant, active plant and realise just how vivid a picture 'Fireworks' is going to make each early summer. A dozen or more small, wide-open spotless flowers have well-recurved petals and are well-posed, down but a little outwards. Altogether graceful and attractive. 90cm (3ft).

'Fuga' 1962 (*L. cernuum* x *L. davidii*) Still offered after over thirty years, this tall hybrid has a lot of glowing-orange, well-spotted turk's-cap flowers. 1.2–1.8m (4–6ft).

Hallmark 1965 (*L. cernuum* x *L. lancifolium*) White, midsummer-flowered turk's caps on tall stems. 1.2m (4ft).

'Hannah North' 1985 ((*L. lankongense* x 'Maxwill') x 'Enchantment') Strongly recurved, cream flowers fading to white with very few dark greenish spots, dark brown pollen and faint scent. 40–75cm (16–30in).

Harlequin strain 1950 Basically of mid-century origin, these downward-facing lilies with *L. cernuum* blood flower in midsummer in various colours from ivory through yellow and gold to salmon and red, with yellow and buff the most common colours today. 1–1.5m (3½–5ft).

Harlequin hybrid

'Iona' (Bred by Dr North) A *lankongense* hybrid with unusually large flowers with recurving petals in shades of coral-pink. 1.2–1.8m (4–6ft).

'Karen North' 1985 ((*L. lankongense* x 'Maxwill') x (('Cardinal' x (*L. lancifolium flaviflorum* x 'Enchantment'))).This lily has up to 20 lightly scented flowers, orangey-pink on the inside with a few darker pink spots, and a dark orange down the centre of each petal on the outside. Dark pollen. Allotriploid. 1.2–1.4m (4–4½ft).

'Lady Bowes Lyon' 1956 (('Maxwill' x 'Edna Kean') x 'Dark Princess') Bred by G. W. Darby, this remains a splendid lily with wide pyramid heads of downward-facing, broad flowers slightly tilted outwards and so making the most of their rich red colouring enlivened with black dots. The petals spread outwards and reflex for the last third. A strong plant. 90cm–1.2m (3–4ft).

'Last Dance' 1987 ((*L. leichtlinii maximowiczii*. 'Unicolor' x white Pastel sdlg) x (*L.l.max.* 'Unicolor' x cream yellow Pastel)). The name gives the clue to one feature of this very attractive and graceful hybrid – it is one of the last of the Asiatics to open in bloom as the Orientals take over. It has a beautifully arranged head of spotless, recurved, wide, lemon flowers with orange anthers, the open blooms overlooked by limey buds with some of the delightful fluffiness of babyhood. The stems are strong and wiry and the foliage is neat. 90cm–1.5m (3–5ft).

'Marie North' 1985 ((*L. lankongense* x 'Maxwill') x (('Cardinal' x (*L. lancifolium flaviflorum* x 'Enchantment'))) A lankongense hybrid with dark buds opening to surprising, pale flowers, white suffused gently with suggestions of pink, it has well-arranged heads of reflexed-petalled flowers. 1.2–1.5m (4–5ft).

'Maxwill' 1932 (*L. leichtlinii maximowiczii* x *L. davidii willmottiae*) Parentage has been queried but I imagine this must be correct. The strong stems can carry up to three dozen orange-red flowers with a scatter of dark spots. 2m (6½ft).

Seedlings raised by the author and at present under trial. They are labelled firstly by sequence for ease of cultivation and their free-flowering habit and secondly by year of selection

No. 25/94

No. 3/94

No. 8/94

No. 25/94

No. 3/94

No. 8/94

No. 10/94

No. 5/93

No. 21/94

No. 10/94

No. 5/93

No. 21/94

114

'**Pegasus**' A very distinctive plant with wiry, near-black stems and a few widely-spaced, narrow, blue-black, arching leaves below widely-spaced flowers hanging from long pedicles. The flowers are almost complete balls formed by recurving petals coloured in soft tones of whispered orange and light buff with spots. It is very fertile, and carries up to a dozen flowers per stem. 90cm–1.2m (3–4ft). (p105)

'**Peggy North**' 1985 ((*L. lankongense* x 'Maxwill') x 'Enchantment') A typically recurved *L. lankongense* hybrid with glowing mid-orange, attractively spotted flowers and good stems. 1.2–1.5m (4–5ft).

'Pegasus'

'**Pink Panther**' Panther or tiger? Large well-formed, many-flowered pyramids of tiger-lily flowers, the petals heavily dark-spotted and curling back. The colour of newly opened blooms is a coppery-orange which quickly takes on a suffused buffy-pink. 90cm (3ft).

'**Red Snappers**' With a mixed parentage including *L. cernuum*, *L. concolor*, *L. davidii* and *L. pumilum*, this lily looks closer to the species than most with graceful, extensive flower heads of many medium-sized, brilliant scarlet-wine-red turk's caps in midsummer. 90cm (3ft).

'**Rosemary North**' 1985 ((*L. lankongense* x 'Maxwill') x 'Enchantment') A pyramid of spaced, hanging flowers in soft tones of buffy orange, reflexed to make them into turk's caps. 1.2–1.5m (4–5ft).

Rosepoint Lace 1988 ((Southern Belle grex x 'Alpenglow' & other pinks)) Southern Belle was a rather virus-prone grex from *L. lankongense* crossed with mixed pink and white Asiatics. An American *L. lankongense* hybrid strain with well-spaced, good-sized, wide blooms with recurving petals arranged in many-headed pyramids, its early-summer blooms compromise between downward and outward pose, a most effective arrangement that makes the most of the ivory-pale-pink colouring that is marbled, lined and speckled with contrasting maroon. As you approach to examine the intricate working of the flowers you will become aware of the fragrance. A strong, fertile triploid. 90cm–1.5m (3–5ft).

'**Sally**' Deservedly popular with wide-recurving flowers held at a 45° angle downwards from dark stems. Many well-spaced, orangey-pink and crushed-strawberry blooms, overlaid a richer, darker orange in the centre, this darker tone-value being taken up by the buds and the petal reverses. 1.2–1.5m (4–5ft).

'**Smiley**' 1986 ('Connecticut Lemonglow' x *L. amabile*) This is a strong-stemmed, luxuriantly-leaved cultivar with multi-headed inflorescences of wide, outward-pointing floors of golden-tangerine enlivened with dark spots in their centres. 90cm–1.2m (3–4ft).

'**Tibetan Snow**' A strong *L. pumilum* hybrid with upright-pointing foliage and a shower of early, shining-white flowers completely without anthers. The stamen filaments point outwards from the recurving petalled blooms. The many small flowers are gently scented. 60–75cm (2–2½ft).

'**Tiger Babies**' 1980 ('Pink Tiger' x mixed pink and white Asiatics) Formidable, strong stems like walking sticks easily capable of carrying two to four dozen nodding pinky-apricot or peach flowers with margins often being a stronger buff perhaps influenced by the stronger reverse colouring of chestnut-pink. Close to the flower centres the colouring is stronger, rather orangey, but this is somewhat lost behind the strong dark spots on more than half of each petal. Dark anthers. Triploid. 90cm (3ft).

'**Viva**' A strong-stemmed lily with dozens of small, lacquered *L. pumilum*-like turk's caps, hanging daintily from extended inflorescences, a composition in glowing orange-red. 1.5m (5ft).

New batches of seedlings are raised by the author each year, making rigorous selection a necessity. At present the majority of Asiatic hybrid seed sown one year provides blossom the next. Downward-facing seedlings are particularly selected for their gracefulness

No. 20/94 (Ic)

No. 14/94 (Ic)

No. 15/94 (Ic)

No. 20/94 (Ic)

No. 14/94 (Ic)

No. 15/94 (Ic)

No. 18/94 (Ic)

No. 6/94 (Ic)

No. 19/94 (Ic)

No. 18/94 (Ic)

No. 6/94 (Ic)

No. 19/94 (Ic)

MARTAGON HYBRIDS (Div II)

Compared in number with the Asiatics these Martagons are very small beer, yet as garden plants and in their beauty they hold their own against any. At present most are the result of cross-breeding *L. martagon* itself with *L. hansonii* but this may be changing as breeders are trying to incorporate the genetic potential of other species. The fact that seed from these plants gives rise to small bulbs that take five, six or seven years to reach flowering size makes these lilies less immediately attractive to breeders, whether professional or amateur.

The martagons are early into blossom and then have a long period of glory. Once planted they are virtually indestructible if left alone. Their downward-hanging flowering pattern is attractive and the narrow columns of flowers distinctive and especially telling in amongst shrubs. They are normally very healthy plants and rarely seem to suffer from virus diseases – there are plantings around a hundred years old still flourishing. Some of the 1957 and other selections from the Backhouse hybrids were of clones that had been living at Sutton Court since the turn of the century – a testament to their health and longevity.

L. medeoloides has been crossed with *L. martagon* and the upward-facing *L. tsingtauense* with *L. x dalhansonii*. Overstepping the division boundaries, *L. martagon album* has been successfully crossed with the North American species *L. kelloggii*.

Backhouse hybrids A series of hybrids reported to have come from *L. hansonii* crossed with *L. martagon* forms including *L. m. album*, it is difficult to imagine that reverse crosses were not also made. Colours range from pink and mauve through the most frequent tan and orange to paler, more creamy flowers. All are more or less dotted. 1.2–1.8m (4–6ft).

'Dairy Maid' 1957 Typical turk's caps, these creamy-buffy-yellow flowers with peppered throats are a selection from the Backhouse hybrids. 1.2–1.8m (4–6ft).

'Dalhanse' 1964 Raised in the Canadian nursery of E. Robinson, a hybrid from *L. x dalhansonii x L. tsingtauense*, this lily has unspotted, lavender flowers with some warmer tones, and is paler in the centre. 90cm–1.5m (3–5ft)

x dalhansonii This is the official name for all the hybrid progeny of *L. martagon* and *L. hansonii*. The original clone is still grown, a fine kind from the dark-flowered *L. m. dalmaticum x L. hansonii*. The flowers are a rich dark tan – a brown shade that sounds dull but is really a pleasing chestnut enlivened with golden spots, veering from a purple cast to a mahogany one. The *L. hansonii* effect is to pull the petals wider than *L. martagon* before they curve back. 90cm–1.5m (3–5ft).

'Early Bird' 1957 selection from the Backhouse hybrids. One of the first lilies to open with bright-coloured, orange-gold, lightly spotted flowers. The pinky-mauve buds keep a suggestion of this colour in the open blooms. 1.2–1.8m (4–6ft).

'Indian Chief' 1949 A sport from 'Marhan' with lacquered, metallic copper-bronze flowers with flashes and dots of deep maroon in proper turk's-cap shapes. 1.2–1.8m (4–6ft).

'Jacques S Dijt' 1950 ((*L.m. album x L. hansonii*) x *L. m. album*) As one might imagine from the parentage, this cultivar favours the *L. martagon* side of the family with traditional turk's-cap flowers of a pleasing creamy-yellow with purple spots. It has enough substance to make two or three flowers from every one. 1.2–1.8m (4–6ft).

'Kelmarsh' (*L. martagon album x L. kelloggii*) Bred by Oliver Wyatt in Britain and named in 1950, officially classified as a Div VIII lily – the awkward-squad division for hybrids not catered for by other divisions – this is listed out of interest and is placed here for convenience as the flowers are described as basically of martagon-form and foliage would also pass muster. It is listed as having recurved, hanging, white flowers suffused maroon-purple. 90cm (3ft).

'Marhan' 1891 (*L.m. album x L. hansonii*) This hybrid was raised in the famous Dutch nurseries of C. G. van Tubergen in the last century. A hundred years old and still growing strong, I think there were several clones originally marketed under this name but now we seem to have a single one that has rich orange-chestnut flowers with much of the tan colouring coming from the spotting. Flowers are a

'Marhan'

good size and have petals curving back and pointing outwards and upwards, but not curled back in the more severe martagon fashion, the wider pose makes more of the flowers. It is a splendid plant, making steady increase. 1.2–1.8m (4–6ft). (photo left and p95)

'Mrs R O Backhouse' 1921 (*L. hansonii* x *L. martagon*) The buds are a mauvey-pink, the open flowers a glowing gold with small, red spots. 1.2–1.8m (4–6ft).

Paisley hybrids 1955 A repeat cross of *L. m. album* with *L. hansonii*, made by Jan de Graaff. The colour range covers amber, lilac, purple and tan shades with some veering towards a rich mahogany. The turk's-cap flowers

have the typical small dots. 1–1.5m (3½–5ft).

'Shantung' 1957 Another of the selections made from the Backhouse hybrids, this lily is closer to *L. martagon* than most in colour – shades of pinky-mauve with dots – and in flower form. 1.5–1.8m (5–6ft).

'Sutton Court' 1925 Named after the home of the Backhouse family in Hereford, England, this typical Backhouse hybrid has warm, golden-tangerine flowers with some mauve shading, especially on buds and outer surfaces, and some darker spots. The petals spread out and curve back but not so far as to lose their fly-away impact. 1.2–1.8m (4–6ft).

CANDIDUM/EUROPEAN HYBRIDS (Div III)

This division is again a small one but one with considerable potential. It includes the oldest European hybrid, *L. x testaceum*. The potential of species such as *L. monadelphum* to breed early-flowering, large-flowered lilies with constitutions that favour long lives has yet to be fully exploited, a possibility made all the more alluring by one or two already on the market.

'June Fragrance' 1971 Sometimes listed as 'Fragrance'. (*L. candidum salonikae* x *L. monadelphum*) As early as late spring the creamy-white flowers of this *L. monadelphum* hybrid begin to delight the eye and intoxicate with their perfume. The wide-open flowers with broad, outwards-pointing petals, recurving, in older blooms are carried on extended heads of perhaps nine or more, held in a nodding pose at 45° to the leafy stem. The foliage is bright green and healthy and with the delicately fringed margins of the species. The pollen is fertile. 1.2–1.4m (4–4½ft).

'Limerick' 1983 ('June Fragrance' x 'Coquet') 'Coquet' was bred from *L. bulbiferum croceum* x 'Connecticut Yankee'. Six to nine nodding flowers not quite fully

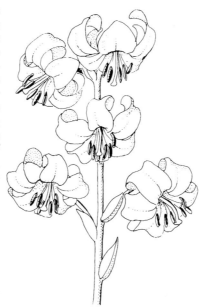

L. x testaceum

pendant are a most pleasing limey colour in which yellow and green vie for mastery, with a light scatter of tiny spots and dark pollen. 90cm–1.2m (3–4ft).

'Peacetime' ((*L. candidum* x *L. monadelphum*) x 'Juliana') 'Juliana' is of involved parentage, a creamy-white Div Ia Asiatic hybrid. A pure-white, very fragrant, large-flowered, early lily with lightly spotted flowers on good heads. 90cm–1.2m (3–4ft).

x testaceum This was an accidental hybrid probably raised as long ago as 1810, from *L. candidum* x *L. chalcedonicum*, a cross that has been repeated since and produced similarly lovely flowers. The original stock was widely spread in gardens but became virus infected. Modern techniques

118

for raising new, clean stock mean that we can again enjoy one of the most pleasing of lilies. The foliage is graded to small leaves below about six large, fully pendant flowers, glowing with a soft pinky-buff colour, uniform except for a few tiny, raised, red spots. Sometimes called the 'Nakeen lily', the

official colour coding description is 'maize yellow' but this colour name does not suggest the right shade – a pale apricot-pink. 90cm–1.2m (3–4ft).

'Uprising' 1983 ('June Fragrance' x 'Burnished Rose') The pollen parent was from L. lancifolium x

(L. davidii willmottiae x L. regale). An unusual hybrid with creamy, upward-facing, long-stalked flowers with a sprinkling of tiny spots. A plant of real distinction with plenty of upward-pointing leaves and dark, almost-black stems. 1.2m (4ft).

AMERICAN GROUP HYBRIDS (Div IV)

One or two of the wild American species make easy garden plants and others respond reasonably to attentive care. As a whole, however, they are plants of the wild and do not always grow easily in cultivation. Hybridised they seem to grow more easily, some obviously having been bred from at least one of the stronger, easier species. Rather like the martagon types, they may take a season to settle then, in suitable spots, they will go from strength to strength, with very little effort from the gardener. After the initial work in 1918 in Los Angeles to breed the Bellingham series the next major advances have been made by Oliver Wyatt and, later, Derek Fox in England.

The hybrids listed below are all more or less vigorous, rhizomatous bulbs and have stems with the typical whorled foliage of the majority of American species.

Bellingham hybrids 1933 This famous series derived from seed purchased from Carl Purdy in California by Dr Griffiths who was working for the United States Department of Agriculture and who named them after Bellingham, the Washington site of the USDA experimental station.

The original series was thought to be derived from L. parryi x L. ocellatum and L. pardalinum x L. ocellatum. Certainly they exhibited heavily spotted flowers. The L. pardalinum role may have expanded as selection and further work went forward. L. bolanderi and L. kelloggii and other species were introduced.

The present range of these West-Coast lily-hybrids covers colours from yellow to orange and orange-red, all with spotting – sometimes looking strongly freckled. There may be a faint scent. 90cm–1.5m (3–5ft).

Bellmaid hybrids 1968 A Derek Fox series from Bellingham hybrids x 'Bridesmaid'. The pollen parent came from (L. pardalinum x L. parryi) x L. parryi, making the flowers a basic rich yellow that is, or becomes, suffused with tangerine and darkens with age to something close to red. They are typical American hybrids with hanging flowers with recurving or more sharply-reflexed petals. 1.5–1.8m (5–6ft).

Bullwood hybrids 1967 (L. pardalinum giganteum x pink Henry Bolander hybrid) Derek Fox's series, named after his nursery in Hockley, Essex, England, has giv-

en gardeners a real treat. These robust plants increase at a satisfactory, steady rate and grow in a variety of soils, doing well even on some apparently uninviting ones. The pink hybrid parent has widened the colour spectrum with peachy-coloured seedlings and others where the orange-red of L. pardalinum has been brightened to a fuller, more crimson-red. 90cm–2.7m (3½–9ft)! (photo right and p95.)

'Cherrywood' 1964 A selection from Bullwood hybrids, this is a distinctive plant and flower with strong, erect stems and classy foliage in whorls below the heads of

nodding flowers on long pedicles. Like the classy, unrelated L. canadense they have very cleanly drawn outlines of sweeping, curved petals coming to sharp points that point out and upwards and are very definitely not clamped back in the restricted L. pardalinum-manner. The shining, polished flowers are a rich red with crimson tones, golden spotted in the centre, blooming in midsummer. 1.8–2.4m (6–8ft).

'Dairy Maid' 1947 ((L. pardalinum x L. parryi) x L. parryi) A Wyatt hybrid not to be confused with the martagon hybrid introduced later under this name.

Tangerine-yellow flowers with well reflexed petals. 1.2–1.8m (4–6ft).

'Lake Tahoe' 1977 ('Peachwood' x *L. bolanderi*) A flower of beautiful outline with long, pointed petals, well-reflexed to show off their strong, red upper halves; towards the centre the white zone is banded gold down towards a green base. Rich, pinky-red spots. 1.8–2.4m (6–8ft).

'Lake Tulare' 1977 (Bullwood hybrid x *L. bolanderi*) Tall, stately plant with flower heads held by ascending, long pedicles so that each large, nodding bloom is clear of the next. The pointed segments sweep out and up with their crimson-red ends shading down to white, with some gold banding and dark red spots. 1.8–2.4m (6–8ft).

'Oliver Wyatt' 1964 (*L. parryi*

hybrid) A lovely, pale tangerine or amber flower with petals pointing outwards and only very gently reflexed. This classic does not need extra adornments, yet it has a light sprinkle of dark red spots on its fragrant, midsummer flowering bloom. 1.8m (6ft).

'Peachwood' 1960 A selection from Bullwood hybrids. The soft, glowing peach tones are best in young flowers or in semi-shade as persistent sun can fade them a little. However, even half a shade paler it remains a very pleasing, lightly spotted flower. 1.8–2.4m (6–8ft).

'Robin' 1965 An involved parentage that can be roughly summarised as *L. kelloggii* x *L. pardalinum* hybrid. A pleasing flower in rich vermilion with orange with slightly recurved petals. 90cm–1.2m (3–4ft).

Bullwood hybrid, one of a series of extremely robust lilies that can be left for years with almost no attention

'Rosewood' 1969 A selection from Bullwood hybrids, this lily offers a distinct change with the glowing pink flowers with a paler, spotted centre. Long, pointed petals sweep cleanly out and up. 1.8–2.4m (6–8ft).

'Shuksan' 1933 (*L. humboldtii* x *L. pardalinum*) One of only a very few of the Bellingham hybrids grown on as named clones, this is a noteworthy plant typifying the best qualities of the series. It is sturdy and healthy, with good-sized, strongly-reflexed petals making rounded tangerine-gold flowers boldly enlivened by the many black spots and the strong red petal tips in early summer. 1.2m (4ft).

(*above*) 'Robin' is a distinct and
excellent example of the relatively
few useful and attractive American
species hybrids (p119)

(*right*) 'Shuksan', dates back to
1924, and is still going strong, more
in the way of these yellow and
golden hybrids would be very
welcome

L. LONGIFLORUM AND *L. FORMOSANUM* HYBRIDS (Div V)

L. longiflorum has had a long history of cultivation for the cut-flower and pot-plant trade. One form became associated with the name 'Easter lily' although now this is used with less precision for most forms of *L. longiflorum*. Over the years there have been, and still are, many named forms varying by fairly small taxonomic details but sometimes important commercial ones. Dwarf forms are useful for pots, ones with distinct foliage can be equally welcome. However, until fairly recently hybridisation has not been an obvious part of the lily's activities. Now this has changed somewhat with a range of hybrids with the rather similar *L. formosanum*, hybrids which certainly grow with vigour and produce good crops of pure white trumpet flowers. These still are on the whole of more interest to commerial growers than the amateur gardener.

L. formosanum is a variable plant in the wild and one could expect selections from the wild population to be dignified by varietal names. This has happened to some extent but few are now in use. G. W. Darby produced a vigorous large hybrid from two tetraploids in about 1955 that had been produced by the use of colchicine. This was 'Welwyn Tetraploid' and comes true from seed. The small form *L. f. pricei* is of course very well established and it is from this small plant that some growers have been tempted to make some efforts at selection. Little Snow White is offered as a very dwarf kind coming more or less true from seed, the plants usually growing only 15cm (6in) high but sometimes making 20cm (8in). Both these trumpet species are very susceptible to virus, *L. formosanum* particularly so.

A more distinct break was the introduction of 'Longistar', the successful result of mating *L. longiflorum* with the Asiatic 'Sterling Star'. This is a sturdy plant, 60–90cm (2–3ft) high, with good, umbel-like heads of upward-facing, spread-open, ivory-white flowers with a suggestion of limey-green. The strong, firm texture of the flowers is immediately noted. Its foliage is a real compromise between the very narrow 'Sterling Star' fashion and the broad one of *L. longiflorum*. If cut, they need handling with care as the petals shatter, making it useless for the commercial cut-flower market. In the garden grow it in a fairly sheltered spot to avoid the blooms getting blown about and losing a lot of petals. It is an interesting hybrid across the division barriers, heralding all sorts of new things.

Other *L. longiflorum* matings with Asiatic kinds have given 'Casa Rosa' a full trumpet in a deep mauvey-pink. 'Arizona' is a large magenta one, while 'Summer Breeze' is a clean, unspotted creamy-peach colouring.

'Longidragon' is a 60–90cm (2–3ft) high, robust trumpet-hybrid that combines the dwarfer size of *L. longiflorum* with some of the dramatic colouring of 'Black Dragon' – beautifully formed trumpets are shining white with dark reverses, held above a lot of healthy foliage.

TRUMPET HYBRIDS (Div VI)

This group divides into two parts: the pure-bred trumpets, derived from the crossing of trumpet species and their hybrids, and the entire range of lilies that have in their breeding some of that tough species *L. henryi* – the antithesis of trumpet-form and a different kind of plant.

The pure trumpet hybrids have been derived from a number of species. These hybrids grown in gardens in temperate zones have been bred from *L. regale*, *L. sargentiae*, *L. leucanthum*, *L. brownii* and *L. sulphureum*. Some species, such as *L. sulphureum* and *L. sargentiae*, have never been plentiful in gardens as they are prone to succumb to virus. *L. regale* is altogether tougher. By a lucky accident on the nursery of R. & J. Farquhar in Boston, Massachusetts, a hybrid between *L. sargentiae* and *L. regale* was raised.

This was named *L. x imperiale* by Ernest Wilson, the plant collector who had found and introduced *L. regale* at the beginning of the century. Miss Preston in Canada had deliberately crossed the two species in 1916, trying to improve strength and quality. At the Ontario Agricultural College she raised a series of which the best was 'George C. Creelman' and, although the name was wrongly used later for a number of clones, the proper plant was an impressive, large bloom of *L. regale*-type with a dark reverse. Both this and *L. x imperiale* improved on the standard *L. regale* by having broader petals that tended to recurve more.

A major advance in breeding took place when the de Graaff breeders raised large numbers of *L. leucanthum centifolium* and exercised a rigorous selection process to keep only those plants that appeared stronger and had wide-petalled flowers in a defined, pyramid-shaped inflorescence. The inner white and the dark purple-mahogany of the buds were both intensified. The selected kinds were then mated with *L. sargentiae*, *L. sulphureum* and *L. brownii*. The selected progeny were originally marketed as Centifolium hybrids but then were renamed in 1955 and launched as the Olympic hybrids – a range of fine trumpets covering all colours from white, cream, lime and yellow to pink. Checking through the white-flowered ones led to further selection and reselection to end with the Black Magic strain with large white blooms with dark reverses. One outstanding plant was cloned and introduced as 'Black Dragon'.

In the breeding of the trumpet lilies genetic factors restrict the golden colouring in white trumpet-species to the throat alone, a factor that was lost or overruled in odd seedlings. The most successful of the yellow trumpets has been the Royal Gold series, sometimes marketed as 'the golden regale'. The progenitor of this was a yellow-flowered plant that turned up in the middle of a block of straight *L. regale* on the de Graaff farms. It was thought that *L. sulphureum* may have had something to do with the parentage and be the obvious reason for the flooding of the whole flower with yellow pigment. Certainly the original plant and the strain developed from it look very much of the *L. regale* stable.

From the progeny of both the cross *L. regale* x *L. sargentiae* and from batches of *L. leucanthum centifolium* appeared individuals with petals with pink margins and/or veining. These were gathered and interbred and suddenly pink flowers were raised which became the basis for the Pink Perfection strain. It is still not clear whether this breaking of the inhibition on the colour zoning in the pinks was due to natural mutation, recombinations of genetic material or the accidental introduction of pollen from Aurelian hybrids which, with their *L. henryi* background, are free of zoning inhibitions.

THE AURELIANS

It was the introduction of *L. henryi* material that enabled breeders to produce a much wider range of lilies that proved to be very hardy and amenable to a wide range of garden conditions. M. E. Debras in France had been trying for some years to cross the white trumpet *L. sargentiae* with the orange turk's-cap-shaped *L. henryi*. Having harvested two seeds in 1925 he managed to bloom the one surviving plant in 1928, christened *L. x aurelianense*. A similar plant had been raised at Kew in 1900 from *L. leucanthum* x *L. henryi* and called *L. x kewense*. In the mid-1930s a further clone was named 'T. A. Havemeyer', the result of crossing *L. sulphureum* with *L. henryi*. This was a wide, deep orange-buff lily with a green throat and pale petal tips. It was a vigorous plant with perhaps twenty wide, recurving flowers, each up to 18cm (7in) across – proving that cross breeding was possible.

In 1938, the de Graaff team had a thousand *L. henryi* and a similar number of *L. leucanthum*

Aurelian hybrids. *L. henryi* is an important influence in breeding, imparting great vigour and resilience. Crossed with trumpet kinds it helped produce the range of flower forms shown here, and crossed with *L. speciosum rubrum* it gave the extraordinarily strong 'Black Beauty' (p133)

L. Sunburst type (VId)

L. Sunburst type (VId)

L. henryi

L. Sunburst type (VId)

L. Sunburst type (VId)

Pendant form (VIc)

Pendant form (VIc)

Bowl-shaped form (VIb)

Bowl-shaped form (VIb)

L. 'Black Beauty' (VIId)
(L. speciosum rubrum × L. henryi)

Trumpet-shaped form (VIa)

Trumpet-shaped form (VIa)

124

centifolium together with useful stocks of *L. sulphureum* and *L. sargentiae*, and some bulbs of 'T. A. Havemeyer' and *L. x aurelianense*. All the *L. henryi* were pollinated with various trumpets; the trumpets were given pollen of the best forms of *L. henryi*. A huge crop of seed resulted and these became collectively known as Aurelians after Debras' *L. aurelianense*. Yellow trumpet-forms were selected and reselected and launched as the Golden Clarion strain. Further work with these and other forms resulted in the naming of various strains and clones. The richly-coloured Golden Splendour strain quickly became entrenched, but the

public were very taken with paler kinds such as the Limelight strain.

The varying forms of these Aurelians necessitated their classification. The 'trumpet'-division was split into four – these four classes have recently been modified so that they are separated by flower form:

VIa Trumpet-shaped flowers such as 'Black Dragon' or 'Pink Perfection'

VIb Bowl-shaped flowers such as Heart's Desire strain or 'Lady Anne'

VIc Flat flowers such as 'Bright Star'

VId Flowers with distinctly recurved petals, such as 'Journey's End'

TRUMPET-SHAPED FLOWERS (Div VIa)

'**African Queen**' 1958 Plants gathered from the Golden Clarion Aurelian hybrids with full trumpets, very dark in bud and with some pink or orange veining in the petals were hybridised to intensify the colour, and a series of rich orange clones was offered as the African Queen strain. Quite soon one good clone was chosen to use the name and it is this clone which is mainly offered for sale. It is a tall strong plant with bamboo-dark stems carrying impressive heads of large, dark purple chocolate buds that open to display flowers at the proper trumpet angle, just slightly below horizontal. The fragrant flowers are a very rich, warm, deep tangerine-apricot, the petal margins outlined in the dark colouring of the buds. 1.2–2m (4–6½ft).

Angelica A fairly new type of genetic dwarf-trumpets, this strain has narrow foliage and relatively large trumpets, maroon-pink in bud, shining white when opened. An engaging plant for pot or border, it seems like a Black Magic flower looked at through the wrong end of a telescope (see also Pink Cherubs). 40–60cm (18–24in).

Blackdown Pink Bred by Derek Gardham, this is a strong series of very rich fuchsia-pink, heavily fragrant trumpets, with large flowers of proper trumpet form on very robust plants. 1.2–1.5m (4–5ft).

'**Black Dragon**' 1959 With *L. leucanthum centifolium* and other species in the background the Black Magic strain was established. This is an outstanding clone from that tall, strong series, with massive heads of large, dramatic, heavily fragrant flowers with well-displayed purple-red dark reverses, shining-white blooms that are shaded into a yellow centre and dark anthers. 1.5–2.5m (5–8ft).

Black Magic 1959 A fairly tightly uniform strain of strong plants with formidable candelabras of pure white trumpets with maroon-brown reverses. 1.2–2m (4–7ft).

Copper King 1958 A number of clones selected originally from the Golden Clarions, this grex has strong, fragrant trumpet flowers of rich apricot or melon-orange with buds and reverses usually showing maroon shading to a

greater or lesser extent. 1.2–1.8m (4–6ft).

Crystal Palace A strain of cooler-coloured trumpets blooming mid- to late summer with large, green buds opening to ivory-white flowers with a suggestion of green that becomes more pronounced in the throat. 1.2–1.5m (4–5ft).

'**Damson**' 1954 The parentage is given as an Aurelian crossed by a form of *L. leucanthum*. This strong plant has remarkable, deep-toned, plum-purple-red flowers like one of the darkest Pink Perfection clones. 1.2–1.5m (4–5ft).

Golden Splendour 1957 These flowers are the result of selecting good forms from the Golden Clarion strain. Once a mix of yellow and gold forms, the bulbs now supplied produce full, golden flowers with a winey-purple stripe down the outside of each petal. 90cm–1.2m (3–4ft). (p126)

'**Green Dragon**' 1955 A clonal selection from the Olympic hybrids with their *L. leucanthum* background, this tall, strong lily has large, proper trumpet-shaped

L. 'Royal Gold' type

L. Olympic White type

L. Blackdown Pink type

L. pale Pink Perfection type

L. Blackdown seedling

L. 'Limelight' type

L. Blackdown seedling

L. Golden Splendour type

L. Heart's Desire type

L. Golden Sceptre type

L. Golden Clarion type

L. 'African Queen' type

126

Golden Splendour

flowers with green buds and reverses. 1.5–2.2m (5–7ft).

Green Magic 1962 A grex with *L.
leucanthum* and probably *L. sargentiae* playing the major roles in
the background breeding, sporting white flowers with greenish
centres, green in bud. 90cm–1.8m
(3–6ft).

'Limelight' 1958 A clone selected
from the Golden Dawn grex that
was originally introduced as the
Limelight strain, this plant soon
found favour with the gardening
public and is still in demand. The
blooms are large, the slender, lem-
ony-yellow trumpet opens neatly
at the mouth and has an alluring
hint of limey-green. One of the
classics. 1–1.5m (3½–5ft). (p125)

'Mabel Violet' 1974 (Pink Pearl x
Pink Perfection) This formidable
plant has dark, maroon buds
opening to dramatic, long trumpet-shaped flowers with evenly
open mouths, the petal tips being
pink while the main flower is a
very deep, unbroken, dark purple-
pink with green shading in the
throats. It has dark foliage and
stems, the heads carrying over a
dozen large flowers. 1.2m (4ft).

Midnight 1963 (Aurelian hybrids
x *L. leucanthum centifolium*) A
number of very deep-coloured
clones were offered under this
name. I rather fancy that those
offered now are one clone, a
particularly dark purple, sometimes looking nearly black! This
lily has long trumpets, well
opened at the mouths, dark leaves
and stems. 1.5–1.8m (5–6ft).

Moonlight From the same breeding as Golden Splendour but
much paler, this series has cool-
coloured trumpets of luminous
chartreuse. A rich perfume adds
to the magic – an amalgam of
colour, habit, scent and well-
drawn form with pointed petals.
90cm–1.5m (3–5ft).

Olympic hybrids (See above for
their derivation) A wide range of
colours was originally marketed
under this name, but it is more
usual now to find only whites,
often with green shading and reverses. 1.2–1.8m (6–8ft). (p125)

Pink Cherubs A strain made up of
dwarf clones with wiry stems well
clothed with slender leaves and
topped with nicely opened
trumpets in glowing tones of rich
fuchsia-pink. 40–60cm (18–24in).

Pink Pearl 1958 These clones of
Aurelian abstraction, have delightful dark pink or purplish buds

Royal Gold

opening to display light pink flowers with a darker pink on the reverses. Strong plants, they flower in late summer. 1.5m (5ft).

Pink Perfection 1960 A strain that is the result of interbreeding the plants of the basic *L. leucanthum centifolium* x *L. sargentiae* mating. When first introduced there was a wide range of pink colourings, yet latterly the plants on offer have produced few of the paler shades, being either a very deep fuchsia-pink or a beetroot shade! As the large blooms can measure 15cm (6in) across and there can be two

or three dozen to a massive stem it is little wonder that the strain is still in demand. Around 1.8m (6ft). (p125)

Royal Gold 1955 A number of closely akin clones often offered as 'Golden Regale', the fully trumpet-shaped, heavily scented blooms have dark maroon buds, opening to wide-petalled, rich golden flowers. This lily has strong dark stems and narrow dark leaves. 1.2–1.8m (4–6ft). (p125)

'White Lady' 1960 Raised in Latvia from *L. x sulphurgale* x white

trumpet lily, Sulphurgale was a pale yellow trumpet raised from *L. sulphureum* x *L. regale* around 1916. 'White Lady' is a large, white flower with a limey throat, opening to 15cm (6in) across and deep. The anthers are a contrasting orange, and the dark foliage is neatly arranged on dark strong stems. 1.5m (5ft).

Winter Palace A series of large-flowered, traditionally-formed trumpets with maroon buds and well-displayed, expanded, warm gold and peachy or apricot flowers. 1.2m (4ft).

BOWL-SHAPED FLOWERS (Div VIb)

First Love 1964 A strain from involved Aurelian breeding, the widely open bowl form is well demonstrated in these flowers of mixed tones of apricot and creamy-yellow, some with pink suffusions. A typical flower would have a rich apricot throat giving way to a golden-flushed central area, with pink-apricot petal edges and tips, the petals curling back at the ends. It is perhaps best seen in semi-shade when the play of colours can be fully appreciated. 1.2–1.5m (4–5ft).

Heart's Desire 1950 Still marketed forty years on, the expanded trumpets approach a wide bowl-shape and are usually creamy-white with tangerine-golden centres, sometimes more yellow or white. It is fragrant and flowers in midsummer. 1.2–1.8m (4–6ft).

'Lady Anne' 1974 (*L. henryi* hybrid x *L. leucanthum centifolium*) A beguiling flower in graded shades of pinky-apricot and pinky-cream, the paler tones of the

pointed petal tips becoming a more glowing colour on the blade of the petals and a richer apricot in the throats. The long, pointed buds are a green-shaded apricot and are held on dark long pedicles. The petals open widely and are only gently recurved looking very smooth and appealing in an outward and slightly downward pose, flowering in midsummer. It has neatly arranged, rather pale foliage on dark stems 1.5m (5ft).

FLAT FLOWERS (Div VIc)

'Bright Star' 1959 A very typical Sunburst-type flower, outward-facing and with widespread petals making a rather flat ivory-white flower with the deep-honey or near-apricot colour of the throat spreading half-way up the centre of each rather oblong-shaped petal, producing a star of colour in the centre of the white, the very centre being a smaller but very definite green star formed by the nectary furrows. The petal tips recurve. It can have six to over a dozen flowers on strong stems that may be sloping. 90cm–1.2m (3–4ft).

'Gold Eagle' 1968 An *L. Woodriff* cultivar, this splendid, strong, tall Sunburst lily has lots of widespread, clean-cut rich lemon-yellow blooms with a green nectary approach and a number of raised points towards the centre base of each petal, these papillae being coloured a rusty-red. Perfumed. 1.5–2.2m (5–7ft).

Golden Sunburst 1960 (*L. henryi* x *L. aurelianense*) Lilies with wide, flat, star-shaped, rich golden-yellow flowers showing some of the raised fleshy points, the papillae, that are a feature of *L.*

henryi. Strong stems and typical, shiny, rather broad and shortish leaves and durable flowers. 1.2–1.8m (4–6ft).

'Henry VIII' ('White Henryi' x *L. regale*) This lily favours the 'White Henryi' parent with wide, white blooms with orange-gold throats, this colour approaching part-way up the centre of each petal. It opens a fortnight earlier than 'White Henryi'. 1.5m (5ft).

'Louis XIV' The Sun-king-god! This tall plant bursts with energy – very wide flowers of Sunburst

128

form with reflexed petal tips, the whole three-quarters pendant, flower in midsummer in vivid golden-yellow becoming darker in the centre leading down to the nectary. It usually lasts into late summer and is one of the last of these types to bloom. 1.8m (6ft).

'Marie Antoinette' Another typical Sunburst flower, this one is ivory white with apricot throats, the colour spreading two-thirds up the centre of each petal. A

sturdy plant, it flowers in late summer and has a half-pendant pose. 1.5m (5ft).

Pink Sunburst 1957. Starry, flat, pink and white flowers with rich honey-gold throats, outward facing and scented, this flower typically has its petals slightly rolled back at the tips and the margin, the pink colouring being strongest in the tipmost half and perhaps giving way to near white before the golden throat. 1.5–1.8m (5–6ft).

'White Henryi' (*L. henryi* x *L. leucanthum centifolium*) An early Woodriff cultivar, held in high esteem since its introduction as far back as 1945, the beautiful, textured, wide Sunburst-type, white flowers have strong orange throats flaring into the petals and tiny, rusty-red papillae radiating from the orange area into the white like sparks from a fire. It is one of the joys of midsummer, a plant of undoubted vigour and disease resistance. 1.5m (5ft).

FLOWERS DISTINCTLY RECURVED (Div VId)

'Lady Bowes Lyon' (('Maxwill' x 'Edna Kean') F3 x 'Dark Princess') A 1956 G. W. Darby hybrid, still featured in catalogues which

is not surprising when one sees the wide pyramid heads of wide, very rich red flowers with their black-dotted centres, widely

spaced in a half-pendant pose. The petals reach out and curve backwards. A strong and pleasing plant. 90cm–1.2m (3–4ft).

ORIENTAL HYBRIDS (Div VII)

There can be few flowers more spectacular than some of these Oriental lilies bred in the main by the cross-breeding of *L. auratum* and *L. speciosum*, although *L. japonicum* and *L. rubellum* have given lovely hybrids and may play a larger part in the future. Historically, the first named hybrid of this range was *L. x parkmanii*, raised in 1869 by the crossing of *L. speciosum* with the newly introduced *L. auratum*. It has been described as a large, crimson flower with white petal edges. Another hybrid was shown the following year, 1870, 'Mrs A. Waterer' from *L. speciosum rubrum* x *L. auratum*, a white lily with crimson spots first called 'Purity' but renamed after the stock passed to Mrs. Waterer. Both these hybrids were lost, but a third one, 'Jillian Wallace', raised by Roy M. Wallace in Victoria, Australia around 1938, is still grown and has been used in further breeding. This plant came from a selected form

of *L. speciosum* called 'Gilrey' crossed by 'Crimson Queen', a form of *L. auratum*. In Oregon, the de Graaff team backcrossed 'Jillian Wallace' onto 'Crimson Queen' to give 'Empress of India', a very rich red flower with white edges. By using 'Jillian Wallace' on *L. auratum virginale* the same firm bred 'Empress of China', a white with red spots, and 'Empress of Japan', a pure white with a yellow band.

Of course these spectacular flowers have attracted breeders all over the world. Very successful work has been undertaken in New Zealand and Australia as well as in the United States, and some work in Europe. One of the main preoccupations of breeders has been the selection of more disease-resistant plants. Both the main species, *L. speciosum* and *L. auratum* are vulnerable to virus which quickly kills them. Some progress has been made with this work. Derek Gardham's strains are particularly

ORIENTAL HYBRIDS, Division VII, DEVON DAWN strain
The Devon Dawn strain was bred by Derek Gardham originally using the
1969 registered 'Red Dragon' as one parent and 'Skyline' as the seed parent

L. 'Red Dragon'

(All shown at ¹/4 life size)

strong. Starting in 1970, he aimed to build on any 'virus resistance' available. As many *L. auratum* and *L. speciosum* forms as possible were collected and propagated until a stock of fifty of each was ready. These were then planted out in fields between rows of 'Enchantment' known to be carrying a cocktail of virus diseases. Within a few years all but a few of the original 10,000 bulbs had succumbed and died. Of the few survivors, two grew into strong clumps and three others did moderately well. Two were chosen to form the basis for a breeding programme. One was named 'Skyline', a seedling from a New Zealand batch. Producing heavy seed which germinated and grew well, this kind was mated with an American-raised kind, 'Red Dragon', bred by H. J. Strahm at the Harbor bulb farm in Oregon and introduced in 1969. This produced a strain of plants growing remarkably quickly from seed to flowering size and with very considerable resistance to viruses or the effects of them. Originally marketed as Pacific hybrids, the name was changed and they are now known as the Devon Dawn strain. The strain has been maintained by repeated crossing of these two selected parents. The results are remarkable plants with very high bud counts, large flowers of good form – better than either parent. The flower pose varies but is usually outward or only semi-pendant.

The main initial work in the USA was undertaken by de Graaff as mentioned above. Not only were clones bred but strains were also built up that are still on the market. Selecting the best forms of many thousands of *L. speciosums* and *L. auratums* and their hybrids the Imperial strains were bred, basically from (*L. speciosum* x *L. auratum*) x *L. auratum*. The strains are of three colour types: Imperial Crimson, Imperial Silver and Imperial Gold.

Various breeders have introduced *L. rubellum* and *L. japonicum* into breeding plans with attractive results. Imperial Pink was a large-flowered lot from (*L. auratum* x *L. speciosum*) F2 x (*L. auratum* x *L. japonicum*) F2.

There is now a wealth of clones on the market in Australasia, the USA and in Europe. Much of the breeding work is paralleled in the different continents, but in Europe growers are at present mainly offering those lilies bred in the States or in Australia or New Zealand. Below, some of this welter of kinds are listed, concentrating on those on offer in Europe. Readers from other continents are advised to look to the suppliers' list at the end of the book. Some nurseries specialise in Orientals and have fantastically alluring collections.

At present the Orientals are an almost inviolate group – they have not strayed outside the confines of their own division to produce hybrid offspring. Almost, but not quite: one exceptional cultivar has been raised and suggests a whole new field for endeavour. In looking for disease resistance perhaps it is not surprising that eyes should fall on the species *L. henryi*, even though it would seem distinct from all the Oriental group. It was the dedicated breeder L. Woodriff working in California who managed to effect a mating and the resulting plant 'Black Beauty' from *L. speciosum rubrum* x *L. henryi* was the amazing result. Its vigour has to be seen to be appreciated. The original was a diploid, but by artificial means a tetraploid form was engineered.

The numbers of these Oriental hybrids led to a division by flower shape for horticultural classification. It started with trumpet-shaped flowers, but these never approach the shapes of the true trumpets, therefore in this division such a classification means that the flowers have petals initially inclined to go forward to make a defined bowl form before expanding like the mouth of a trumpet. In Div VIIb, the flowers are defined as bowl-shaped. This means that the petals again come forward from the base at an angle to leave a concave area around the ovary but in not quite so pronounced a manner. It can be almost a matter of caprice into which of the four sections many flowers are placed, certainly the boundaries are very much less clearly marked than in Div VI. As far as the amateur gardener is concerned, it can often be a matter of very little concern.

TRUMPET-SHAPED FLOWERS (Div VIIa)

'**Alliance**' 1958 A large, clear pink lily of involved parentage, with white tips and throat and green midvein. There is red spotting on about two-thirds of each petal of this erect-flowered kind. 1m (3ft).

'Angelo' A most appealing lily with an extended head of nine or more large, wide, trumpet-shaped flowers looking upwards, with petal ends curving back. All are a soft, rosy-pink, and a shade darker half-way down the petal centre until taken up by a salmony zone towards the green nectary lines. At least two-thirds of each petal have crimson-painted papillae. 90cm (3ft).

'**Joy**' (syn. 'Le Reve') A good plant with large, spreading flowers in glowing, soft pink with the centres marked green in the nectary channels to the bases, and with a light sprinkle of small red spots. 90cm (3ft).

'**Mr Ed**' ((Little Rascals) x (Little Rascals)) This and the following two cultivars are US-bred genetic dwarfs, of which there are now a considerable series. Very good pot and container plants, they bloom for several weeks in late summer and early autumn. Sturdy plants, they have plenty of neat, broad foliage held at right angles and several pure, shining, white, widespread flowers to a stem, lightly

sprinkled with tiny, orange-pink flecks. 30–60cm (1–2ft).

'**Mr Sam**' As in the other two dwarfs listed this has outward-facing, large flowers with pleasing perfume. The broad-petalled blooms are predominantly crimson-pink with white margins and dark crimson dotting. 30–50cm (1–2ft).

'**Mr Rudd**' Each stem holds several large flowers with overlapping widespread, white petals, with a golden-yellow throat with this colouring moving up the centre of each petal to give a starry effect behind the protruding, orange anthers. 30–60cm (1–2ft).

BOWL-SHAPED FLOWERS (Div VIIb)

'**Bonfire**' 1962 ('Empress of China' x 'Empress of India') A striking, rather starry, deep crimson flower with even darker spots, the petals rather narrowly edged silvery-white, the buds and reverses polished white blushing pale pink. Stocks allow this still to be marketed; although showy, nowadays selectors would want smoother flowers with wider petals. 1.2–1.5m (4–5ft).

'**Casa Blanca**' 1987 One of the successes of the past decade, this has an important place in the cut-flower trade and is a lily prized by gardeners. This is little wonder – some of our blooms have measured 25cm (10in) across! The flowers are a glistening snow-white with sometimes just a light touch of green from the style and nectary furrows. The papillae add restrained ornamentation to the wide, outward-spreading petals which recurve at the tips. The heavily scented flowers appear in mid- to late summer in good numbers. 1.2m (4ft). (p149)

Devon Dawn 1987 Derek Gardham's remarkable strain bred from 'Skyline' x 'Red Dragon', this covers a wide range of flowers and plants. Their health and disease resistance is second to none amongst those of this vulnerable division. Large numbers of strong flowers, often over fifty, ensure a very long blossom time, normally starting in midsummer and lasting

Devon Dawn

through until autumn. The rich crimson-pink flowers have white petal margins, varying in the width of the margins and the strength of the central colour. There are also plenty of good, paler pinks. The flowers are a good size and vary in pose from a more or less horizontal arrangement, some slightly inclined upwards and some held a few degrees below the horizontal. The pyramid heads may carry up to three flowers per pedicle. 90cm–1.4cm (3–4½ft). (p129)

'Dominique' A full, red lily with some darker spots in throat, a limey-yellow-green nectary, a slightly declined outward pose and short stems. 40–50cm (15–20in).

'Hitparade' 1990 ('Star Gazer' x pink seedling) A distinct, rosy-pink kind with a white centre that extends some way up the petal centres to form a misty area with a green nectary base, all behind the protruding orange anthers. While having a bowl-formed centre, the petals are very widely spread and recurve at the tips. The flowers are outward and slightly upward-facing and so make a real impact. 90cm (3ft).

'Kyota' 1989 ((Little Rascal x 'Star Gazer') x 'Freedom')) Six to twelve large, broad-petalled, snowy-white blooms prettily dotted with small, crimson-pink spots. 90cm–1.2m (3–4ft).

'Little Girl' One of the dwarf kinds, with silvery-pink buds opening to starry, pointed, rosy-pink flowers well spotted crimson in the throat and looking outwards. 45cm (18in).

'Midnight Star' Huge, wide-petalled flowers with terrific dramatic impact, the wide, white bowl dominated by the very deep red band from the throat to the end of the petals. Each bloom has a deep chocolate-coloured throat and crimson spots. It blooms freely so that the stems may be displaying a dozen 15cm (10in) blossoms. 1.5m (5ft).

'Red Dragon' 1969 (*L. speciosum* x *L. auratum*) A medium-sized, deep crimson-pink flower with white throat and petal margins and pink petal tips. It is heavily spotted crimson and has bright orange pollen. This strong plant enjoys a topping up of its diet which will make its bulbs expand significantly and larger flowers develop richer tones with the white areas tending to blush. This is one of the parents of the Devon Dawn series. 90cm (3ft). (p129)

'Trance' Strong floriferous plant. Large, outward-facing blooms of glowing dog-rose pinks and pale crimson. 90cm–1.2m (3–4ft).

FLAT FLOWERS (Div VIIc)

'Carmen' 1971 (*L. auratum platyphyllum* x *L. speciosum* 'Gilrey') A New Zealand lily with up to a dozen 17cm (7in) rich crimson flowers heavily freckled with darker spots. 90cm–1.2m (3–4ft).

'Early Rose' Wide open, flat flowers, flooded with glowing pink, darker towards the centre of each petal blade and freely dotted with crimson papillae. These bold, outward-facing blooms are neatly arranged in pyramid heads on the top of sturdy stems. It is a good container or garden plant. 75cm (2½ft).

'Friendship' An upward-facing cultivar on the 'Star Gazer' model, it has warm, rich crimson-red flowers with clean white petal margins. 1–1.5m (3–5ft).

'Furore' 1984 Large, pure white, heavily scented flowers, 20cm (8in) across, with pale primrose midrib and noticeable raised points all over. The nectary is a violet-shaded green, the pollen a contrasting rusty-red. 1.2m (4ft).

Imperial Crimson 1960 ((*L. speciosum* x *L. auratum*) x *L. auratum*)) An impressive grex of richly-coloured clones, most flowers are almost uniformly covered with rich crimson but maintain a white margin. Its midsummer blooms are held horizontally or slightly upwards in well-arranged heads. 90cm–1.5m (3–5ft). (p134)

Imperial Gold 1960 From the same breeding lines as above but composed of clones with silvery- or ivory-white flowers with a conspicuous, golden-yellow band down the centre of each petal. It is normally well endowed with crimson spots, and flowers in midsummer. 1.8m (6ft).

Imperial Pink ((*L. auratum* x *L. speciosum*) x (*L. auratum* x *L. japonicum*)) Impressive 20cm (8in) flowers of glowing shades of pink usually marked with a darker line down each petal centre and with a greenish approach to nectary. The strength of the pink of different clones and of the tones within individual flowers varies considerably. The very impressive, gracefully arranged, outward-facing flowers make considerable heads, 12–25 to a stem. 1.5–1.8m (5–6ft).

Imperial Silver 1960 ((*L. speciosum* x *L. auratum*) x *L. auratum*) The clones gathered together under this name have shining, white flowers, up to 25cm (10in) across. Some clones have flowers with the papillae just caught with a tiny fleck of crimson. 1.5m (5ft). (p134)

'Mona Lisa' The very flat, open flowers are broad-petalled, rich pink-shaded to white edges, with darker spots. Outward-facing on sturdy stems. 75–90cm (2½–3ft).

'Olivia' This strong-growing lily has pure white, flat flowers with recurved tips, greenish nectary furrows, and all set off well by the dark orange pollen. 75cm (2½ft).

'Pink Beauty' 1956 (*L. auratum platyphyllum* x 'Jillian Wallace') One of the older New Zealanders that is still grown and offered for sale, it is a dog-rose pink flower paling at the petal margins, well-endowed with dark crimson, raised spots. The large blooms are over 25cm (10in) across and numerous. 1.5–1.8m (5–6ft).

'Red Jewel' Outward-facing, dark crimson flowers with parts of the petal edges pencilled white and with darkest crimson, raised spots. 90cm (3ft).

'Star Gazer' 1975 (Unknown parents) A world-beating Woodriff cultivar now grown in record numbers for the cut-flower trade, this is the first of the upward-facing Orientals. As a pot plant it is usually artificially dwarfed by chemical inhibitors. A good, early-flowering kind, but prone to virus. Dark crimson flowers with narrow, white margins to the petals are produced in good numbers by even very small bulbs. 1.5m (5ft). (p147)

'Troubadour' 1984 (*L. rubellum* seedling x *L. rubellum* seedling) An impressive number of large, outward-facing blooms, their flat, outward-stretching feel losing any sense of rigidity with the waved margins and the reflexed tips. The

long flash of rich crimson on each petal is graded down to pale pink at the edges. The throat is paler and marked with lemony nectary furrows. Almost the whole flower is decorated with raised flecks of crimson. 90cm–1.2m (3–4ft).

'White Mountain' Impressive, 20–25cm (8–10in), sparkling white flowers with greeny nectary furrows towards the bases, dominated by the bold yellow band radiating from the flower centres to the recurved petal tips. The petal margins are pleasingly waved. To this bold design is added a restrained sprinkle of pale pink, raised spots. The pollen is a rich rusty colour. 90cm (3ft).

RECURVED FLOWERS (Div VIId)

'Black Beauty' 1958 (*L. speciosum rubrum* x *L. henryi*) Another magic plant from L. Woodriff, this is quite one of the most extraordinary of all hybrids, a prodigy of vigour and floral performance and virtually unkillable. The flowers are of a rather flattened *L. speciosum*-shape, the petals recurving and somewhat incurved at the margins, all a very dark crimson looking almost black in some lights. Although this pales towards the petal edges, the overall effect is of a brooding colour, with a matt rather than a gloss finish. This is not a complaint, how can one when stems carry dozens, or even over 150 flowers? The pedicles hold flowers more or less horizontally and make a pyramid head, each pedicle dividing into two or three to cope with the number of flowers that open and last over a period of eight to ten weeks, from midsummer into autumn. There's value for you! The bulbs increase well in almost every kind of soil – this lily could almost be used to make hedges!

The original is a diploid, but an artificially-induced tetraploid form is available. The tetraploid form has been used by breeders to help raise a new army of giants. Many of the progeny tend to favour the 'Black Beauty' looks – almost too closely. The tetraploid form of 'Black Beauty' is altogether bigger, the flowers are almost half as big again, with wider and perhaps smoother petals. 1.2–1.8m (4–6ft). (pp123 and 135)

'Everest' 1962 ((*L. speciosum* x *L. auratum*) x *L. speciosum*) Still on offer, the shining, pure white flowers spread flat, with only a modicum of very small, maroon dots. 1.2–1.5m (4–5ft).

Jamboree 1960 ((*L. speciosum* x *L. auratum*) x *L. speciosum*) A de Graaff strain that is still listed, the wide flowers are flooded with crimson-red, highlighted by thin, white petal margins and plenty of darker spots. The flowers, up to 20cm (8in) across, are carried in large numbers. 1.2–2.4m (4–8ft).

'Journey's End' 1957 ('Phillipa' x *L. speciosum* 'Gilrey') An indestructible New Zealand lily that each year justifies its place in a collection by bringing forth a good number of durable flowers towards the end of the Oriental season, for several weeks from late summer into the beginning of autumn. A rich, glowing crimson-pink spreads all over the petals, perhaps just paling to white at the edges and attractively dotted maroon-crimson overall. Petal tips curving back. 1.2–1.8m (4–6ft). There is a tetraploid form of 'Journey's End', a strong plant and larger flower, used in breeding work. Dutch growers market a lighter coloured clone.

'Omega' 1984 ((*L. x parkmanii* x 'Pink Delight') x 'Red Bank' hybrid) A striking, large cultivar with six to nine wide, white star-shaped blooms with bold, salmon-on-pink stripe down the centre of each petal up to the tip, reinforced by evenly scattered, darker, raised spots. 90cm (3ft).

'Black Beauty'

Imperial Crimson

'Sans Souci'

Imperial Silver

'**Sans Souci**' 1971 A Woodriff hybrid, from *L. speciosum rubrum* possibly with *L. rubellum*, this has done well over the world as a garden and pot plant. The broad-petalled, flat flowers are recurved at the tips and measure up to 18cm (7in) across. Posed to look boldly outwards, half to a dozen blooms are carried per stem. The white is centred a rosy-pink that gently suffuses most of the surface, but leaves the tips and margins quite broadly white. There is a pleasing number of small, crimson, raised spots. It is in bloom for a good stretch through mid- and late summer. 90cm (3ft). (p135)

'**Scarlett Delight**' Bred by L. Freimann in the USA, this comes from tetraploid forms of 'Journey's End' and 'Black Beauty'. One to two dozen, 20cm (8in) wide blooms look out and down, each in its allotted airspace and the whole extended tall pyramid head looking very grand indeed. The flowers favour the seed parent 'Journeys End' – for once the influence of 'Black Beauty' is less evident. The flowers are rich rosy-crimson-pink with yellowish centres and darker, pink, raised spots. The tetraploid revolution is certainly with us. 1.8m (6ft).

'**White Journey's End**' This is one of the later-flowering lilies with very large, shining, white blossoms on sturdy stems, reflexing petals and a typical, strong scent. 1.2–1.5m (4–5ft).

8

BREEDING YOUR OWN LILIES

Lilies are exciting plants. Their life cycles are dynamic; their blossoms are normally spectacular, certainly always beautiful; and they can be grown in all types of garden. How much more exciting would it be to raise your own new lilies and to know that each plant is unique due to your own efforts! Many kinds are very easy and quick to raise from seed to flowering specimens. Your hobby could be blooming within a year. You do not need acres of space nor any special expertise; you hardly need to invest any money – just some time and interest.

IS IT DIFFICULT?

Most species and hybrid lilies are fertile and give plenty of seed – from one pod, 20–100 seeds can be expected. Fresh seed germinates quickly, and seedlings of many popular kinds can be grown on to bloom in one or two years. The bulbs of particularly good lilies can be propagated rapidly. You will not find it difficult to place what you feel were 'also-ran' seedlings. Fanciers with only modest plots have bred lilies that have been named and sent all over the world, for their flowers to be enjoyed.

It is worth having a go for the excitement and enjoyment of finding your own winners. There is another good reason: your seedlings are likely to be free from disease and may well outdo standard cultivars in performance.

TECHNIQUES FOR PRODUCING HYBRID SEED

Almost all lilies produce an abundance of pollen on large easily detached anthers. Ideally, once you have chosen a flower as prospective seed parent, you should remove its anthers before the pollen has been shed, perhaps already on the stigma. Fingers will do this job, but a pair of tweezers is helpful – holding the anther(s) with a pair of tweezers is easier and keeps your hands clean. If you are ultra-cautious, you could protect the stigma with a little contraceptive cap made out of a twist of foil or sticky tape. However, the stigma becomes sticky and receptive soon after the flower has opened and this is the time to introduce the pollen from your male parent. You can bring an anther taken from this cultivar into contact with the stigma so that pollen is plastered evenly over all three lobes.

After pollination some fanciers enclose the bloom in a paper bag or cover the stigma to prevent strange pollen, carried by wind or insect, from entering. It rarely matters. However, if you were dealing with a very rare kind extra caution maybe justified. Working with flowers other than lilies the familiar method to ply a stigma with pollen is to transfer it using a small watercolour brush. This is normally a pointless exercise with lilies. It is easier and more efficient to offer the anther directly to the stigma. If the pollen has been stored for some while, a small brush is a useful tool – too large a brush will waste pollen and is too clumsy.

Once a cross has been made, it is important to label the flower immediately. It is no good thinking you are going to remember what you have done – you can easily get confused with other crosses and flowers within a few minutes. You will need a tie-on label of card or plastic for it to survive for several weeks while the

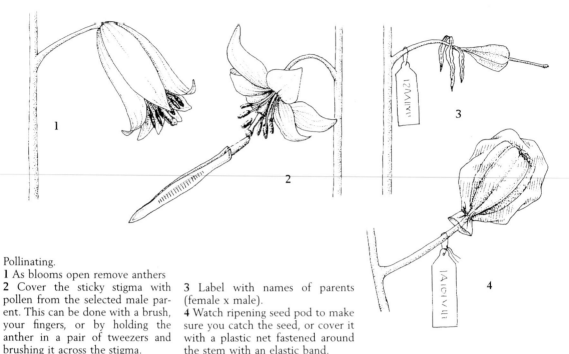

Pollinating.

1 As blooms open remove anthers
2 Cover the sticky stigma with pollen from the selected male parent. This can be done with a brush, your fingers, or by holding the anther in a pair of tweezers and brushing it across the stigma.

3 Label with names of parents (female x male).
4 Watch ripening seed pod to make sure you catch the seed, or cover it with a plastic net fastened around the stem with an elastic band.

seedpod ripens. The parents should be noted on the label in indelible, waterproof pencil or ink. The convention is to write the parents in this manner: 'Enchantment' x 'Connecticut King', where the first name is the seed (female) parent and the second the pollen (male) parent.

Should you plan to mate two flowers that are not in bloom at the same time, there are two approaches: you can artificially change the flowering time of one by retarding it or, more easily, bringing the later one into bloom earlier by gentle forcing. The alternative is to store pollen until such time as the female parent opens blooms. You can take anthers just before they have split and spilt their pollen. Place them in a plastic pill box and leave them in a safe, warm, dry spot until the anthers have split and dried out. Label the container with the cultivar name – one lot of pollen looks much like another – and only clamp the container lid on when the anther is dried and the pollen free. Now keep the container in a domestic refrigerator until such time as the pollen is needed.

This procedure suffices when the pollen is only to be stored for a few days. If you need to keep it for several weeks or even months, you will need to take a little more care to ensure that it is kept dry and will not become mouldy. You can easily do this by enclosing with it in the container a deliquescent chemical or manufactured gel that will absorb the small amount of moisture that may be present. Calcium chloride is one such chemical. Place a small amount in the bottom of the container, cover it with gauze or cotton wool and then store the pollen on top of a small piece of blotting or tissue paper. Such an arrangement can keep pollen vital for half a year in the refrigerator.

HARVESTING SEED

Hopefully the cross proves fertile, the seedpod swells and becomes upright. Infertile ones remain small and shrivel. As the seeds mature and begin to ripen, the seedpod starts to dry out and may begin to split at the top prior to allowing the ripe seed to escape. At this stage you need to either harvest the complete pod or to make sure that no seed escapes. You can take the pods away, complete with their label, and lay them on clean paper in a dry, airy spot where the seed will be safe and the final ripening can take place. Alternatively you could place a square of muslin or fine-mesh plastic net over the pod and secure it with a small rubber band to prevent any seed falling. I use this method fairly frequently, with lilies and other plants. If you are away for a few days or have no time to check the ripening pods regularly you will at least know that all is safe and that your earlier work was not in vain.

Later-ripening pods may well have to be cut off towards the end of autumn when they will not ripen any further. Hang such pods upside down over paper in a warmer, dry spot so ripening can continue and ripe seed can be safely gathered. It is a sensible precaution to spray developing pods with fungicide in the autumn to prevent infection and destruction. Again, be careful to label all batches of seed very carefully at all times.

WHY BREED LILIES?

Each fancier will have a different set of aims. It could be simply a matter of raising a series of pretty plants to augment the garden display. Having raised a pleasing number, the programme can be shut down. This, however, is the exception. Once started, the process becomes addictive, further possibilities become obvious, more crosses are made. It keeps you young – plant breeders live next to forever!

Raising flowers with new or improved colours or combinations of colours is the obvious first aim. Larger flowers or wider-petalled ones may be desired. It could well be that more blooms to a head or, perhaps more importantly, their more pleasing disposition is a top priority. Serious growers may well put disease-resistance at the top of their particular list of criteria – health is certainly something all fanciers should bear in mind.

Other aims could be to extend the flowering period of a particular group of flowers – later Martagons, earlier Orientals for example. Breeding cultivars that last a week or more

longer would be a very big bonus. Most, but not all Asiatics, are without scent – something the newcomer to lily-breeding is quick to want to change. While many species have little perfume, this does not invalidate the idea that a range of good garden Asiatics with pleasing perfumes would be welcomed by everyone. Commercial breeders have welcomed Orientals with less perfume in the belief that flowers with extrovert scents are not so much in demand as less endowed ones.

Some short-stemmed lilies suitable for pots have already been bred but there is a huge need for a wider selection of colours and types. The preoccupation of many breeders with raising flowers suitable for the cut-flower trade has led to a plethora of upright-facing ones, a perfectly acceptable form but perhaps not a pose that encapsulates the essential grace of the genus. Graceful, semi-pendant poses are very appealing and seem right for lilies. There are so many elegant species and hybrids that opportunities beckon from all sides.

It could be worth jotting down your own aims. Once the flowers are out there is a big temptation to distribute pollen all over. You could find yourself with a huge harvest of seed, needing half a county to sow and rear the resulting plants. On the other hand, if you are trying more extreme crosses, the pods may shrivel up and you are left with nothing until the next season. A balance has to be struck so that you are working within your own resources of time, space and energy. Some fanciers pollinate a single bloom of one particular cross. This is something I would try to avoid. Three is usually the fewest number I pollinate of any cross so allowing for a degree of failure. Any surplus seed can always be given away.

There are one or two guidelines that are worth following. First, as you are investing time and space, you might as well be sure that the cross you make is correct and no foreign pollen makes contact by wind or insect carrier. Remove anthers of the seed parents before they drop any pollen, and cover the stigma with a foil cap. Second, having made your cross and

140

flowered the seedlings, try to go to the F2 generation. Self-pollinate the best seedlings, or back-cross these to the parents. This ensures that you stand some chance of benefitting from recessively-governed factors. Third, raise as many seedlings as you practically can from a particular cross. Only thus can you get any idea of the genetic potential of the cross.

SELECTING PARENTS

Usually, the closer two lilies are related the more certain they are to mate easily. Some kinds are very fertile to their own pollen but many are fully or partially inhibited. When one of the parents is a plant of questionable fertility it is sensible to use this as the male parent, other things being equal. An ovary can hold only perhaps a hundred plus gametes as ovules but there can be many thousands of pollen grains, giving a higher chance of fertile gametes.

Crosses between widely-different types of lily may prove impossible or very close to this. However, it is the exceptional occasion which might give just the odd seed or two that could begin a new range of types. Crosses between species and hybrids belonging to different specific groups or hybrid divisions can take place, although one must not expect a high success rate and any pods harvested may well be full of chaff. Yet there could be the odd seed!

The barriers between the divisions seem to be tumbling all the time, due in part to the techniques described below. Perhaps the most exciting series of crosses are those between the trumpet lilies of the 6a group and the Oriental lilies. They seem possessed of huge vigour; this strength with size and colours promises great things for our gardens. This series is currently called 'Orienpets' – not perhaps the prettiest of names! The other trumpets, those like *L. longiflorum* of the 6b group, are now also kicking over the traces, and a series of *L. longiflorum* x Asiatic hybrids is already on the market.

FERTILITY AND INFERTILITY

There may be a number of reasons why certain crosses do not give seed. There could be a problem with the chromosome count – an approach to this is outlined below. The problem could be a relatively simple one: the pollen parent may have pollen that has been genetically engineered to travel a certain distance down the parent style to the ovary, and this distance could be less than required for the chosen seed parent. The answer could be to complete the reverse cross which should give you the same genetic mix.

Alternatively, if we suspect that style length is the problem, we can resort to surgery and cut off a part of the style and introduce the pollen to the reduced style. You could cut to leave a 1cm (½in) length of style. You will of course not have the nice, wide stigma to plaster pollen on, but a lot of pollen grains can be massed on a very small area. Some breeders moisten the cut surface with the juices present on the ripe stigma surface; this may well help the pollen germinate quickly and get growing down to the ovary.

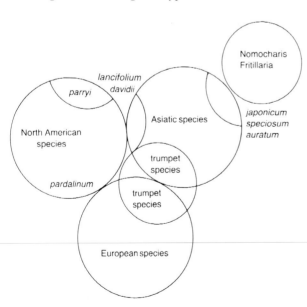

The relationship of lily groups

The soft colouring of 'Menton' is easy to place in any border scheme (p104)

The wider the cross, the more disparate the parents, the greater the likelihood of problems for the pollen. Crosses between different divisions can prove difficult. At one time, crossing trumpet lilies with Orientals would have been thought impossible. The problem is to overcome the inhibiting mechanisms in the seed parent that bar the progress of pollen from undesirable suitors causing the pollen to die.

A solution to this problem is the so-called 'Mentor pollination method'. Professional breeders place an amount of irradiated pollen on the stigma of the seed parent and this grows down and triggers the 'intruder-alarm system' but cannot fertilise the ovules. The alarm having being turned off, the real pollen is introduced about 24 hours later and all should go according to plan. A variation of this method is suitable for all amateurs and seems to work. Place a very small amount of pollen known to be compatible with the seed parent on the stigma. This should be only a very small amount. The vanguard pollen advances down the style, switches off the rejection mechanism and should allow a free run for the real pollen parent to follow within a 24- or 48-hour period. It may well mean that there is a small percentage of 'unwanted' seed amongst that which is eventually harvested, but this is not a big price to pay – and who knows this seed may give you something good!

142

EMBRYO CULTURE

Sometimes pods swell, evenly or unevenly, and when they are opened the expected seed appears to be all chaff. You may think that pollination has failed. This may not be so. Embryos may have formed but be left high and dry by the failure of the supporting endosperm cells to develop. It is perfectly possible for the amateur to 'untimely rip' the embryos from the developing seed pod and to culture them in sterile nutrient mediums until they make small plantlets that can be transferred to normal cultural methods. The job has three main stages:

● to prepare the nutrient solution
● to deliver the embryo from the seed and place it in the medium
● to transfer the plantlets from the medium into growing compost.

The embryos can be seen in the transparent seed, especially easily on a light box. The best time to complete the job is while the seed pod is still green yet the embryos are already clearly developed; this could be about eight weeks after pollination, that is 56–60 days. Conditions need to be as sterile as possible. It is something that can be managed by amateurs without expensive equipment. The procedure is simply explained in an article in the 1990 supplement to *Lilies and Related Plants* published by the Lily group of the RHS.

TETRAPLOID BREEDING

We are now at the beginning of a whole new chapter in breeding, with strong new tetraploid plants being bred in several divisions. The normal complement of chromosomes of a lily is 24. These are the diploids, usually noted down as 2n=24. The reproductive gametes, the egg and pollen cells, carry one set of chromosomes, that is n=12. Occasionally in nature and in cultivation, individuals mutate to become triploids, with three sets of chromosomes (3n=36) or become tetraploids (4n=48). Except in very rare cases of mutations, when diploids are crossed diploids are bred. Similarly tetraploids bred together will reproduce plants of similar polyploidy. If a triploid is crossed with a tetraploid and it produces seed one may get both triploids and tetraploids. Diploids crossed with tetraploids can give both triploids and tetraploids. These polyploids vary in their fertility. Pods may have only a few seed. If you wish to mate plants of different chromosome counts, you should plan to use the higher polyploid for the pollen parent.

The difference between diploid and tetraploid plants can be dramatic. Benefits include:

● plant growth more energetic, resulting in stronger stems and foliage
● larger flowers, wider petals, all of thicker texture
● more disease resistance
● longer period of bloom
● more productive bulbs
● easier breeding with triploids which should lead to an ever-larger bank of tetraploids.

Dangers could include:
● loss of some of the grace of the flower?
● in some tetraploids, a tendency for buds to be more brittle, something that hopefully will be bred out as selection takes place.

INHERITANCE OF CHARACTERISTICS

Characteristics are inherited through the influence of genes in the DNA of the two parents. Some features are simply governed by a single gene in two forms, so-called alleles. Thus the spots of Asiatic lilies are governed by a single gene, one allele of the gene favours spots and the other favours spot-free flowers. One allele, the dominant one, swamps the influence of the other, the recessive one; in this case the one favouring spots outdoes the one favouring no spots. So if a cultivar carries either two alleles favouring spots or one of each, all the flowers will be spotted; only those plants carrying two recessive alleles of the gene will have unspotted flowers.

While many characteristics are governed by two, several or many genes, there are quite a number that are the result of one gene with two alleles. The main ones are:

CHARACTERISTICS GOVERNED BY SINGLE GENES WITH TWO ALLELES

Dominant allele effect	Recessive allele effect
1 spots in Asiatics	no spots
2 spots on papillae of Asiatics	no spots (no papillae)
3 brush marks in Asiatics	no brush marks
4 deep orange in Asiatics	yellow
5 rich yellow or orange in Asiatics	pale yellow or orange
6 gold in Asiatics	no gold
7 gold released over entire petal in Asiatics	gold 'blotch'
8 anthers in Asiatics	no anthers
9 no stem bulbils on mature Asiatics	stem bulbils
10 pink or red in Orientals	white
11 no band in Orientals	gold band
12 spots in Orientals	no spots
13 normal height in Orientals	dwarf form
14 yellow or orange confined to throat in Aurelians	throat colour released over entire petal
15 gold 'blotch' in North Americans	gold released over petal
16 normal seed colour in *L. martagon* and some Asiatics	albino seed

Amateur growers have less pressure on them than the professionals whose livelihood depends on getting things right and producing a product the public wants. The Martagon and Candidum groups are not ones that can be revolutionised overnight and so do not attract much professional interest. Their seedlings take too long to reach flowering size. The amateur, however, has more time, and new series of both these two groups would certainly be welcome in gardens – they bloom early and, once established, will last a lifetime. The use of upright-facing *L. tsingtauense* with the other martagons has been shown to be possible. Eventually its use could provide a range of flowers with different flower forms and poses. The relatively new hybrids of *L. monadelphum* and *L. candidum* point the way forward for early flowers larger than the Martagons in a variety of soft colourings.

The wide range of types amongst the North-American species would seem to indicate that the possibilities of raising more amenable garden plants are still wide open. We want the easy-going habit of *L. pardalinum* married to the varied colours, shapes and habits of many other appealing species. There could be a useful bit of inter-division dalliance. 'Kelmarsh', bred in England by Oliver Wyatt and named in 1950, came from *L. martagon album* crossed with the American species, *L. kelloggii*, to prove that such things are possible. It gained an Award of Merit from the Royal Horticultural Society in 1951. What are we waiting for?

The Asiatics are such a melting pot of genetic influences that almost anything could happen. The increased influence of *L. concolor* and *L. pumilum* as well as *L. leichtlinii maximowiczii* are all adding permutations that stretch the range of possibilities to infinity. We could certainly do with a scented series.

The leading edge of hybridising at present, however, is probably the use of tetraploid plants. Some hugely vigorous cultivars have been bred, performing feats of growth and blooming that have only been dreamt of in the past.

9

LILIES IN AMERICA

The earliest days of hybridising in the USA are shrouded in the mists of time. Could some of the early pioneers have played with the pollen of the exciting flowers they found growing as they moved and settled in the west? Certainly quite early it would seem that bulbs of the *L. pardalinum* persuasion were being moved around widely from homestead to homestead. The wild American species have undergone some hybridisation although relatively little as yet compared with the larger divisions. Mention has been made of the work that resulted in the Bellingham Hybrids (p118).

A huge impetus was given to lily breeding by the work undertaken at Oregon Bulb Farms – hereafter OBF – under the direction of Jan de Graaff who had bought the place in 1934. Once growing and breeding other plants including daffodils, the decision was taken in the late 1940s to specialise in lilies. A collection was made of as many species in their best forms and of all available hybrids so that a start could be made of evaluation and breeding on a major scale. To begin with, almost every division was given rigorous attention and hybrid seed grown. It soon became apparent that certain areas were going to be vastly more productive of good garden lilies than others – and much more quickly. By the early 1950s a substantial start had been made with most hybrid types, and the species were not neglected either. Thereafter the work concentrated more and more on the Asiatics, the Aurelians and the Orientals. Some indication of this is included in chapter 7.

In the earlier years, Jan de Graaff's team had a leader in Earl Hornback to whom must be given much of the credit for the implementation of the mammoth hybridising programme.

Later, in the early 1960s, Ed. McRae joined the team. Nowadays Mr McRae's independent enterprise is looked to each season for exciting new flowers and new breeding departures.

The Mid-Century Asiatic Hybrids bulldozed their way into the attention of gardeners in the USA and worldwide. The OBF became famous. Led by 'Enchantment', bred as early as the late 1930s, and joined by the famous yellows, 'Destiny' and 'Prosperity', this series went from strength to strength. 'Harmony' in soft tangerine and 'Cinnabar' in rich maroon shades widened the colour spectrum and are still grown; the names of all these cultivars feature in the pedigree of many of today's newest hybrids. This series had been bred from the species and derivatives of *L. amabile*, *L. bulbiferum*, *L. dauricum*, *L. davidii*, *L. lancifolium*, *L. leichtlinii* and *L. maculatum* (*wilsonii*) together with the mongrel lot known under various names, often as *L. x hollandicum*.

It was not long before *L. cernuum* was added to the breeding to widen the colour range extensively. Prof. C. F. Patterson of Saskatoon University had already produced fine kinds by mating *L. davidii* with *L. cernuum*. A good second-generation seedling of this breeding was named by Prof. Patterson 'Edith Cecilia' in about 1944, a buffy, orange, pendant lily. It appears in the ancestry of very many cultivars as it was used very extensively at OBF. 'Edith Cecilia' crossed with Ia yellows brought forth a big breakthrough series of white and pink upward-facing Asiatics. Some of the 'Edith Cecilia' seedlings were mated with Mid-Cen-

'Connecticut King' is an Asiatic hybrid famous for decades as a commercial cut flower, garden plant and parent (p102)

tury kinds to give such important cultivars as 'Pirate', 'Sterling Star' and 'Discovery'. 'Gypsy' was another, the first really pink one. 'Pirate' in particular has proved a most useful parent for Dutch breeders.

The David Stone and Henry Payne partnership worked for years on the famous Connecticut cultivars. 'Connecticut Yankee' and the fantastically successful 'Connecticut King' are only two examples of the spotless yellows they were aiming for and managed to produce. While most selected kinds were upward-facing and so useful for the cut-flower market, others, such as the outward-facing 'Connecticut Lemon Glow' and 'Sunray', were to make their major impact on the garden scene and in breeding.

The strengths of the three main series – the Mid-Centuries, the Connecticuts, and the Patterson hybrids – became more and more fused in OBF and other breeding. 'Enchantment' x 'Connecticut Lemon Glow', for instance, gave a fine range including the strong plant 'Matchless' with its unspotted, orange-red flowers. 'Firecracker' came from 'Byam's Ruby' and 'Harmony'.

In a conscious move to further improve virus resistance the very tolerant *L. leichtlinii maximowszii* 'Unicolor' was crossed with *L. dauricum* to give strong plants with outward-facing blooms, and these were taken to a further generation. These F2-generation plants included some very attractive flowers, with one showing the beginnings of a brushmark. Once crossed with 'Connecticut King', a series with clearly defined brushmarks appeared. This type of flower has been worked with by Dr Withers in Australia and by Julius Wadekamper in Minnesota whose hobby became a business, called Borbeleta Gardens. After having introduced over 70 new cultivars, Mr Wadekamper decided to retire. This specialist nursery is now owned by Mr David Campbell who continues the good work.

The range of trumpets and Aurelians bred at OBF led the field for some decades and many are still amongst the world leaders. It is difficult to imagine anything better than a good stand of 'Black Dragon', a kind dating from 1950! The Orientals were very successful and, although huge advances and diversification has taken place in the USA and other continents, the early OBF Imperial Crimson, Imperial Gold, Imperial Pink and Imperial Silver strains are still grown with great success and pleasure by gardeners, each grex breeding true within quite tight limits – one of the many successes engineered by Harold Coomber.

Len Marshall and Judith McRae are two leading exponents of the art of involving some new species into the breeding game. The *L. pumilum* multi-headed hybrids in all colours are now a growing, admired reality. This species may be making its contribution alone, as does *L. concolor*, or it can be working in tandem with *L. concolor*. Not all of these hybrids are small-flowered or dwarf, but there are some that have huge vitality, terrific freedom of bloom and enchanting daintiness. *L. lankongense* has also been used, and Len Marshall has used *L. cernuum* and *L. callosum* to produce a series of extraordinarily strong plants with many dainty flowers.

With the attention of most breeders turning with ever greater urgency to the tetraploids, the pioneer work and very fine flowers of Le Vern Freimann have naturally come centre stage. His 'Apricot Supreme' is only one of the new actors at the start of a revolution, and what a plant! Registered as an Asiatic Ib, it was in fact bred from an Aurelian VId by an Oriental VII which in its turn was from Imperial Crimson VIIc crossed with 'Black Beauty' VIId. It may look like an Asiatic – a glaring example of the difficulty of maintaining the present classification.

Leslie Woodriff has been busy adding to the complexity of classifications! Exercising magic and loving dedication over many years, he has managed to produce worldbeaters in most divisions and to cross division barriers frequently. His 'White Henryi' is still leading amongst the Sunburst-type Aurelians; his 'Star Gazer' has beaten all records as a cut flower and pot plant with over 400 acres being grown at present in Holland, and his 'Black Beauty' has confounded all as the highly successful result of mating *L. speciosum* with *L. henryii*. Well established as a leading garden plant with a huge future ahead of it, its name must live for ever, with its tetraploid form leading the way to a whole series of Orientals that will be easy and dramatic garden plants. The health of lily breeding and culture in the USA is in the capable hands of many keen fanciers, a growing number, too many to mention here. All power to their pollen dabbing!

Oriental 'Star Gazer', a uniquely successful cut flower and pot plant (p133)

(All shown at ¹/4 life size)

L. 'Casa Blanca'

10

LILIES IN AUSTRALIA AND NEW ZEALAND

There has been a long and distinguished history of lily culture in both Australia and New Zealand. Europeans tend to think of New Zealand as a country where anything grows easily – anything that the sheep do not eat! Certainly almost every lily can be grown in some part of the islands with their varied climates and conditions and most flourish in all parts. On a visit a few years ago I was very impressed by the availability and quality of bulbs, especially the Orientals. The same applied to the parts of Australia we visited, New South Wales, Victoria, Tasmania. I should not have been surprised – we have had bulbs growing in our garden in the West Midlands that were raised in both these countries.

It is in Australia that some lilies have felt so at home that they have gone walkabout. In fact the trumpet species *L. longiflorum*, *L. formosanum*, *L. philippinense* and *L. wallichianum* together with their hybrid progeny are not only seen in many gardens, especially in New South Wales, but are to be found in the bush from the coastline up to the top of the wonderful Blue Mountains. They have found a home from home, rather like *L. longiflorum* has done in parts of South Africa. The outstanding *L. longiflorum* form 'Melbourne Market' grows with great gusto. They are so easy that they are

almost overlooked by the more involved lily grower. As might be expected, the martagons prefer cooler conditions and it is the trumpet lilies and the Aurelians that have really proved splendid Australian plants – with the Orientals of course. The introduced Asiatic hybrids have not proved as successful as might have been guessed, but now home-grown cultivars are overcoming this slightly tarnished reputation.

Orientals in both Australia and New Zealand have been hugely successful. Through the decades of the 1950s, 1960s and into the 1970s their kinds clearly led the world and now they are still up there with the best. It was not long after the breeding of *L. x parkmanii* from *L. auratum* x *L. speciosum* in Boston in 1869 that breeding work got underway in Australia, and the name Parkman is still associated with these Orientals. One of the most important of this group still grown today was bred by Roy Wallace as far back as 1938, 'Jillian Wallace', and features in the ancestry of a huge lot of the modern hybrids all over the world. The important Lavender Lady strain came from 'Jillian Wallace' x *L. auratum platyphyllum*, a New Zealand-raised strain that finds a second home in Australia. *L. rubellum* and *L. japonicum* have entered the breeding of some of the newer Australian kinds such as the pale pink 'Stella Crozier' and 'Pink Lace'. 'Taj Mahal' is a wonderful, large white lily, a shallow bowl with petals pointing outwards with just the slightest tilt backwards at the ends. Its blooms can measure 28cm (11in) across.

European growers can only gasp with admiration and feel green with envy when they

ORIENTAL HYBRIDS, Division VII, SILVER SWAN strain plus 'Casa Blanca'
Selection of flowers taken from this strong strain with a bloom of well-known 'Casa Blanca' for comparison. 'Casa Blanca' is usually at least 20cm (8in) across. This strain was bred mainly from Imperial Silver x 'Swan Lake'

see how *L. speciosum* can run riot in gardens both in Australia and New Zealand. The lovely trumpet *L. wallichianum*, which we have to cosset in the greenhouse to protect its very late blooms, grows like a very handsome weed, as too does the wonderful species *L. wardii* in some gardens.

Of course the Asiatics are such a huge clan that they had to be tackled by Australian breeders. 'Wattle Bird' bred by B. G. Hayler of Golden Ray Gardens, Victoria, has established an enviable reputation, as an unspotted, yellow, upward-facing lily with numerous – up to 40 – flowers on strongly-held heads. From a seedling x 'Connecticut King' it has plenty of good foliage and all-round vigour. It is being used with good effect to breed pale creamy flowers and limey-toned ones. Brushmarks have found quite a bit of favour. 'Windahloo', bred by Dr Withers, is a I (a) in brilliant yellow with a dark, well-defined brushmark, altogether a gutsy flower with wide petals and supported by robust stems and foliage. 'Ayers Rock' is a strong, outward-facing kind from R. J. Sinclair of Lilium Vale Nursery, New South Wales, a flower of those mixed reds, oranges and pinky-buffs like those of the famous feature after which it is named. 'Winterset' is a strong, white lily with spots and petals pointing straight outwards. 'Byjingo' is a wide-petalled red and 'Black Satin' an exceptional, deep-coloured one.

'Trenwell' is another prodigy bred by the late Gordon Chandler, with pyramid heads of 30 or more, upward-facing, bright lemon, lightly spotted flowers. From the same raiser, but introduced by Bob Nelson, came the trumpet 'Uranus', a very strong plant with about 25 large, non-fading, limey-yellow flowers with golden throats, able to grow to over 3m (9ft). There are stems reported as having had over a hundred blooms. Rex and Robert Myers have established their Oakville strain of trumpets and Aurelians.

J. S. Yeates started working in Palmerston North at the beginning of the 1940s and produced in 1952 the famous Lavender Lady Oriental strain. This proved hugely successful in New Zealand and Australia. Worldwide the cultivar most associated with the Yeates name is the late-flowering 'Journey's End' which remains one of the most popular and reliable of all. From 'Phillipa' x *L. speciosum* 'Gilrey', this kind has gone its all-conquering way for decades, and its journey has not ended, the tetraploid form ensuring an even longer life for this flagship lily. 'Phillipa' was an auratum-type flower, a Yeates selection from 'Crimson Queen'. There have been and are a bevy of energetic fanciers working in New Zealand – Wm. Doreen of Lilies International, Levin, North Island, has worked as a grower, hybridiser and exporter of lilies. Happily there are many other energetic, dedicated lily growers and breeders who will see to it that New Zealand stays up there with the world's best.

The New Zealand Lily Society was founded as long ago as 1932 and so is well past its half century. They have 700–800 members and are very active. Their seed list has about 14 pages and over 700 offerings including up to 500 lilies. An unusual and enterprising feature is the pollen bank which the society maintains for the benefit of its members. There are other active organisations, such as the Auckland Lily Society, with a full programme of activities.

11

SPECIES CHECKLIST

The chart gives information as follows:

(1) Page reference to full plant description

(2) Division number (see p60–2 for classification)

(3) Seed germination (see p21–2): h=hypogeal; e=epigeal; i=immediate; d=delayed

(4) Bulb: c=concentric (normal form); s=stoloniferous; c/s=concentric bulb with stoloniferous stem; r=rhizomatous; sr=subrhizomatous

(5) Foliage: s=scattered; w=whorled; sp=spirally arranged; a=alternate; n=numerous

(6) Stem rooting: sr=stem rooting

(7) Height given in metres, e.g. .4=40cms

(8) Flower colour: w=white; r=red; o=orange; gr=green; y=yellow; p=pink; pu=purple; m=mauve; o/r=orange and red on same flower; o.r=some clones orange, some clones red

(9) Flower pose: h=horizontally held; p=pendant; s=semi; u=upright

(10) Soil: lt=lime tolerant (bulbs either will take some lime or enjoy lime); a=acid (bulbs prefer acid soil); n=neutral, t=tolerant of wide range

Species name	(1) Page	(2) Division	(3) Seed germination	(4) Bulb	(5) Foliage	(6) Stem rooting	(7) Height	(8) Flower colour	(9) Flower pose	(10) Soil
alexandrae	79	4c	hd	c	s	sr	1	w	h	a
amabile	84	5b	ei	c	s	sr	.8	r	p	lt
amoenum	85	5c	ei	c	s	sr	.3	p	sp	a
arboricola	85	5c	ei	c	s	sr	.5	gr	sp	a
auratum	79	4b	hd	c	s	sr	.7–2	w+r	h	a
bakerianum	85	5c	ei	s/s	s	sr	.5	w	p	a
bolanderi	65	2a	hd	c	w		.4–.9	r	h/sp	lt
brownii	80	4d	ei	c	s	sr	1–1.2	w	h	a
bulbiferum	77	3d	hd	c	s	sr	1	o	u	t
callosum	84	5b	ei	c	s	sr	1	o.r	p	lt
canadense	69	2c	hd	s	w	sr	1.5–2	r.y.	p	lt
candidum	73	3a	ei	c	s		1.2–2	w	h	lt
carniolicum	74	3b	hd	c	s		.9	r	p	lt
catesbaei	73	2d	ei	c	w		.3–.6	y+r	u	a
cernuum	84	5b	ei	c	s	sr	.5–.7	p	p	a
chalcedonicum	75	3b	ed/ei	c	s		1–1.2	o/r	p	lt
cilatum		3	hd	c	sp	sr	.6–1.5	c	p	a

152

Species name	(1) Page	(2) Division	(3) Seed germination	(4) Bulb	(5) Foliage	(6) Stem rooting	(7) Height	(8) Flower colour	(9) Flower pose	(10) Soil
columbianum	65	2a	hd	c	w		.6–1.5	o	p	a
concolor	84	5b	ei	c	s		.2–.6	o/r	u	t
dauricum	92	7	ei	c/st	s	sr	.1–1	r/o/y	u	t
davidii	81	5a	ei	c/st	s	sr	1.2	o	p	a
distichum	64	1	hd	c	w	sr	.8	o	h/sp	a
duchartrei	81	5a	ei	c/st	s	sr	1	w	p	lt
fargesii		5b	?	c	s	sr	.2–.5	w	p	a?
formosanum	90	6b	ei	c	s	sr	.1–2	w	h	lt
georgei		5c	?	c	w/s		.1–.4	m	p	a
grayi	70	2c	hd	s	w		1.7	r	p	a
hansonii	63	1	hd	c	w	sr	1–1.5	o	p	lt
henricii	86	5c	ei	c	s		.8–1.2	w/p	sp	a
henryi	82	5a	ei	c	s	sr	2–3	o	p	lt
humboldtii	66	2a	hd	c/s	w		2	p	p	lt
iridollae	71	2c	hi	s	s	sr	.5–2	y	p	a
japonicum	79	4c	hd	c	s	sr	1	p	h	a
kelloggii	66	2a	hd	c	w		.3–1.2	w+p	p	lt?
kesselringianum	76	3c	hd	c	sp		1–1.4	y	sp	lt?
lancifolium	82	5a	ei	c	s	sr	1.2–1.8	o	p	a
lankongense	83	5a	ei	c/s	s	sr	1.2	p	p	lt
ledebourii	76	3c	hd	c	s/sp	sr	1.2–1.4	w+y	sp	lt?
leichtlinii	83	5a	ei	c	s	sr	1.2–1.8	y	p	a
leucanthemum	89	6a	ei/ed	c	s	sr	1–2	w	h/sp	lt
longiflorum	91	6b	ei	c	s	sr	1	w	h	lt
lophophorum	86	5c	ei?	c	s		.1–.4	y	p	a
mackliniae	86	5c	ei	c	s	sr	.2–1	p	sp	n/a
maculatum	93	7	ei	c/s	s	sr	.3–1	y.o	u	lt
maritimum	67	2b	hd	rc	s/w		.1–2	r/o	sp	a
martagon	63	1	hd	c	w	sr	1–2	m	p	lt
medeoloides	64	1	hd	c	w	sr	.8	r	p	a
michauxii	71	2c	hd	s	w	sr	1	o	sp	a
michiganense	71	2c	hd	s	w		1–1.8	o.r.	o	a
monadelphum	76	3c	hd	c	sp		1–1.2	y	p	lt
nanum	86	5c	ei	c	s		.1–.4	w	p	a
neilgherrense	91	6b	ei	c/s	s	sr	.6–1.4	w	h	a
nepalense	87	5c	ei	c/s	s/a	sr	.9	w.m	p	a
nevadense	67	2b	hd	r	w		.8	o/r	p	a
nobilissimum	79	4c	hi	c	s	sr	.6	w	u	a
ocellatum	67	2a	hd	r	w	sr	1–1.8	o	p	lt
occidentale	67	2b	hd	r	w		.6–2	r/o	p	a

Species name	(1) Page	(2) Division	(3) Seed germination	(4) Bulb	(5) Foliage	(6) Stem rooting	(7) Height	(8) Flower colour	(9) Flower pose	(10) Soil
ochraceum	87	5c	ei	c/s	a	sr	1–1.2	y	p	a
oxypetalum	87	5c	ei	c	s/w		.2–.3	y	h	a
papilliferum	84	5a	ei	c/s	s	sr	.7–.9		p	lt
paradoxum		5c	?	c	s/w	sr	.4	pu	u	a?
pardalinum	68	2b	hd	r	w		1.5–2	o.r	p	lt
parryi	68	2b	hd	r	w/s		.5–1.8	y	h	lt
parvum	68	2b	hd	r	w/s		1.5	o.r.y.	h/su	a
philadelphicum	73	2d	ei	s	w		1	y.o.	u	a
philippinense	92	6b	ei	c	s	sr	.5–1	w	h	a
pitkinense		2b	hd	r	s/w		1–2	o	p	a
polyphyllum	77	3c	hd	c	s		1–2	w	p	a
pomponium	75	3b	ei/ed	c	s		.8	o/r	p	t
ponticum	77	3	ed	c	sp	sr	.3–.7	y.o	p	a
primulinum	87	5c	ei	c/s	a	sr	1–1.8	y	p	lt
pumilum	85	5b	ei	c	ns	sr	.3–.6	o	p	t
pyrenaicum	76	3b	ed	c	ns		.6–1.2	y	p	lt
regale	90	6a	ei	c	s	sr	1–1.5	w	h	lt
rhodopeum		3	?	c	na		.8–1	y	p	t?
rubellum	80	4d	hd	c	s	sr	.3–.8	p	h	a
rubescens	67	2a	hd	r/sr	w		1.5–2	p	u	a
sargentiae	89	6a	ei/ed	c	s	sr	1–2	w	h/sp	a
sempervivoi-deum	88	5c	ei	c	s	sr	.1–.2	w	sp	a
sherriffiae	88	5c	ei	c	s	sr	.3–.9	pu	p	a
souliei	88	5c	ei?	c	s		.2–.4	pu	p	a
speciosum	78	4a	hd	c	s	sr	.8–1.5	w.r	p	a
sulphureum	90	6a	ei	c	s	sr	1.2–3	y	h/sp	lt
superbum	71	2c	hd	s	w	sr	1.5–3	r.o.y	p	a
szovitsianum	77	3c	hd	c	sp		.6–1.5	y	p	lt
taliense	88	5c	ei	c/s	s	sr	1.5–2	m/pu	p	lt
tsingtauense	64	1	hd	c	w	sr	.5–1	o	u	t/a
vollmeri	69	2b	hd	r	w/s		.5–1.2	o	p	a
wallichianum	92	6b	ei	c/s	ns	sr	1–2	w	h	lt?
wardii	89	5c	ei	c/s	s	sr	1–1.5	m	p	lt?
washingtonia-num	67	2a	hd	sr	w		1–2	w	h	a
wigginsii	69	2b	hd	r	w/s	sr	.6–1.5	y	p	a

Note: Those species listed here but not given a full description within the book are felt to be too rare in cultivation to be featured at the present time.

12

FALSE LILIES

Common name	Genus (and species)	Family
African corn lily	Ixia	Iridaceae
African lily	Agapanthus	Liliaceae/Alliaceae
Arum lily	⎰ Zantedeschia	Aracea
	⎱ Arum	Aracea
Belladonna lily	Amaryllis bella-donna	Liliaceae/Amaryllidaceae
Bethlehem lily	Eucharis grandiflora	Liliaceae/Amaryllidaceae
Bluebead lily	Clintonia borealis	Liliaceae/Convallariaceae
Bugle lily	Watsonia	Iridaceae
Canna lily	Canna	Cannaceae
Cape lily	Crinum	Liliaceae/Amaryllidaceae
Day lily	Hemerocallis	Liliaceae/Hemerocallidaceae
Eucharis lily	Eucharis	Liliaceae/Amaryllidaceae
Foxtail lily	Eremurus	Liliaceae/Asphodelaceae
Giant lily	Cardiocrinum	Liliaceae/Liliaceae
Glory lily	Gloriosa	Liliaceae/Colchicaceae
Guernsey lily	Nerine sarniensis	Liliaceae/Amaryllidaceae
Kaffir lily	Schizostylis	Iridaceae
Lent lily	Narcissus pseudonarcissus	Liliaceae/Amaryllidaceae
Lily-of-the-valley	Convallaria	Liliaceae/Convallariaceae
Lily pink	Aphyllanthes	Liliaceae/Aphyllanthaceae
Lily thorn	Catesbaea	Rubiacea
Peruvian lily	Alstroemeria	Liliaceae/Alstromeriaceae
Plantain lily	Hosta	Liliaceae/Funkiaceae
St. Bernard's Lily	Anthericum lilago	Liliaceae/Anthericaceae
St. Bruno's lily	Paradisea lilastrum	Liliaceae/Asphodelaceae
Scarborough lily	Cyrtanthus purpureus (Vallota speciosa)	Liliaceae/Amaryllidaceae
Snake's-head lily	Fritillaria meleagris	Liliaceae/Liliaceae
Toad lily	Tricyrtis	Liliaceae/Convallariaceae
Torch lily	Kniphofia	Liliaceae/Asphodelaceae
Trout lily	Erythronium	Liliaceae/Liliaceae
Voodoo lily	Sauromatum guttatum	Araceae
Water lily	⎰ Nuphar	Nymphaeaceae
	⎱ Nymphaea	
Wood lily	Trillium	Liliaceae/Trilliaceae

APPENDIX

WHERE TO SEE LILIES

In Britain the largest number of lilies will be on view at flower shows. There are likely to be some at most of the major shows from spring through to autumn, including the regular shows of the Royal Horticultural Society at their halls off Vincent Square, Westminster and the Chelsea show. To see lilies growing is a little more difficult. Some general nurseries grow a few and these may be traced through *The Plantfinder*. This will also give you the addresses of specialists. The Lily group of the RHS puts on a cooperative exhibit at one of the RHS midsummer shows which is well worth seeing. It will give you an opportunity to meet other enthusiasts, ask questions and to join, if you are not already a member. The group organises trips to gardens in different parts of the country where lilies are grown, often places not open to the general public.

Edinburgh Botanic Gardens grow some species beautifully that southern gardens struggle with or abandon. Other botanic gardens are also likely to grow some. There is no national collection at present.

National Garden Scheme lists over 3,500 private gardens open for charities supported by the scheme. These are found in the yellow book published annually, *Gardens of England and Wales*. Many of these will have some lilies in the summertime. Two are worth special mention. Please consult the current yellow book for opening dates.

Evenley Wood Garden, Brackley, Northants. A woodland garden spread over 60 acres of mature wood. Trees, shrubs and many bulbous plants including lilies.

Old Rectory Cottage, Tidmarsh, Nr Pangbourne, Berks. A two acre garden crammed with unusual plants of all kinds. Lilies are of special interest.

In the USA, New Zealand and Australia there are very active societies that run shows and visits. The commercial growers are usually happy to see prospective buyers, too.

WHERE TO BUY LILIES

You may have to go to several sources to get all the lilies you want. You are likely to find some of the main Asiatic and trumpet hybrids, together with a few species, on offer at the local garden centre or store. These can be good value if you purchase them before they have been hanging about too long. It might be an idea to ask your local garden centre when they expect to get their lilies in and to buy them as soon as they unpack their newly arrived cartons.

Bulb merchants and growers that produce mail-order catalogues and lists fall into different categories – lily-specialist firms, especially in the United States, may have splendid catalogues and lists. Some nurseries may list some groups of lilies that are difficult to find elsewhere. The following list of suppliers is not exhaustive; ask the secretaries of lily societies for other sources.

UNITED KINGDOM

Jacques Amand Ltd, The Nurseries, Clamp Hill, Stanmore, Middx HA7 3JS. Wide range of all types of bulbs; a good general list of lilies with some species rarely offered elsewhere.
Walter Blom & Son Ltd, Coombelands Nurseries, Leavesden, Watford, WD2 7BH. Long-

established bulb merchants; useful range of kinds from all the main divisions, a range that gets updated regularly.

Blackdown Lilies, Venn Ottery Road, Newton Poppleford, Devon. The nursery of Derek Gardham, breeder of the fine Devon Dawn Orientals and other lilies. A range of main division kinds and species offered from his own grown stock.

Bridgemere Nurseries, Bridgemere, Nr Nantwich, Cheshire CW5 7QB. Huge selection of all types of plants to take away; wider range of bulbs and lilies than in most garden centres. [No mail order.]

Bullwood Nursery, 54 Woodlands Road, Hockley, Essex SS5 4PY. The nursery of Derek Fox, breeder of some very lovely hybrids and grower of lilies, related plants and other interesting plants.

Paul Christian, PO Box 468, Wrexham, Clwydd LL13 9XR. Grower of rare plants, especially bulbs; lists some rare, small lily species. [Mail order only.]

P de Jager and Sons Ltd, Staplehurst Road, Marden, Kent TN12 9BP. Long-established family bulb business; good range of lilies from main divisions and species.

J. Parker Bulbs Ltd, 452 Chester Road, Old Trafford, Manchester M16 9HL. Large-scale supplier of popular bulbs; lilies listed include popular kinds but also some interesting ones not on offer elsewhere in Britain.

R V Roger Ltd, The Nurseries, Pickering, N. Yorkshire YO18 7HG. Large nursery supplying all kinds of plants; their lily list includes a good range of species grown for them by a British grower with Asiatics and other hybrids.

Van Tubergen UK Ltd, Bressingham, Diss, Norfolk IP22 2AB. Wide range of all kinds of bulbs; lilies listed include all main divisions and a reasonable number of species.

USA

US lily fanciers are well served by many nurseries and garden centres together with specialist growers. Membership of the North American Lily Society will give details of others.

B & D Lilies, 330 P Street, Port Townsend, Washington 98368. Excellent catalogue of new and tried kinds in all divisions, with new introductions from leading breeders. [No export.]

Van der Salm Bulb Farm, 35306 N W Toenjes Road, Woodland, Washington 98674. Wholesale growers and breeders of wide range of new types. The firm supplies the leading distributors.

David Campbell, Borbeleta Gardens, 15890 Canby Ave, Faribault, MN 55021. Growing modern cultivars and introducing new kinds, some derived from unusual species backgrounds.

Judith McRae, The Lily Garden, 36752 S E Bluff Road, Boring, OR 97009. A leading breeder and technologist grower with an attractive catalogue of many types including species hybrids.

READING ABOUT LILIES

This list is a selection of books that might be useful for amateur growers.

Fox, Derek, *Growing Lilies* (Christopher Helm, 1985) Excellent book covering all main aspects of the lily cult, but especially strong on reviewing the species. Includes a three-page bibliography.

Fox, Derek, *Lilies* (Wisley handbook series, RHS + Cassell, 1985) Concentrates on educa-tion, advice and review of all types of lilies.

Jefferson-Brown M., *The Lily* (David & Charles 1988) One of the author's attempts at a review of lilies and the cult.

Woodcock H. B. D., and Stearn W. T., *Lilies of the World* (Country Life Ltd., 1950) Still an excellent reference book about lily culture and the species. Only very limited reference to hybrids.

Matthews, Victoria, *Lilies* (Kew Gardening

Guides, Kew with Collingridge, 1989) Covers all aspects of lily culture, including a review of hybrids.

Lily Yearbooks (North American Lily Society, annually) Covers activities of society and affiliated bodies with up-to-date information and thoughts on lilies.

Lilies and Related Plants (RHS Lily Group, annually) Replaces former RHS publications, such as *Lily Year Books*. Excellent, wide-ranging articles on all aspects of the lily cult.

International Lily Register (RHS, 1982 plus supplements to present) Lists all known lily species and cultivars with classification, derivation and short descriptions.

Synge, P. M., *Lilies* (Batsford, 1980) A monograph of the genus. Exhaustive cover of all wild forms.

SPECIALIST SOCIETIES

UNITED KINGDOM

The RHS Lily Group General Secretary: Dr Ian Boyd, 14 Marshalls Way, Wheathamstead, St Albans, Herts AL4 8HY. Produces a yearbook, newsletters, a cooperative display in the summer, meetings, visits, bulb auctions and seed lists.

USA

North American Lily Society Inc. Executive Secretary: Robert Gilman, PO Box 272, Owatonna, MN 55060. Produces yearbook, newsletters, seedlist. Regional and state societies are affiliated. Organises shows, visits, and meetings. With membership comes a book, *Lily Disease Handbook*, by Edward A McRae.

AUSTRALIA AND NEW ZEALAND

Auckland Lily Society
New Zealand Lily Society PO Box 1394, Christchurch
Otago Lily Society

CANADA

Ontario Regional Lily Society
The Canadian Prairie Lily Society

SOUTH AFRICA

South African Lilium Society

The addresses of the above societies can be found in current directories of the region concerned.

INDEX

Page numbers in *italic* refer to illustrations
Lily species will also feature in the species checklist, pages 151–3